Proud to Be:
Writing by American Warriors

Southeast Missouri State Univer

Proud to Be:
Writing by
American Warriors
Volume 1

Edited by Susan Swartwout

Partners in the Writing By and About Warriors Series

WITHDRAWN WARRIORS
ARTS ALLIANCE

ISBN: 978-0-9883103-0-8

First Published in the United States of America, 2012

Southeast Missouri State University Press
One University Plaza, MS 2650
Cape Girardeau, MO 63701
http://www6.semo.edu/universitypress

Southeast Missouri State University Press, founded in 2001, serves as a first-rate publisher in our region and offers internships for Southeast students interested in learning about literary publishing. The Press produces books, *Big Muddy: Journal of the Mississippi River Valley, The Cape Rock* poetry journal, the Faulkner Conference Series, *Journey* student magazine, and five national writing competitions.

The Missouri Humanities Council (MHC) is a 510 (c)(3) non-profit organization that was created in 1971 under authorizing legislation from the U.S. Congress to serve as one of the 56 state and territorial humanities councils that are affiliated with the National Endowment for the Humanities.

The Warriors Arts Alliance is composed of organizations and individuals dedicated to building communication and understanding between veterans, families, and communities through creative writing and visual arts.

Table of Contents

Acknowledgements

This work would not be possible without the support and contributions of several individuals and organizations. My gratitude to the Board of Directors of the Missouri Humanities Council and Executive Director Geoffrey Giglierano, Southeast Missouri State University Press and Editor Susan Swartwout, and especially to the writing Warriors—our veterans and their family members. Without each of you, these voices would be whispers into the darkness.

Peace,
Deborah Marshall
Director, Warriors Arts Alliance

When I was working in an historical society library back in the mid-1970s, one of our librarians was the widow of man who had served in WWI. I asked her if her husband had ever told her much about his experiences in France in 1918. She replied that no, he had only told her a funny story about stealing a chicken when he and his buddies were short on rations. It was then that I began to understand how many of our citizen soldiers aren't inclined to talk much about their experiences in war. This was further confirmed for me about 15 years later, when I did over 100 oral history interviews with WWII veterans for a museum exhibit. Again, the majority of these veterans told me that they had not talked very much with anyone about their experiences. In many cases, I was literally the first person to hear their stories, almost five decades after the events had taken place.

The prose and poetry pieces in this anthology represent stories and perspectives that need to be shared for two reasons: first of all, it is vital for the veterans themselves to experience the process of self-expression, to not keep these things bottled up; secondly, it is essential for the good of our society and our nation that the rest of us listen to what these men and women have to say.

The content of this book is important, and we want to thank the various and organizations and individuals who have made it happen. All of us are particularly grateful to Deborah Marshall for setting this project in motion. And we especially want to thank the veterans who shared some of what they had to say.

—Geoff Giglierano, Executive Director, Missouri Humanities Council

Foreword

It is an honor for an old veteran of a long-ago war (WWII) to be asked to write a foreword to an anthology of writings by American veterans and their families. It is also a welcome opportunity to reach across the years and identify with these veterans.

The circumstances and characteristics of our wars may be markedly different, and society and times are decidedly dissimilar. Yet there is much in common that brings us all together. We share a common pride in service to our country and feel a warm stirring in our hearts when we see the Stars and Stripes. We have known a unique kind of camaraderie not to be found in any civilian relationship. And, on the down side, many of us with combat experience are obliged to endure some of the traumatic residue of war. Finally, those of us who encountered danger and death often came home to experience difficulty in adjusting to a strangely different social setting. Admittedly, I had the advantage of returning to a society of nearly universal support and sacrifice for the war. I can only imagine how returning Iraq and Afghanistan veterans must feel. Coincidentally, on the very day I wrote the foregoing, the *St. Louis Post Dispatch* carried an article on the problems veterans are having in trying to fit into the environment of area colleges and universities.

At the outset I want to assure the contributors to this anthology that in writing their stories they have performed a commendable public service. Later I will turn to what I hope it has done for them personally. As one who has spent his professional life studying, teaching, and writing history, I can attest to the value of this service.

As a war ends and recedes from view, the impression left behind in the public mind may simply associate it with a well-publicized name: an Eisenhower or Marshall, a Patton or MacArthur, a Westmoreland, Schwarzkopf, or Petraeus. The exception, of course, is the knowledge that a family member or friend served in the conflict. Yet we know that these "names" were often miles away from the real action. Untold numbers of men and women were performing the essential services, the grunt work as it were, and just generally doing the heavy lifting. In creating Willie and Joe, two of the most ordinary G.I.s in WWII, and following their trials and tribulations, the late cartoonist Bill Mauldin lifted ordinary servicemen from their normal obscurity. The more we know about the "Willie and Joes" of any war, the better we understand that war. Likewise, while the individual contributor to this anthology may consider his or her story of little consequence to the reading public, when added to the whole, we get a better understanding of war, including those currently in Iran and Afghanistan. Anyone with an interest in the history of these conflicts is beholden.

Thus as an American citizen I am appreciative of the contributors' military service to our country, and as a professional historian I am grateful to them for their written contribution to the historical record.

Turning from my role as an emeritus professor of history to that of a combat veteran, I submit that the most valuable reason for writing a war memoir comes from the personal, often therapeutic, benefits it can bring. I recommend that all veterans, no matter their role but most particularly if they have been left with any residual problems, examine themselves and give written expression to their feelings and experiences. The result can be most beneficial.

My wife Alice has always helped with the editing and polishing of my writing, including the memoir of my service years. In looking back at my first draft, I realized that I had examined and exposed things never previously shared with her or anyone else. This sharing helped both of us better understand the occasional panic/anxiety attacks and accompanying depression I still feel occasionally, though mercifully less frequently. She credits the writing experience with bringing me, in her words, a "catharsis of spirit." She also uses two terms that aptly describe the process of writing a war memoir: reaching in and reaching out. These can be illustrated with reference to my own writing. My main purpose was to reach out to share my past with my children. To do that necessitated reaching in to my innermost feelings and memories. Reaching out to old comrades, with letters and telephone calls, completed the picture of my war experience and the meaning of the events. Putting it all together meant reaching out by sharing and discussing it all with my wife. The result has proven beneficial to me and those dear to me, and from the comments I have received, the work has proved interesting, thought-provoking, and useful to others.

Although a veteran of my generation shares much with contemporary veterans, there are some things that are strikingly different. One that stands out so very vividly to me is the difference in communication between the homefront and the battlefront.

When I was in Europe, 1944–45, the only means of communicating with my parents was by letter. The delivery of a letter could take place anywhere from many days into weeks. All my letters had to pass through a censor. Since I did not want my parents to know what war—close up— was like for me, my letters would have been uninteresting to the censor and uninformative to an enemy who perchance found one.

My parents got their information and their perception of the war mainly from a local newspaper and the radio. The nature and means of information dissemination changed dramatically in subsequent decades. Television, computers, and satellite communications have brought the face of war directly into the homes of service people.

I am thankful it was never so immediately and graphically available to my parents back in 1944–45, as our unit entered the Hurtgen Forest, endured the Battle of the Bulge, crossed the bridge at Remagen, and fought through the Ruhr pocket. Knowing of that possibility would have made it all the more worrisome and difficult for me. On the other hand, perhaps a later generation has become so habituated to change and immediacy of everything, that it can be seen more as a normal expectation than a problem.

A more significant difference in our experiences lies in the nature of our respective enemies. My enemy presented itself in a formal and uniformed army. I can only imagine facing an enemy of insurrectionary and terrorist makeup, neither easily identifiable nor readily distinguishable from the civilian mass within which it moves.

A rumor floated through our ranks in mid-to-late April 1945 that as the German army collapsed in front of us (my division alone captured over 47,000 enemy soldiers that month), fanatical elements would flee to the mountainous south and from there wage guerrilla warfare. Fortunately, this proved no more than a rumor, and we settled into an orderly occupation role.

Unfortunately, no such role was ever available for the most contemporary contributors to this volume. The armed forces of Iraq were dispatched with military efficiency and the forces representing the Afghan government were bested. But then our forces became engaged in a long enduring struggle without a discernible end in sight. With the nation depending entirely upon a professional military service (of small size relative to my day), the same people are called upon to make repeated tours in hellish situations.

From some limited experience, I know that is not good for morale. Having survived the war in Europe as a member of an infantry regiment, my morale plummeted when we began training for a different enemy and expected to be in Japan later in the year 1945.

While I had a strong feeling, throughout our three battle campaigns in Germany, that I would survive, I had an equally strong premonition of dying in Japan. On a warm August day, my infantry company took time off from training to listen to reports from Radio Luxembourg. When I heard the nearly unbelievable news of the Japanese surrender, I knew I had been granted a future after all.

Like many veterans of previous wars, some veterans of Iraq and Afghanistan experienced psychological problems in varying degrees of intensity. But unlike my day and earlier times, the military has made more of a serious effort to acknowledge the existence of these problems and to treat them.

After only a short time as a soldier, I began to perceive the army as a distinct entity in itself, with a life and will of its own quite apart from that which even the highest ranking officer might impose. The will of the army was inflexible, implacable, and often impervious to logic and reason. One of the more disturbing examples of this, to me as a combat infantryman, was its attitude toward the mental and emotional damage that war inflicts upon its participants. From war to war, the army made remarkable advances in the evacuation and treatment of the physically wounded. Yet the army long held fast to the position that there was no such thing as an emotional/psychological injury that might be and should be treatable. Instead, any such behavior was seen as a flaw in the soldier himself that caused him to behave as less than a man. Soldiers of the First World War who exhibited signs of psychological damage were described as victims of "shell shock" and frowned upon more as objects of pity rather than subject for treatment.

In the Second World War, the army seemed to feel the need to soften this phrase which had come to be interpreted as a stigmatic description, so the term "battle fatigue" was adopted. Even so, the army position on emotional injury had so permeated military culture that no soldier wanted to be tagged with this label. I know, for I was one of them!

Thankfully, in subsequent years and with more conflicts, the military lost its once solid grip on censorship. The veritable revolution in communications and dissemination of information mentioned above obliged the military to take a more reasoned approach to emotional problems. Just as it was understood that horrible situations inflict severe traumatic damage upon civilians, the same could apply to military personnel. The adjustment problems experienced by many Vietnam veterans, for example, led to the use of the term "post-traumatic stress."

In Iraq and Afghanistan the military has treated both physical and psychological harm, using the term Post-Traumatic Stress Disorder (PTSD) in diagnosing the latter. Both the military and the media have given much attention to PTSD. With greater public awareness, one would like to see the once belittling atmosphere surrounding psychological wounds gradually fade away. Hopefully, it will be understood that it is still possible for most of us to live productive and fulfilling lives. News reports indicate, however, that some veterans seeking employment are finding little societal change.

Veterans have responded to the invitation by the Warriors Arts Alliance and the Missouri Humanities Council to share their war experiences with submission in a variety of forms, including poetry.

Historically, there is abundant evidence that both poetry and fiction give readers understanding and feel for a particular war. When I was a school boy from the late 20s through the 30s, the Great War (1914–1918) was still a subject of great interest. I listened with fascination and sometimes horror to the many stories told by the men in the small town near our farm in northwest Missouri. We studied this war in history, and I read avidly everything I could find. My much-respected high school math teacher had seen combat in France. My English teacher introduced me to war poems and war fiction. She had the class memorize one of her favorite poems, one that made a profound and everlasting impression on me: "In Flanders Field," by John McCrea, 1915. This Canadian army officer was inspired to write this very moving poem after a fellow officer was killed by a German artillery shell and buried in a military cemetery in Flanders. I have visited similar cemeteries in Belgium and the Netherlands, where some of my combat buddies are buried, and McCrea's poem touches me deeply.

In addition to poetry, the Great War (sadly later it had to be renamed World War I) inspired many novels, and some of these added to my understanding of the war. One of the great war novels of all time, published in 1929, was written by a wounded veteran of the German army, Erich Remarque. Translated into English as *All Quiet on the Western Front*, it helped fuel anti-war sentiment in the postwar world. Unfortunately, it did nothing to deter his fellow countrymen from launching an even larger conflagration exactly a decade after its publication. Even so, Remarque's work remains a classic in depicting the folly and waste of war. And it remains a beacon to those who choose fiction as a way of expressing what war has done to them and those around them.

In addition to compelling and descriptive contributions in both prose and poetry by veterans themselves, the anthology adds another dimension to make it even richer and more rewarding to the reader: accounts provided by family members. These not only tell us more about the veteran, they offer insight into the effects of war upon the family at home and those left behind when a loved one dies in service to our flag and country.

Families sometimes find it hard to learn about the experiences of their veteran. Some veterans, especially those in combat units, are unable to talk to loved ones about the alien and irrational kind of world they have had to endure. From my own experience back in 1946, I know that happy as they are to be at home, they cannot help feeling uncomfortably different from their former selves and perhaps even out of place back in the civilian world. I was greatly relieved that my parents never delved into the grim details of that difficult winter and spring of 1944–45.

Eventually, some family members deserve and want to know more. I am grateful to a good friend for persuading me, a half century after my discharge, to write a memoir for the benefit of my children. Even now, it is not uncommon to read letters in the quarterly journal of the 78th Infantry Association from children, nephews, nieces, and grandchildren, seeking information about a loved one.

To add another point before closing out this foreword and allowing the reader to get to what this anthology is all about, I turn to the connection between service people and the general populace. As noted earlier, my generation of servicemen and women enjoyed an ideal relationship with the nation. Beginning with Korea, however, there were signs of an emerging disconnection, and to their misfortune, the veterans of Vietnam were hit with the full force of this.

In relieving the nation of any legal sense of obligatory service, we have fought our recent wars with all volunteer personnel. Some disconnection between much of the nation and those who choose to serve remains evident. In giving the veterans and their families a chance to speak to us, this book offers readers an opportunity to connect with these men and women who have chosen to serve under our flag and in the name of our nation. At the same time, these contributions offer quality reading and the history of each war represented here will be all the more complete because of them.

Lawrence E. Breeze, PhD
Emeritus Professor of History
Southeast Missouri State University

Introduction

All books come to us through a journey combined with a quest. The author or authors write to explore a topic and to bring their vision to light; they're often driven to do so, because writing is not always easy. It's a quest complete with its own versions of dragons, villains, sidekicks, and characters, and its pathway to victory is on the slippery slopes of human language. When the writer's quest becomes a mission accomplished, the fledgling book, still a manuscript, embarks upon a journey toward the light, toward being brought to light and to a wider audience by the fluid and finicky business we call "publishing."

This anthology you hold is no exception regarding quest and journey, but it is in many ways exceptional.

The writers' voices you will hear are many, as are their quests. Each voice has accomplished a mission: becoming a completed work by or about exceptional Americans who have served their country. Each work has travelled miles to reach you, both in actual distance and the metaphoric distance of someone else's life lived—in this case—on the tough road of wartime experience. The writers were moved to share what they have seen and heard, what they know and feel in heart and gut. And it takes a lot of both heart and guts to share these stories and thoughts.

The book journeyed to you by way of organizations that believe in thanking and supporting our veterans. It started with Geoff Giglierano, Executive Director of the Missouri Humanities Council, and Deb Marshall, President of The Missouri Writers' Guild, pairing up to launch a pilot program: The Missouri Warrior Writers Project. The Project, coordinated by occupational therapist Rita Reichert, featured creative writing workshops in veterans hospitals to promote self-expression and confidence, with laptops provided by Missouri Humanities Council and writing instruction by Deb Marshall.

The workshops metamorphosed into a new organization called Warriors Arts Alliance and into a new project that would be an extension of the workshops: a published anthology. The Missouri Humanities Council and Warriors Arts Alliance extended their partnership to include Southeast Missouri State University Press and its director Dr. Susan Swartwout, who edited and published the anthology with funding from the Missouri Humanities Council. The project blossomed further to include writing from veterans and their families from across the nation and a writing contest, judged by stellar writers Mark Bowden (*Black Hawk Down*), William Trent Pancoast (*WILDCAT*), and soldier-poet Brian Turner (*Here, Bullet* and *Phantom Noise*). And finally, the title of the anthology emerged, from veterans' comments about the pride they feel in serving their country, as *Proud To Be: Writing by American Warriors*. While the 2012 anthology's journey has reached its destination in your hands, this important, reaffirming project continues to grow.

The Missouri Humanities Council and Warriors Arts Alliance will continue to both offer and expand the confidence-building work of the writing workshops. The anthology will become an annual series published by Southeast Missouri State University Press, with the mission to increase its reach to an even larger audience, and a dedicated, informational website is in the works. The Missouri Humanities Council hopes to expand the partnership to include additional organizations that are both concerned and supportive of American veterans.

Thank you to all our veterans, from everyone involved, for allowing us the privilege of hearing your voices.

—Susan Swartwout

Winners of the Warriors Anthology
Writing Competition

Nonfiction
Judged by Mark Bowden, author of *Black Hawk Down*

Winner: Paul Mims for "Rockhappy 1944-45"
From Mark Bowden:
An account of the writer's experiences deployed to Midway Island during World War II, it is very skillfully written and thus a delight to read. There is no hint of cliché or cloying sentiment here, just wit, careful observation, and concise storytelling. It captures the author's predicament not by turning inward but with deft portraits of those around him—the foolhardy pilot who gets himself and others killed flying a stunt over the airstrip, the male friend who makes a pass at him, the master sergeant who goes mad, the bawdy female USO entertainer who triggers a riot by alluding a little too directly to the men's volcanic sexual frustration. A joy to read.

Finalists: Jarrod L. Taylor for "Sadr City" and Jimmy Castellanos for "Desert Snow"

Poetry
Judged by Brian Turner, author of *Here, Bullet* and *Phantom Noise*

Winner: Gerardo Mena for "Baring the Trees"
"Baring the Trees" shows great economy of language, a sure sense of line and rhythm, and features a timeless voice. It is a highly memorable poem—in the tradition of Carl Sandburg's "Grass" and Matsuo Basho's "Summer grasses— / All that remains / Of soldiers' visions." This is wisdom poetry, the poetry of warning, in the vein of the Hungarian poet János Pilinszky's, "Harbach, 1944." It is a poem of recognition, of desolation, of resignation—one in which the use of repetition and tone underlines the poem's theme at a musical level. I look forward to reading more of this poet's work in the future.

Finalists: Carol Alexander for "Rewind" and Bill Glose for "Desert Moon"

Fiction
Judged by William Trent Pancoast, author of *WILDCAT*

Winner: Monty Joynes for "First Day at An Khe"
"First Day at An Khe" is an odyssey of a medic's first days in Viet Nam: Phil Warren working to exhaustion in triage in the biggest fire fight the base hospital has had to deal with thus far in the war. He was put on duty by the First Sergeant and never logged in, never relieved in triage for over two and a half days because no one even knew he was there. The story builds tremendous momentum, and in the course of the odyssey, the author compacts the elements of a tour of duty into Phil's triage experience—battle, religion, life, death, comradeship, service, courage, compassion, anger, duty, humor, and the loss of self. This is a fine story and I thank the author for the experience of reading it.

Finalists: Edie Cottrell Kreisler for "Remembering Cu Chi" and Ryan Smithson for "Tap Shoes"

Best Writing from a Missouri Writer
Judged by Missouri Humanities Council

Winner: Jay Harden for "Between Wives"

Fiction Winner

Monty Joynes

First Day at An Khe

The 270-mile flight to An Khe in the rolling coastal plains was hot on the crowded Air Force C-130. Phil and the other replacements assigned to the flight found seats around the cargo that was lashed down in the huge plane's bay. There was no way to see the country below, so Phil leaned against his duffel bag and tried not to think of what he might do if the aircraft took hits from ground fire. In the thirty hours that Phil had waited for his hop to the 1st Cav base, he had seen the lightning of shellfire around the Saigon airbase.

When the ramp opened, Phil and the others filed off into a hot, dusty afternoon. The heat and humidity were exceeded only by the dust clouds kicked up by the helicopters. Phil had never seen so much helicopter activity. The sound of them was everywhere. He was used to the Hueys used for medevacs, but the Cav had huge Chinooks and Cranes and gun ships of every description.

A sergeant was yelling at him. "Get your gear on that truck, goddamn it! Let's clear this area."

The truck made two stops in a tent city that seemed to cover acres of the landscape before Phil's turn came. Two other replacements got off at Phil's stop; one was a medical records specialist, and the other was a cook. The pyramidal orderly room tent had a dirt floor and a makeshift arrangement of field desks, typewriter tables, filing cabinets, and chairs. The lights were bare bulbs strung from the roof poles. The only reassuring color in the room was the red glow of the light on a coffee urn sitting atop an artillery shell crate.

"I guess you're the replacements," a clerk said to them. "You've arrived at a hell of a moment. I don't have time to process you in right now. Find a seat and stay out of the way."

"What's going on?"

"The Division is in a hell of a fire fight up country. We're taking mass casualties, and the hospital is pure chaos."

The new men, out of place in their class-A uniforms, looked at each other and then found seats in the hot orderly room tent.

Suddenly, a large man rushed into the tent. Phil recognized the abundance of stripes on his sleeve and guessed that he was the First Sergeant of the Hospital Company.

"Who are these people?" he demanded from his clerks.

"They're replacements, First Sergeant. Just got in. I haven't even had time to look at their orders."

"Any medics? Is either one of you a medic? I need a medic."

"I'm a corpsman, Sergeant," Phil admitted.

"Good. You're coming with me."

Then he turned to the clerks. "We need medics, and we need blood. Get me some volunteers. You can start with these two. March them down to the hospital as soon as you can."

Phil could smell the carnage before he could see it. The First Sergeant trotted ahead of him, leading them through a maze of tents. Phil recognized medevac choppers landing above the tents just ahead, and then they rounded a large hospital tent and Phil saw the triage. Doctors and medics worked among the wounded on the ground while litter carriers shuffled the bodies in and out of the confusion. Everyone except the wounded seemed to be yelling. The closer Phil got, the more horrible details came into focus. The First Sergeant gripped him roughly by the arm when he stopped in awe of the scene.

"This is what you're here for, goddamn it. Now shake it off. You've got to go to work."

Phil was handed over to a master sergeant who was too busy to do anything but push him toward a doctor who had just risen from a litter.

"Here's some more help, sir."

There were no introductions. Someone passed Phil and pushed a canvas bag of supplies into his chest. He knelt beside the doctor and, for the first time, got the full view of a traumatic casualty. The soldier on the litter was missing his right leg below the knee. Fragments of white bone could be seen protruding from the pulpy mass of bloody flesh at the stump.

"Give him 75 milligrams of Demerol. I need a fresh pressure bandage and something to elevate the leg. Get me an IV started."

Phil found the Demerol in the supply bag. Fortunately, as he looked up from preparing the injection, he saw an IV team, and he, too, became part of the clamor.

"IV! IV! Over here."

Phil cut the sleeve off the private's uniform and hesitated before plunging the needle into the arm. The doctor had found the pressure bandage and was tying it off around the wound. Phil was surprised at how little blood was actually oozing from the stump. He used the soldier's pistol belt with its two canteens still attached as a wedge to raise the limb.

"Get him to surgery," the doctor said as he moved to the next litter.

Phil rose to one knee and searched for a litter team.

"Litter! Litter!" he shouted to no one specifically.

A bloody hand gripped his shirt. Phil jerked away in fright. Then his eyes followed the arm until he saw the patient's face for the first time. The face was filthy with dust and streaks of blood that had been transferred from the bloody hands. His eyes were dazed in shock and from the morphine he had received in the field.

"I know it's gone. They couldn't even find my boot. It was a mortar. They got a lot of us, didn't they? Those goddamn Charlies."

Phil tried to remember what he had been taught to say to a patient in shock. What were some of the reassuring phrases they learned at Fort Sam?

"Litter! Litter!" was all that came to his lips.

"Did PJ make it?" the bloody hand asked.

"PJ?" Phil said absently.

"My buddy. PJ. He got hit, too. I'm going to make it. I sure hope PJ makes it. I'm going to make it, ain't I?"

"Sure you're going to make it. I'm going to get you a ride here in a minute. Litter! Litter! And you're going to be fine."

A litter team finally responded to Phil's frantic waving and carried the infantry private to the surgery.

Phil lost track of his doctor but saw another calling for a corpsman. He picked up his supply bag and stepped between the bodies to reach the doctor's side.

"Get me a cut-down set and some fluids."

Phil saw the doctor holding the remains of a hand. The fingers were gnarled and charred a dry lamp-black. Twisted bones and flesh, torn by some cataclysmic event, communicated a sudden queasiness to his stomach. He was glad to run for the nearest IV team to collect the needed supplies.

While the doctor worked to start the IV, he told Phil to look for other wounds. There were tears in the pants, and as he cut away the cloth, he revealed many small but nasty wounds. The pieces of shrapnel were still visible in punctures and lacerations. Phil found others above the waist.

"That's debridement room stuff. Don't worry about that now. Mark him for surgery, first on the hand."

Phil noted four fat black bulges on the exposed leg and brought them to the doctor's attention.

"Are these hematomas, sir?"

"Hematomas? For Christ sake, how long have you been around here? Those are goddamn leeches."

The stench of the wounded was making Phil nauseated, as if the sights he had already seen inches away from his face were not enough to induce vomiting. An odor he came to identify as the smell of burned flesh was a new, piercing sensation. It was mixed with the more familiar emanations of human sweat, urine, and feces.

Phil did not know where to focus his vision when he was not giving a shot, holding up an IV bottle, or updating a medevac tag. The only thing he dreaded more than facing the wounds was looking into the faces of the wounded. He was afraid of what they might see on his face. He was initially so sick to his stomach that he could hardly walk. Then an ambulatory trooper with a bullet wound in the shoulder vomited on him as he helped the doctor make an examination. Phil turned as if he had been shot, fell to his knees, and retched until his stomach had nothing else to offer up. No one other than the wounded trooper seemed to notice.

"I'm sorry," he said to Phil as the medic regained his composure.

"I'm sorry, too," Phil said, still shaking involuntarily from his protesting abdominal muscles. "This is my first day."

"I wondered why you were in your class-A's."

"Yeah. Well, I think I'll burn these tomorrow. Can I have some of your water?"

The trooper used his good arm to offer Phil his canteen. The water was hot, but Phil welcomed it to rinse his mouth of the foul bile taste. He looked up to see the young staff sergeant nodding at him.

"Go ahead, drink your fill. I'll get some more. The doc said you would show me to the debriding room, or something. I guess they've got to probe for whatever hit me. I hope that morphine I got in the field lasts until they finish."

For a second, standing amid the dying and the maimed, they exchanged a smile and soon parted, never knowing each other's name.

Phil continued to be intimidated by each new patient, although he was giving shots without hesitation, directing cases from the triage to other areas of the hospital, and putting his hands on the supplies the doctors called for. As soon as he had carried out the doctor's orders on a patient and had seen him dispatched to surgery or another service, he would respond to the nearest doctor and help with a new case. The doctors did not wait for Phil to finish before they moved to another body. Phil knew that *they* had the harder job. They had to make the decisions about who went to surgery first. The assignment in triage was to save lives by rapid diagnosis and by-the-book screening. Wounded who could be saved by immediate surgery went first. Cases that required surgery, but were not life-threatened by waiting, were given a lower priority. Pain was not a factor.

Phil's uniform lost all identity when viewed from the front. It could have been any color or hidden any rank. There was no part of it left unstained by blood or worse. Phil's hands were dark and sticky with clotted blood. He still put his dirty hands over raw wounds to stop the outpouring of blood that sometimes happened when the doctor probed a wound or removed a pressure dressing.

There was no way that his training at Fort Sam, or his ward experiences at Fort Dix, could have prepared him for mass casualties and the horror of the triage. Phil wanted to scream. His head was splitting in a sharp blade of pain that dominated the space above his eyes. His mouth tasted like a field shithouse. He was sure that he had already had the runs in his pants. He still fought off waves of nausea. Just when he thought that his nose had had its olfactory senses blocked out by the constant assault of stench, a new threshold would be established with another piercing, ugly aroma.

If he had been able to scrape the crystal on his watch, he would have been aware that he had worked over fifteen hours, throughout the night, and still the helicopters landed and disgorged the dead, the dying, and the disfigured. Already he hated the sound of them. The *wop-wop-wopping* of their blades, and the dust and sand whirlwinds associated with their landing.

He was weak from hunger and thirst, but he felt he could never eat again until he was clean of the gore on his body. His hair and brows were matted with it. His three-day beard captured it and bound it to his face.

He found a moment to rest, and someone handed him a paper cup full of steaming coffee. It was late morning. Already 90 degrees. There were flies everywhere. He sat in the dirt and leaned against a tent pole. In spite of his tense stomach, he began to drink the coffee. Ants and unnamed insect creatures crawled across his outstretched legs and paused to feast off the products of war. Phil did not even attempt to brush them away. He wondered if he himself was going into shock. Sometime last night, he shot 50 milligrams of Thorazine into the arm of a hysterical young rifleman. Phil considered giving himself a similar shot.

The next hours were more of the same organized chaos. Phil saw many of the same types of wounds over and over. He began to anticipate what the doctors needed, and they worked better as a team.

Phil saw many sucking chest wounds where a shell had penetrated a man's chest cavity, causing the lung to collapse. The entry and exit wounds had to be sealed with a Vaseline gauze dressing. The sound of the air being sucked through the wound made a whistling sound. Frothy blood sputtered from the ragged holes. Phil assisted in the placing of a

Kelly clamp on several cases. The fact that most of the patients were conscious—and even talkative—during the procedure made him wince every time the probe ripped through the chest-cavity membrane with a pop, and blood shot out its top. The Kelly clamp provided chest drainage so that the patient would not drown in his own fluids. It was held in place with a few quick sutures, and a drainage tube was attached.

Phil learned rapidly the significance of fixed dilated pupils. He saw the remains of boys who looked more like a bundle of rags than mortals. He got angry when he saw them being brought into the triage on the canvas litters.

"Don't put that down there," he finally shouted at a litter team just about to lower the stump of a body. It had no arms or legs visible.

"Fuck you," said the young private who was obviously a Cav rifleman. "Everybody that comes off those choppers is going to see a doctor. We ain't taking no wounded straight to Graves. Do you understand me? I'll get my fucking M-16 if I have to!"

"Hey, easy, man. We're not fucking over anybody. We're on your side," Phil reassured him.

"You a doctor?"

"No. I'm a corpsman."

"Well, do something then. At least see if he's alive, for God's sake!" the nervous soldier said in passion.

Phil did not want to face the pitiful remains of the man at his feet, but he realized that he could not run from the confrontation with the litter bearer. As he started to his knees, he caught sight of a metallic cross hanging around the belligerent soldier's neck. The man had been constantly fingering it since he had put the body down.

Phil searched for the remnants of the victim's head and placed his hand on what had been the neck. There was no pulsation. The medevac tag said KIA, initials scrawled on the form by a medic far away in the elephant grass of the highlands. Phil paused, head down, still on his knees, wondering how he was going to console them. Then he straightened his back and made the sign of the cross. He was not a Catholic, and he hoped that he had gotten the directions of the sign in the right order. Then he looked up into the faces of the infantrymen.

"I'm sorry, he's gone."

The one with the neck chain crossed himself devoutly.

"Shit," he said in dejection, "I knew he was dead. But it just ain't right to rush him over to Graves without somebody doing something. He was a man. Maybe he was a Catholic, like us. A priest, somebody, ought to say something. Anything."

"I can't stay here, guys. I've got to help the doctors. Why don't you say a 'Hail Mary' while you're taking him over to Graves. I'll say one as soon as I can."

The two litter carriers picked up their load and began the "Hail Mary" as they walked away. Phil saw a doctor beckon to him, and as he moved, he tried to remember the Catholic prayer without success. Maybe it was the wrong prayer anyway. Wasn't there a prayer, a special prayer, that Catholics say at the time of their death? Phil was raised a Baptist; how should he know? But he felt no pride in having deceived the litter bearers. For one of the few times in the last mad hours, he had actually given comfort to another human being. Comfort that was not dispensed from the tip of a syringe. He wished he could give himself the comfort of religion. A religion that could explain the waste and slaughter of humanity.

Sometime during that night, Phil fainted from extreme fatigue. He was not the first to falter because of the long hours without rest or relief. Some 20 hours before Phil collapsed, the hospital Sergeant Major had established 15-hour shifts for enlisted hospital personnel. But since Phil's name was not on the Sergeant Major's duty roster, he was never relieved. A few doctors and medics knew Phil's face from the two and a half days he had been in the triage, but no one knew his name or claimed responsibility for him.

The First Sergeant had forgotten about Phil, and as far as the orderly room was concerned, he was AWOL.

Phil woke on a canvas litter suspended by its wooden poles between two crates of medical supplies. He had been put out of harm's way in a supply tent and forgotten again. As his sensibilities recovered from their somnambulistic flight, he became acutely aware of the outrageous stench of his own body and uniform. A close second to this indignity was the parched ugliness inside his mouth. His entire frame ached, and it was with balancing difficulty that he managed to free himself from the litter without falling face down on the dirt floor.

Phil did not recognize his whereabouts nor did he remember how he came to be there. His last recollection was calling for an IV team. He was dazed as if drunk. He stumbled toward the tent flap and the sound of a driving rain making pools beyond the door.

Outside, he found himself behind the main hospital. Whoever stacked him in the supply tent had had a long carry. The rain was refreshing. Phil suddenly had the urge to rid his body of its filth. He could not find his shirt buttons under the hardened globs of blood and muck so in desperation he ripped the garment away from his chest and flung it away from his body. He walked a few yards away from the shirt and plopped down in the mud like a drunk. His shoelaces were caked in dried blood, so he kicked at the heels until they were forced off his feet. Next came the socks and the khaki pants. He flung them away. He used mud by the handfuls as an abrasive to wash away the clotted black blood from his hands and arms. The process was a slow one, but finally he saw his own flesh appearing from under its ghoulish covering. He mud-scrubbed his face and neck, and then lay back on the ground to let the rainwater fill his gaping mouth. He lay soaking, rinsing in the heavy monsoon rain until he was no longer thirsty.

His formerly white-boxer, army-issue shorts were blood stained around the waistband. The seat contained the results of Phil's diarrhea. Two days' worth. He peeled the repugnant garment away from his back-side—and was going to cast it away—but reconsidered. He turned them inside out and washed them in the nearest mud hole. By the time he finished scrubbing the cloth against itself and the gritty mud, the stains of blood and diarrhea looked alike. Malevolent brown. He held the pants in front of him to rinse in the rain and then put them on to cover his nakedness.

If anyone observed Phil during his antics in the rain, they never reported it or mentioned it to him.

Phil searched for the nearest army authority. He was disoriented but heard voices from a tent and found an NCO.

"I'm reporting back to duty," he said to the astounded sergeant as he walked into the tent out of the rain.

The sergeant paused, seeking a reference in his mind, and then said in carefully measured, almost melodic tones, "That's fine, son. I think I know where you belong. Wait a minute, and I'll take you over there myself."

Phil nodded. The sergeant found his poncho and turned the ward tent over to a medic who had been smiling unnaturally at Phil since his arrival.

Phil followed the sergeant through a maze of large, dark tents until the NCO opened the door flap of one and ushered him inside.

"Somebody's ass is going to be in a sling," the sergeant said to the Psychiatric Ward attendant who greeted them. "I just found one of your patients wandering around the area."

It took little explaining and a bed check of the Psych patients to convince two sergeants that Phil was newly assigned to the hospital company.

"All my gear is still at the orderly room. I haven't even signed in yet," Phil reminded them.

"Your ass is in a world of shit, trooper," said one sergeant.

"I told you, I've been in the triage ever since I got here. The First Shirt put me to work over there and then never came back. I was never relieved. Is the battle still going on?"

The rain had stopped the major combat assaults by the First Cav. Helicopters don't fly well in heavy rains. So things were caught up in triage, and the hospital was in a state of exhaustion. Those still on duty prayed for continuing rain so they could get their turns at sleep.

They gave Phil directions to the orderly room; and before he departed the Psych Ward, one of the sergeants said with a leer, "The First Shirt is going to love this."

On his way to the orderly room, Phil wanted to avoid being seen out of uniform. Staying off the main streets of the hospital area, which had become soupy mud flats, Phil picked his way over tent ropes and around tent pegs toward his destination. Behind one of the tents, he discovered a pile of cast-off field gear. From the damaged condition of the webbing, pistol belts, canteens, ammo pouches, and packs, he guessed that the equipment had accumulated from the battle casualties.

Seeing no on-lookers, Phil began to pick among the packs in search of food. There were many cans of C-rations undamaged. Phil may not have known the location of the mess tent, but he was not going to be hungry any longer. The tiny metal can opener with its collapsible blade opened first a can of peaches and then a can of soda crackers. Phil found peaches in three different packs. The First Cav must sure like peaches, he thought, as he found a comfortable backrest amid the discarded equipment.

Phil did not feel ridiculous sitting in his underwear, eating three cans of peaches in the rain. The peaches were sweet, with just a hint of pucker. He drank the heavy syrup, and it changed the vile taste in his mouth to nectar. He forgot with the pleasure in his mouth that the men who had carried the peaches were probably dead.

When Phil appeared in the orderly room tent, the First Sergeant was startled enough by the sight to spill his coffee.

"Who the hell are you?" he demanded, after inspecting Phil at close range.

"I'm Warren, the new replacement."

"Well, Warren, the new replacement, you sure as hell need a shave, and you are definitely out of uniform."

"He's AWOL, too, Sarge," one of the clerks said.

"I am not AWOL, either," Phil shot back. "Don't you remember me? The day I arrived, you dragged me over to triage."

"Don't point your finger at me, boy," the Sergeant replied. "Is this your gear over here?"

Phil saw his duffel bag and service cap in a corner of the tent. "It looks like it."

"Well, where the hell have you been, Warren? And where is your goddamn uniform?"

Phil erupted.

"It's so fucking covered with blood and brains and shit, real human shit from gut wounds, and vomit, and sweat . . . it's so fucking foul that I couldn't stand to wear it! You left me in that Godforsaken triage until I dropped, Sergeant. I don't even know what day of the week it is! I'm no fucking trainee. I'm a goddamn medic, and I've been proving it over and over and over again on your mass casualties. Where in the fuck were you when I was up to my ass in other people's blood and guts? Your uniform looks too fucking clean to me. You want to see my uniform? You want to smell it? I'll get the goddamn thing for you if you're so concerned about my uniform." Phil turned and started walking for the door.

"Wait a minute. Calm down. Wait a minute, goddamn it!"

Phil stopped and turned at the doorway. The First Sergeant's voice softened.

"I remember something now. I guess I did put you into the triage." The Sergeant paused. "I guess I forgot about you, too. Come over here and sit down . . . please."

Phil went limp again after the injection of anger that had caused him to stiffen. He limped across the tent floor and dropped into a metal folding chair that the sergeant offered.

"Have you had any chow?" the NCO asked.

"I don't even know where the mess tent is," Phil answered without looking up.

"Look, Warren," the Sergeant said quietly bending over him, "we just fought the biggest battle of the war, and we took a lot of casualties. No one was prepared for it. Things got a little crazy around here. You got the shaft. I'm sorry."

Phil continued to slump in his chair and remained silent. He seemed to have no more energy to move or to speak.

The Sergeant ordered his clerks to assign Phil a bed in one of the enlisted hooches and to find him some food. Then he poured the near-naked Private First Class a cup of coffee.

"The hospital CO wants to put all the men who worked the triage up for the Army Commendation Medal," the top kick said as he handed Phil the coffee mug. "You might get yourself a decoration on your first day here."

"Can't do it, Top," the remaining clerk in the tent said. "According to the Morning Report, Warren was not a member of the unit during the Plei Me action. We've been carrying him AWOL for the last three days."

"Shut up Dozier, will you?" the First Sergeant snarled over his shoulder.

"We'll pick him up on the Morning Report tomorrow, Sarge. But until then, he's not officially here, so he can't qualify for any. . ."

The Sergeant interrupted his studious company clerk who was cleaning his government-issued, brown-framed glasses over the keys of his typewriter. "Didn't I tell you to cut it off?"

Then to Phil he said, "Warren, I want you to take the rest of the day off. Take your time getting settled and report back here tomorrow after midday chow. Why don't you get into your gear there and find yourself a pair of fatigues. The company commander might wander in here, and we'd have a lot of explaining to do. Aren't you a little chilly? Being wet, and all? Wouldn't you feel better in your uniform?"

One of the clerks returned out of the rain with a small box in his hands.

"The cooks wouldn't give me any A-rations until chow call, Top, but I got a box of C's."

The Sergeant opened the box, examined the labels on the cans, and selected one to open.

"You're in luck, Warren," he said as he opened the can. "Here's the best thing they ever put into a C-ration carton. One of these in the field will get you three or four of anything else. I know this is going to taste real good to you about now."

He handed the open can to Phil. "They're peaches, son. Sliced peaches. Go ahead. You can drink them right out of the can."

Monty Joynes (www.montyjoynes.com) began a writing career under the mentorship of George Garrett at the University of Virginia. As a graduate student in Sweden, Monty made movies instead of grades and was drafted into the Vietnam War-era Army where he served with the 91st Evacuation Hospital. After a career as an editor and publisher of magazines and books, he began to write novels and non-fiction. Eighteen of his books have been published.

Edie Cottrell Kreisler

Remembering Cu Chi
August, 1968

The soldiers of the 25th Infantry Division, the ones who made it back to the base at Cu Chi, all had their rituals to perform. Private Henry Loomis always dumped out the contents of his rucksack so that he could make a list of what he would need before his next mission. *LifeSavers, a carton of Camels, a tube of Colgate.* Even a pack of Wrigley's spearmint gum took up space and added weight.

The trick was to wedge in not only the canteens and C-rations but also the things that helped you keep your head screwed on. In his last letter, Johnny had told him to sneak in a pair of light wool gloves to protect his hands against the cold of night. Since his best friend always knew what he was talking about, Henry tucked the right-hand glove around the flashlight. He lodged the left one between the first-aid kit his mother had fashioned in an old bandage tin and the eight-bladed Swiss army knife he'd discovered in Louie's Secondhand Bonanza when he was eleven.

Unlike almost every other grunt, Henry did not have to pack a stick of bug repellant. Even as a boy in Red Wolf, Texas, he could run around the Moonlight Camper Park in cut-off jeans and a sleeveless T-shirt, and the pesky blood suckers never targeted his bare arms and legs the way they did his sister Dolores. With that small space freed up, Henry could squeeze in the sterling silver ID bracelet. He turned it over now and traced the single word engraved on the back, *DIANA.*

"It's a hunk of silver, man," Paul Hines said.

Henry eyed the big, sandy-haired man lying on the bunk to his left. "Shove it, Paul, or someone might think you're jealous."

"Yeah, like I want to save myself for some broad back home. No thanks, I'll take my R&R."

Henry crammed the bracelet back into its place. His eyes were growing heavy as he finished jotting down the list. Three days in the field, and he'd swear he'd never been so tired. Heaven, that's what it would be, to stretch out on his cot. He stripped to the waist, barely flinching when he peeled back his fatigues from the dried-up layer matted to his chest. How much was mud and how much sweat and blood, Henry couldn't tell you, and right now, he didn't much care.

Ah, Diana.

Paul was a jerk. What did he know about love?

Please stay by me, Diana, Henry mouthed the words to their song.

He shut his eyes and let the waves of exhaustion roll over him. If only he could sleep. He knew he couldn't dwell on what had happened out there on patrol, not for a second.

Ah, too late, too damn late.

He was back in the trench, the men on either side so close they could barely point their weapons outward. Even if his life depended on it, he wouldn't be able to grab the hand grenades or rounds of ammo lodged at his feet. It was twilight, yet still so hot the sweat rolled down from under his helmet.

What the—?

He could swear the shrubs beyond the perimeter had just inched closer. Fire jetted out from the sparse branches and landed all around. RAT-A-TAT-TAT! The enemy towered over him, shooting into the trench. Henry pulled the trigger, too, without taking aim. RAT-A-TAT-TAT! He felt something hot and sticky soaking through his fatigues. Chrissake, what a smell!

When the barrage finally stopped, except for a single PING here and there, Henry heard voices at the far end of the bunker. He opened his mouth to call out but discovered his voice had frozen. As the jabbering got louder, he tried to make out the words. Ah, of course. Gook-talk! Friggin' gook-talk. Closer now, the high-pitched voices combined with an odd thumping sound. Motherofgod, the SOBs must be poking their rifle butts into the Americans.

He craned his neck, but his helmet had lodged at an odd angle that covered his eyes. An arm from the soldier on his left jutted across his mouth and chin. Only the tip of Henry's nose, by some stroke of luck, protruded from the carnage. He reckoned he had one chance to convince the enemy they'd done their job.

He heard the ZING of the bullet before it grazed his helmet.

Screw this!

A second shot thumped hard right into the sandbag in front of him. Shock waves coursed through his neck and down his spine. Another and another, faster and faster, until a spray of bullets rained down.

So now it was his turn. What had been the good of living those extra minutes? Would someone *please* tell him that? Why not just get it over with? Quick and easy, like it had happened to Johnny.

Finally, everything was still.

Then a new sound: footsteps.

And again, silence.

Was he alive? He took stock of his immobilized body. And slowly, he understood. Somehow the remains of the men around him had taken the bullets meant for him.

He waited for a long while until the dark of night made the earlier blackness even darker. The soldiers who had saved his life were weighing him down. He twisted his hips and freed his right arm. Disentangling his limbs was not as difficult as he'd imagined. There, he could move his left arm, too. The liquid that poured out of the other men was cooler now. The smell was different, still nauseating, but different. Henry grabbed the arm lodged across his mouth. When he saw it was just a piece of blood-soaked tissue and bone, he finally found his voice.

He hustled now, clawing his way out of the trench.

Whoever was screaming like that?

Once he'd freed his legs, he stood there in the sand that had spilled out of the bullet-riddled bags and examined what he could of his body. The hot blood had long since congealed, but none of it seemed to be his own. When he ran his fingers across his face and discovered his mouth wide open, he forced it shut. So *that*'s what all the screaming was about. The Lord have mercy.

He walked halfway down the trench.

"Hey, soldier," he called. "Is someone alive in there?"

When he heard a soft moan, he grabbed at the half-empty bags and started digging.

All told, there were twelve who walked away, twelve out of fifty-seven.

Why twelve? That's what Henry asked himself as he lay there on the cot and the smell of hot blood came back to him. Twelve months of the year. Twelve hours of the day and of the night. Twelve eggs to the carton. Even twelve signs of the zodiac, if you believed in that stuff. Twelve knights of the Round Table and twelve disciples.

Whatever magic the number possessed didn't last long. By the time they made it back to the base, two of the dozen had died, and Lieutenant Campbell had cut off Spike Monroe's leg when they couldn't stop the bleeding.

Enough!

Let it go, man.

Please stay by me, Diana.

He felt himself drifting off, but then he heard Sarge yell MAIL CALL and was suddenly wide awake.

It had been a week since Diana's last letter made its way to Cu Chi.

34

Henry never got used to the waiting. With all his heart, he wished she'd write more often. What he longed for even more was that she'd let herself go. Just a little mush, what could be wrong with that? Instead, it was all about her kitties or her stupid brother or, worse, the courses she was going to take in her sophomore year at UT. Whatever was *macroeconomics*? And those friggin' cats! Who the hell cared!

Funny thing was that he was so damn grateful to hear from Diana, he always forgave her. When the letters finally came, time stood still. The sight of the schoolgirl handwriting that had penned his address was all it took. He forgot about the invisible enemy he was forever pursuing. Not even the rumble of distant artillery intruded on his thoughts.

Long before the officer reached him, Henry could see the familiar pink envelope. Once he had the treasure in hand, he waited until Sarge had passed him. His fingers glided over the envelope, like a blind man's deciphering Braille. The packet seemed light, a small disappointment but, hey, no big deal. He held the letter to his face so that he could breathe in the faint whiff of Shalimar that smelled like Diana. From his footlocker, he retrieved the small stack of pink envelopes bound with a long red ribbon. Next came Diana's picture, the one where she'd posed in her bikini, oh yeah, the Saturday before he'd left for boot camp. His beautiful, beautiful girl. God, how he loved her. *Please stay by me, Diana.* The time had come to ease open the seal and spread out the pages.

It took only a minute to read what she'd written. Henry tried to make sense of the words while the damp, stinking air closed in around him. I knew it, I knew it, was all he could think. He crumpled the single pink sheet and hurled it to the ground.

Hot tears blurred the tangle of reeking bodies and muddy gear as he stumbled to the front of the barracks. The slightest provocation, and he would've slugged any one of these men. Buddies? Hell, they were nothing but poor, dumb bastards, just like him. Not a one of them could hold a candle to Johnny, and he'd been dead and gone since February.

Outside, Henry gazed up at the angry, lead-gray sky. The wind whipped through the scorched-out peanut fields, looped along the row of latrines, and then slammed him against the drab olive tent. He tried to put distance between himself and the men he'd rushed past, but with every step, the muddy field sucked his boots deep below ground level. Even here in camp, the earth had turned to a thick orange sludge, the color of the taffy he used to eat back home.

Henry jumped as a metallic clap of thunder announced the first big drops of rain. The instant cascade struck his body in waves, drenching him in an instant. Though he'd cursed the monsoons for weeks, the shimmering sheets of water, slicing sideways at his bare chest, seemed to cleanse him now.

Saigon: average annual rainfall, 81 inches. Hue: 116 inches. The statistics in the Compton's *Pictured Encyclopedia* came back to him while the deluge pelted his body like thousands of dummy bullets. He could just as well stand here forever. All those flooded rice paddies he'd trudged through, all those hours immobilized in that bloody trench— what the hell did this lousy war matter? What did anything matter? First Johnny, and now Diana. His life was over, plain and simple.

Back inside, he yanked open his footlocker. A lot of good the Polaroid snapshot taped to the lid would do him now. Johnny, standing there in full-dress uniform with his arm around Dolores, who was dressed in a white wedding gown like she was still a virgin. Henry and Diana, flanking them—all four beaming like idiots. What a fool he'd been to think the magic of that moment could last.

He slammed the lid shut.

Yeah, a big fat lot of good.

Johnny Ramos, the best friend the likes of Henry was ever going to have on this earth. By the time he got to high school, Johnny could step foot into a room, and you'd think he was Moses parting the Red Sea. Men, women, children—to a person, they marched to his command. And now? Gone. Poof! Just like that.

And Henry? He might just as well have died with the others out there on patrol, all right. Every guy in the company would be all over him the minute word spread that his girl had sent him a friggin' *Dear John*. It wouldn't matter one drop that he'd just helped dig the others out of that trench. Or that he'd been the one to hold down Spike so the lieutenant could do what he had to do with that leg. No, he'd be right back to square one, a dumb spic from Texas.

He smoothed out the wrinkled pink stationery.

Dear Henry,

I'm sorry to tell you this way, but I won't be writing anymore. It's not because I've met someone. It's just too hard being apart. Before you left, you said you didn't want to be just friends when I told you that's what I feel we should be. I never said I'd marry you, but that's all you write about. It's like we don't have anything in common. You let yourself get drafted, and now you're stuck there in Vietnam.

Don't get me wrong—I'm sorry you're there. But here I've been getting ready to go back to UT in the fall. Remember Natalie, my friend in Boston? She sent me this anti-war literature from the protests there. Please don't hate me. I can't help it if I think the war's wrong.

Maybe we can be friends again some day. But right now, I don't feel I should be writing you. It won't make any difference if you write or call; I've made up my mind.

I really hope and pray the best for you.

Diana

I never said I'd marry you! He honestly couldn't say whether or not those words were true. He *thought* she'd said she'd marry him. Or was he simply remembering what he wanted to hear? After all, she'd never once written *I love you*. Not once! *Love always*, that's how she'd signed every damn letter before this one. It drove him crazy because he knew it wasn't the same. And she'd never mentioned the kisses, those kisses he couldn't imagine living without. He'd always thought she felt the same. Hell, he'd *swear* to that. They may have been fully dressed—she in those skimpy little short shorts; he in his tight blue jeans—but she'd pressed her body to his the same as he did to hers. He wasn't imagining a damn thing. But maybe the sad truth was nothing more than that *he'd* wed himself to her every time he held her in his arms.

He untied the red ribbon and slapped the pink envelopes down one at a time on top of the footlocker. What did Diana *think*? That she was too good for the sorry likes of him? He should've known better than to hope for one single moment that someone like him could end up with a girl like her. Yeah, he was a fool, all right. A damn fool in love.

Edie Cottrell Kreisler recently retired from a more than thirty-year career teaching English and humanities at Merritt College in Oakland, California. She grew up in San Antonio, Texas, and received her BA from the University of Texas and her MA from the University of California, Berkeley. She is the daughter of an army nurse who served during WWII, while her own coming-of-age was during the Vietnam. "Remembering Cu Chi" is based on an excerpt from "This Thin Line," her novel-in-progress.

Ryan Smithson

Tap Shoes

I carry my tap shoes in my rucksack.

They're comfortable there, in their little black bag with the gold pull-string. They sit nicely among the green socks and brown t-shirts. Rucksacks are bottomless—you might not know that—so there's always room for my tap shoes. There's a little spot for them right behind my little bag of toiletries, my picture of Dad. They look good there, in their little black bag. They've traveled the world with me.

At first they stayed in the States, my tap shoes.

My first pair was little. I was five years old, and they felt unnatural.

I practiced, and they got better. I learned ballet, too. A little bit of jazz. Some ballroom. I did recitals, competitions. Mom and Dad were proud. Well, Mom was proud. Dad was a cop, real man's man. I guess my leotard embarrassed him.

I stuck with tap the longest. Tapped all the way through middle school. Out of all the styles, it was the most fun, the way you almost hover above the floor. It's not so much about "inspiration" or "interpretation," like the other styles. It's raw. It's you and the floor and the beat between them. I loved it, that feeling. All those people watching me from their seats, watching me hover around the stage. I was alive. Really alive.

I could have been a professional, said my teacher. She wasn't lying either.

Once I entered high school, the stigma of a boy tapping around in cute little circles, shuffling and prancing about in flashy outfits, became too much.

I mean, I was thirteen. *Time to grow up*, I thought.

So I tried out for football. My footwork was incredible.

"You're a natural running back," said my coach. "Where'd you learn to be so fluid on your feet?"

"Dance class," I said, and the other guys laughed.

I made varsity my freshman year. Went out for basketball, too. Then track in the spring. I excelled in all of them. Guys would find out about my dancing, then laugh. And then they'd watch my magic out on the field or the court or the track. Some of them got into dance. They learned ballet. They learned how to tap. They learned jazz. And the jitterbug. All just to keep up with me.

Myself? I was too busy for dancing anymore.

My dad died in '01, shortly after graduation.

The last time I talked to him, he called me from his hotel in Boston where he was staying for some sort of conference. He'd be leaving for Los Angeles soon, he said, and then off to Dallas for some training that would help him earn his captain bars. I wouldn't see him for a couple months. Welcome to my childhood.

He was always working, always traveling; always missing football games, dance recitals, Christmas. . .

I said, "Speaking of Boston, Dad, I've been thinking of going to Boston College for fine arts."

He laughed easily and said he "wasn't sure about me." He laughed like he was joking. But a young man gets to a point in life when he can tell whether or not his father is joking.

I never saw Dad again, never got to say goodbye.

I didn't go to college. I joined the army. Don't really know why. Dad always talked about his time in the service. It sounded fun and hard and exciting. He never saw combat, but he traveled the world before he met my mom.

I joined the military police. Don't really know why. Thought I might like the police as a career afterward.

Then the war started.

My tap shoes go everywhere I do in Iraq, comfortable there in my rucksack.

They've been to Samarra and Fallujah. They've been to Mosul and Tikrit. They hate the cities, love the villages. They lie anxiously in my rucksack during fire fights. And rest quietly on perimeter guard.

Once in a while, they come out of my rucksack, my tap shoes. I try them on. Late in the stillness of night when no one will see, the worn leather hugging my feet like a blanket.

Once in a while, I swing them off the edge of my cot, let them hover above the plywood floor of our tent. Touch down softly: *Tip-tap, tip-tap.* And I look around to see if no one noticed.

Once in a while, I make real contact. *Toe, shuffle, heel, toe-stamp, heel, stomp. Tip, clack-clack, thud, tip-tap, thud, knock.* Until someone stirs in their sleeping bag.

Then I stop.

We hit an IED.

That's how it happens. Out of nowhere. Always unexpected. Picture a hijacked jetliner. Picture men in business suits on their way to meetings, women in floral dresses on their way to leisure. Then bam—out of nowhere—a man with a trigger.

We flip. My rucksack goes flying from the Humvee. I climb from the wreckage. Dust everywhere. And blood. And Private Grange.

I try to keep my head straight. All that training crammed in there. Convoy live-fire exercises. Some infantry sergeant back in the States and his speech about PTSD. Some training NCO who warned us that they'll plant an obvious bomb, then plant another where they think we'll regroup. Don't remain complacent, they said. And all the rest of it.

Well, let me tell you, it all goes out the window when you see one of your soldiers, your gunner, your brother, blown apart. I grab my weapon, yank it from the Humvee, and scream at the top of my lungs.

"You fucking coward!" I yell.

I'm yelling at Haji, the asshole who flipped the switch. I'm yelling at my dad. I'm yelling at . . . myself.

I charge to the road, stand in the center—the summit of a mountain. I stand like I own the place. Fire burns behind my skull. The Humvee that was riding behind us pulls up. I can hear their engine and their radio crackling orders to some QRF team somewhere.

"You alright?" asks Staff Sergeant Miller.

I stare into the vast desert, turning to see . . . anything.

"Sarge," says Miller. "You hurt?"

"No," I hear myself say. I am numb, disassociated. "Grange is . . . Grange is fucked up."

I hear Miller run to our toppled Humvee. I hear myself howl "you fucking coward!" into the air again. I hear gunshots from my own rifle. The sky swallows the bullets. There's nothing around for miles. All I see is the curve of the earth. This ugly, brown thing.

Miller yells for a tourniquet. Someone comes running, a CLS with all that kind of medical shit in a bag around his waist. It's no use. Grange is a goner. I can hear him choking on his own, hot blood. I sprint to the edge of the road and dive, head first, into the bushes.

If you didn't know better, you'd think I was being heroic.

I scramble around on my hands and knees, patting the ground for any signs of my rucksack.

Someone yells my name. *One minute*, I say to myself. *I have to find them.*

Dust is everywhere. And jungle-like foliage in my face. The dense thud of the blood pumping through my head. Someone yells my name again. It's my dad's voice.

Forget it. Find the rucksack.

I spot a strap. There in the dried up irrigation ditch, like it's been there for centuries, my ruck sits comfortably. I crawl over and set it free. I pat the dust off. It coats the olive green pack like dust coats everything in Iraq.

Hell isn't full of fire and brimstone. It's full of dust.

I rip the top of the ruck open like a Christmas present, and inside there are socks and underwear. There's brown t-shirts and deodorant. There's a CliffsNotes copy of *Hamlet* and a laminated picture of Dad.

From somewhere in the bushes—peculiar—the sound of an airplane. Within my rucksack, the black bag with a gold pull-string. I yank it open and feel the sting of hot metal. The bottom of the tap shoes—the thing that gives them life—feels, under this Iraqi sun, like jet fuel igniting.

For the first time, I empathize with Dad. For the very first time, I feel the fear he felt. The intimate fear of watching Manhattan pass so closely beneath his window seat in business class. The brutal fear of seeing a streak of dark smoke in the skyline, a sign of things to come. The dark smoke rolling like eternity.

Somewhere in the bushes, Dad yells my name. I grab tightly the hot metal of my tap shoes, that comforting sting of home, of childhood.

The dusty air settles a bit. And I see the wires now. Off to the right, trailing into the bushes.

From an airplane window, from Eternity, finally, Dad says, "I'm proud of you."

Just before the second explosion.

Ryan Smithson was 17 when he joined the Army Reserve. He was deployed to Iraq from 2004-2005 and published his memoir, *Ghosts of War: The True Story of a 19-Year-Old GI*, HarperCollins, in 2009. He lives in upstate New York with his wife and son.

Nonfiction Winner

Paul C. Mims

Rockhappy 1944-45

Think of Midway Island after the great sea battle as a quasi-penal colony of young men without women. With that in mind, our Flight Surgeon, Navy Lieutenant Goldfarb, aka the Cock Scalper, has the enlisted men of Marine fighter squadron VMF 324 line up alongside the runway for a talk on cerebral sex, i.e., enlightened masturbation. "Men," says he, "regardless of what you may have heard, hair will not grow on your palms if you masturbate, nor will the whites of your eyes turn yellow, nor will you go insane or become sterile. If you don't, however, relieve sexual tension you may become temporarily queer. For best results," says he, "imagine you are with the woman of your dreams. The down side," he admits, "is that the real thing when encountered may not live up to expectation."

If you go to sickbay when Doc Goldfarb is on duty, say for an aspirin or a laxative, you get a short-arm inspection and a lecture on the health benefits of circumcision. "Let the Navy pay for it," he advises. Except for this obsession, the doctor is one of the more pleasant officers in the squadron.

Before leaving San Diego, one of the pilots, a tall, pale, freckle-faced, dour Second Lieutenant named Norton, acquires a wild bobcat kitten. His buddies name him Junior. When we ship out, Junior is smuggled aboard ship in a sack. This bush baby is no pussycat. He needs red meat and plenty of it. He gets table scraps. The second day at sea Major Nickels, our CO, discovers Junior. Short of throwing the cat overboard, there isn't much he can do, except raise a little hell with the malefactors. By the time we reach Midway, the novelty of Junior has worn thin. His masters stake him to a chain in back of their BOQ. Occasionally, they poke him with a stick to hear him hiss. They feed him sweets until his teeth rot. Cataracts form over his eyes from the intense sun exposure. His temper, bad to begin with, worsens, and he bites, as best he can, any who come close enough to tease him. Out of pity, Major Nickels orders Doctor Goldfarb to end the cat's misery. Junior is buried on the side of a dune, in a box that shortly before contained Johnny Walker scotch.

Bored, Lt. Norton and his fellow fighter pilots long to test themselves against the enemy, but the nearest Japanese bases are Iwo Jima and Wake Island. Thirty miles west of us is a shoal called Curie, desolate, all but submerged and home to birds and rats. This bit of coral serves as their target on navigation and gunnery runs. Otherwise, when not flying, the pilots play volleyball or lounge on the beach or shoot skeet or hang out in the ready room. At night they drink and wish there were nurses on the island to play with. In their dreams, they fancy themselves warriors the equal of fighter ace Pappy Boynton and his Black Sheep squadron. To demonstrate prowess, they roar down the runway in groups of three, seeing who has the balls to retract his landing-gear first, causing his F4U Corsair, bomb-racks loaded, to settle dangerously near the tarmac. Another sport of theirs is to see who can hold a dive the longest before pulling out.

One noon Second Lieutenant Norton decides to demonstrate his mettle. I am alive to tell the tale because that day I linger at the messhall, chatting with my friend Brownie. Otherwise, I would have been crossing the parking pad in front of the Group repair hangar and ammunition depot when Lt. Norton came crashing through the roof. Instead, I am half way there when I hear the scream of an F4U pulling out of a long dive. Glancing up, I see it roaring in over north beach, maybe a hundred feet off the deck and fifty yards in front of me. Within seconds, it rolls into a split S. Norton must have momentarily blacked out. For an instant before crashing, the plane's nose comes up; vapor trails appear off its wing tips and ***BOOM!*** it slams through the hangar roof, just aft of the entrance. A huge fireball shoots straight up. The hangar door is wide open, allowing most of the blast to escape. Even so, the corrugated metal roof lifts off its foundation for a moment and the sides bulge out without collapsing. Like one caught in a dream, I run toward the inferno. Considering the bombs, ammunition, and high-octane gasoline stored there, the whole place can go up in a flash. This possibility does not occur to me. In the moment, an excitement I can't explain draws me to the sound of men trapped in the hangar, screaming, the smoke and flames, and the live ammunition popping like firecrackers.

Dunes surround the hangar. It is not until I clear them that I see the wall of flames that seals off the hangar entrance. Running toward the parking apron, I pass a corrugated storage hut. I hear sharp sounds like hail hitting metal, and I realize fifty-caliber machine gun bullets are exploding in the flaming wreckage, lacing the air, kicking up little puffs of coral sand, slamming into the tin shack. Still running, it occurs to me that I am in some danger. It is a passing thought. Bullets are firing sporadically when I stop beside an undamaged SPD dive-bomber. Under its wing, face down on the macadam, is a Marine, probably a mechanic blown there by the explosion, his left leg unnaturally twisted over his right shoulder, the jagged edge of a femur bone protruding from the flesh.

The top of his head looks spongy. A small, blue gasoline flame flickers on his butt. There is an odd yellow sheen to his skin. His facial muscles twitch. As though bewitched, I squat beside him, hesitant to touch for fear of doing harm. In the background men inside the hangar scream in one continuous shriek.

Leaning against a strut of the same dive-bomber is a second man. He sits in shock, staring straight ahead, motionless, muttering: "My god! My god!" From behind me someone shouts. Turning, I see a Marine major. "Get the hell out of there before you're killed!" he yells. I do just that, walk behind a dune. The screaming continues.

From that inferno, one man emerges a hero. A private from VMF 324, a kid whose name I forget, drives his burning gasoline tanker out of the area, jumps out of the cab, grabs the fire extinguisher from its rack, and saves his blazing truck. Major Nickels recommends him for a Bronze Star. Nothing is said about Lieutenant Norton. What is left of him is bagged and buried at sea. The following day, when the last of the wreckage is scooped from the pit his plane blasted in the concrete, more of Norton is found. He is given a second burial at sea. The crash site is sealed off and despite all the screaming, supposedly no one inside was seriously injured. The whole thing is hushed up and never spoken of again, at least not in public.

In the spring of 1945, Major Nickels is promoted to lieutenant colonel. In a gesture of largesse, I suppose, he promotes everybody in the squadron, except me. So I request permission to speak to him. Permission is granted. Inside his office all the shades are drawn, creating a twilight zone effect. Taking a seat in front of his desk, I see from his smug expression that Nickels is enjoying what he perceives to be my discomfort. Sensing that he expects me to protest, I sit silently waiting for him to speak.

"You know," he smiles, "your job only calls for a buck sergeant. I don't have to promote you."

"I haven't come to complain, sir."

"No? Then why are you here?"

"To request a transfer, sir."

He seems genuinely surprised. A defensive note creeps into his voice. "Sergeant, I'm doing you a favor by keeping you in the squadron. I could have dumped you into the 6th Defense Battalion, and you'd never get off this island."

I do not for a moment believe him. What would the 6th Defense Battalion's commander say about Nickels using his outfit as a dumping ground? Anyway, the 6th Defense Battalion is a line unit. It takes a very special situation to switch personnel from air to line or vice-versa. Of this I say nothing.

Instead, I say, "I appreciate that, sir. Back at Kingston I tried to show you I could do a good job for you."

"I'm aware of that, Sergeant. That's why you're still with us. But the T.O. doesn't call for more than a buck sergeant to do your job."

"Yes, sir, I know. All I really want is to get out of the Marines and go to college. Not being promoted doesn't bother me that much. It's just embarrassing being the only one in the squadron passed over."

"Well, I don't know what I can do about that," he says. "I'm afraid you're going to have to do the best you can where you are."

And that is the end of our meeting until two days later. I am summoned back to the office and asked if I still want a transfer. I do. "Okay you're going to 3rd Air Wing, Service Squadron." That same morning I pack my gear, bid my friend Brownie farewell, and move across the airstrip to Service Squadron. The Executive Officer, 2nd Lieutenant Nullity, is expecting me. Nullity is old for a 2nd Lieutenant, a reservist called back to duty. He was VMF 324's top sergeant until Nickels promoted him to sergeant major, then warrant officer, and finally second lieutenant.

Nullity appears to be a pleasant fellow. When I tell him I am reporting for duty, he says he has just the job for me. They need a property sergeant. I will have my own room. I should move right in and make myself at home. My driver takes me to a weather-beaten barracks, one of many jammed together in a small area. The thought of playing janitor again is unappealing. Brownie tipped me off earlier about an opening in a guard unit. Guard duty beats issuing bed linen and toilet paper. Lt. Nullity is surprised to see me back so soon.

"I hear there's an opening in the guard," I say.

"Oh yeah, we do need another sergeant there. You want the job?"

"Yes, sir."

"Okay, it's yours."

This time the driver drops me in front of a Quonset hut snuggled against a dune, alongside the lagoon, at the south end of the airstrip. Three sergeants greet me. In charge is a master sergeant named Carlton. Second in charge is technical sergeant Weaver. The third is a buck sergeant, a kid my age, called Bud. That is the whole outfit, three men. There was a fourth, but he has been rotated to the States. I am his replacement. First thing, they ask me if I play Pinochle. No. They will teach me. We play for matches, Carlton says. He is moody, well over six feet, well-muscled, and a judo expert.

"Come on in back," he says. "I'll show you where to bunk."

As soon as my gear is stowed, I join their Pinochle game. I am part-nered with Weaver, a tall, easygoing guy with great patience.

Compared to my old job, permanent sergeant of the guard is a cinch. It is the best duty I have had since glider school. No one bothers you. When not on duty, your time is your own. There is an OD (Officer of the Day), but he alternates daily. Duty is divided into four two-hour shifts, from 10 PM until 6 AM. The work is simple: patrol the Marine Corps portion of the atoll in a jeep from dusk to dawn. Our living quarters are Spartan. The front fourth of the Quonset hut is a day room, furnished with a wooden bench, four chairs, and a card table. The rear section is walled off and filled with double-decker bunks. That is where everybody sleeps. Sentries rotate daily. They are for the most part privates armed with an M1 rifle. We sergeants carry forty-five automatic pistols. As the new man, I ride shotgun while learning the routine. This being spring, the nights are often rainy and chilled. We wear ponchos over our khakis. Earlier in the war, guards were on the lookout for infiltrators. Now we mainly look for curfew violators. No one is supposed to be out after ten o'clock. There are exceptions: cooks and bakers and Seabees. Thus, if we desire to eat in the officers mess kitchen, we walk right in and help ourselves. The same goes for the Seabee's messhall. They have the best cooks and bakers.

Most nights not much happens. We do our two-hour stint and hand over the jeep. One night there is a break in the routine. Carlton spots a man crossing a field and orders him to halt. It turned out he knows the guy from Guadalcanal, a Corporal Mullein, called Moon. Moon looks like a young boxer out for a jog—a boxer with an attitude. Carlton orders him into the jeep. Mullein refuses. He tells us to fuck off and walks away.

Sergeant Carlton does not try to stop him. Instead, we rouse out the Officer of the Day. With him aboard, we drive to the offender's barracks. Carlton knows where the man lives, knows him from way back as a chronic hot-head. On the way to make the arrest, Sergeant Carlton fills the lieutenant in on the pertinent details. The three of us enter the sleep-ing barrack, flashlight in hand. We do not really need a flashlight. Moon-light reflecting off the coral-sand floods the room. Carlton knows exactly where the man sleeps. He shakes him awake. Until Corporal Mullein sees the lieutenant, he is ready to make a fight of it. Then his attitude changes from belligerency to sullen resignation. Mullein whispers, "Carlton, you're gonna regret this." Carlton says nothing, just watches him dress. By the time we leave, half the barrack is awake. Silently the four of us climb into the jeep and drive to the brig. I wait outside while Carlton and the OD fill out the arrest sheet. By then our tour of duty is over. Although Carlton does not say anything, I sense he is upset. What, I wonder, will I do if something like this happens on my watch? What if he attacks me? I will be strictly on my own.

Master Sergeant Carlton is a brooder. After the encounter with Moon Mullein, he is never quite the same. One night when Carlton has the early watch, he stops by the hut for no apparent reason. Weaver, Bud, and I are playing three-handed Pinochle. Later Weaver says Carlton just stood in the doorway, glowering with a mad gleam in his eye. Weaver asks him if he wants to take a hand in the game and gets no reply. My back is to him, but I hear the big man walk across the room, away from us. I can sense something is wrong. Suddenly, Weaver springs to his feet, yelling, watch out! He's gonna thrown that thing! Instinctively, we jump up and turn in time to see Carlton in the far corner, a wooden ammunition box raised over his head, ready to heave it. We are out the door before the ammo box crashes into the card table, splintering it. Carlton stays in the hut, pacing the floor, talking to the light bulb dangling from the ceiling, appealing, it seems, to his mother, asking her forgiveness. "I've tried," he says, "and I just can't make it. Forgive me." He rattles on like that for some while before becoming aware of us listening.

"You bastards, what do you think you're doing out there? Trying to make a fool of me?" With that he charges out the door and we take off in different directions. I sprint along a gully between dunes. Figuring I can out-climb him, I turn sharply up the side of the mound behind the sick-bay. Climbing in sand is tough. At the crest I fall exhausted among the scaveola. Looking back, I see I am alone. All I have to is slide down the other side and walk into the sickbay. The corpsman on duty calls the OD. When I get back to the hut, Weaver and Bud are standing in the road. I tell them the corpsman phoned the duty officer. Sergeant Carlton is still on the porch, brandishing a table leg, mumbling nonsense.

The OD pleads with him to turn himself in to the hospital. Finally, he agrees to go. Three days later the lieutenant stops by our hut. Sergeant Carlton, he says, is feeling much better and is sorry for all the trouble he caused. Will we take him back? It is up to us. We feel sorry for Carlton, but vote no. We like him but are afraid of him. The last we hear, Carlton is shipped to the psycho ward in Honolulu. Sergeant Weaver is our new Commander. Two weeks later, orders arrive for him and Bud to return stateside. Their time overseas is up. I am the new Commander of the Guard.

As their replacement, Lt. Nullity assigns me one buck sergeant. He and I will split the duty. Instead of four two-hour tours, we will do two four-hour tours. As NCO in charge, I decide to take up landscaping as a hobby. The lagoon has lost its allure and with only the two of us, Pinochle is out. To keep busy, adding ground cover to desolation seems the way to go. Midway Island's Commanding Officer, Commodore Windmore, an amateur ornithologist and gourmet, employs a horticulturist, Chief Petty Officer Lackland, to manage a vegetable and fruit oasis in the midst of an Ironwood grove. The first time I visit the Chief, he invites me to sample a freshly cut papaya. I have never eaten anything that smelled so foul and tasted so delicious. I am impressed by the variety of fruits and vegetables he and his crew grow in their tiny sanctuary, no more than an acre or so in size. When I explain my mission, the Chief agrees to have a cart of topsoil dumped in my front yard. Since grass seed is not available, I go about the atoll collecting wild grass cuttings. All I have to do is water them and keep sand from burying them. To that end, I bum railroad ties from Seabees to build a low wall along the base of the coral dune. The Chief also gives me a young banana tree. For me, though, wind is problematic, as is proper soil. The best I can do for the tree is place it between our Quonset hut and a scaveola thicket. That provides some shelter, but even there, random winds shred its leaves.

Saturday night I get a phone call from the staff NCO club. The bartender tells me there is a guy there named John Brown who says he's a pal of mine.

"Yeah, I know him."

"Well, come get him. He's too drunk to make it home."

"Sure, I'll be right over."

When I pull up in front of the club, he and two other Marines are waiting for me. When they help him into the jeep, I notice Brownie is wearing new staff sergeant chevrons.

"What happened?" I ask.

"Can't hold my liquor," Brownie says.

"So I notice. I thought you didn't go in for NCO clubs."

"You got that right, pal. I don't."

While crossing the runway, I hold on to his shirt to keep him from tumbling out of the jeep.

"Now that I'm a staff sergeant," he says, with some dignity, "I thought I ought to see what I was missing. I went to this chicken shit staff NCO club and got totally pissed before I knew what the hell was happening. So here I am, your old pal, pissed to the gills."

"Why'd they throw you out?" I ask.

"The bartender said I was talking too loud," Brownie explains. "He said I was causing a disturbance. Well, fuck 'em all. Right, pal? Who needs the pricks? I told that smart ass-bartender you were a chum of mine. He gave you a buzz. Knew you wouldn't let old Brownie down. It's just you and me, right, kid?"

Back at his hut, Brownie refuses to go inside. The fresh air seems to sober him up. "Let's climb that hill over there," he says, pointing to a dune across the road. "Sure, why not," I say. I have an hour to kill before patrol. There is a feverish quality to the night; moon glow is so bright you can read by it. Coral glistens and shadows are deep purple. Overhead the sky is indigo, almost black. Along the far horizon, stars glitter. With Brownie clinging to me, we make it to the top of the dune. Standing there, with him on my arm, a goofy smile on his face, swaying slightly, I feel unreal. When I look him straight in the face he appears uncannily girlish. The transformation is bizarre.

"Paul," he says, "kiss me."

"What?" I say.

"Kiss me," he repeats in a whisper. "Kiss me, Paul, please."

Gently, I lead him down the dune to his hut and leave him at the door. We don't speak.

I never see Brownie again. That night he slashes his wrists. Maxie finds him stumbling around the compound, befuddled, bleeding. From sickbay to psycho ward in Honolulu is a short hop. Later, news drifts back that he makes a second unsuccessful attempt on his life.

Shortly thereafter I break up with my girlfriend, Sally Carter. I expect her to protest. She doesn't even answer my letter. A week later I change my mind. I write, telling her I love her and want to see her as soon as possible. This letter she answers. Already she is engaged to a soldier, a medic stationed in Spokane. There is a note of relief in her letter. I, too, am secretly relieved.

There is a rumor that the sergeant who drives the **FOLLOW ME** jeep is going home. His is a simple job. Other than maintaining radio contact with the airport tower and guiding cargo and passenger planes to disembarkation points, all he does is check on sailors guarding runway crossings. These men halt traffic by waving a red flag when planes are landing or taking off. The Commander of the Field Police, as he is called, sees that they do not sleep on the job. Otherwise he just tours the field, waiting for word from the tower on incoming or outgoing traffic.

Lt. Nullity says, okay, the job is yours. Pack your seabag. You're temporarily assigned to the Navy. I am the only Marine in a barracks full of sailors. One of my bunk mates is a third-class petty officer (equivalent to a Marine buck sergeant) named James F. Beard, son of Major Beard, my old commanding officer in Headquarters Company, Fifth Amphibious

Force at Camp Elliott, California. James is a thoroughly nice guy with artistic ambitions. I still have a portrait he did of me, using colored pencils. My four other bunkmates are members of an Air-Sea Rescue Squadron. They crew a PBY, H-340, dubbed GOONEY CHASER. The GOONEY CHASER is parked in a revetment behind the airport tower. When not on patrol, I see a lot of the crew. We eat together at the Seabee messhall, see movies together, and even occasionally fly together. I ask their flight engineer if I can go on a patrol with them. He says sure. When my free time coincides with their schedule, I climb aboard for a flight that passes from today into tomorrow and back again, as we crisscross the international dateline, searching for Japanese submarines, downed pilots, ships in distress, or anything suspicious. All we find is tedium.

On my first flight Lieutenant Rammer, the chief pilot, invites me into the cockpit.

"Want to fly this bird?" he asks.

"No thanks."

"Go on," he insists. "Take the wheel. She practically flies herself."

The instant I touch the controls, I tense up. There is a stick but no rudder pedals in this bird. The stick has a steering wheel attached that takes the place of foot pedals. As for throttle, I am not sure how that works. There are so many dials, switches, toggles, buttons, and lights on the instrument panel that I do not know where to look. My confusion amuses Lt. Rammer. When he tells me to hold her nose up, I pull back on the wheel too hard and started climbing, without benefit of additional power. "Watch it. You'll stall her," he cautions. A slight turn of the wheel and we bank to the right. "You're off course," he says. "That's it, bring her back. Watch your horizon. Keep her nose up and wings level. You're doing fine. See, nothing to it. After a while, you can do it in your sleep."

"In fact, we have, several times," he adds.

"Please, take the controls," I say.

"Hey, you're doing a great job," the copilot tells me. "I think you got a feel for it. The bird likes you. Stick with it while I take a nap."

"You're kidding," I say. They are nice guys, these officers, and not arrogant sons-of-bitches like fighter pilots. Between themselves and their crew there is little formality. Long hours together cruising an empty quadrant of the Pacific Ocean acts as an equalizer.

On most of these flights I sit in a side bubble, staring down at the ocean. The engines are too noisy for conversation. The flight engineer and radio operator have desks in cubicles directly behind the pilots. I do not have headphones. To get anyone's attention, I have to shout. After a while, just staying alert is a challenge.

Tedium is part of our lives on Midway. Most days I just sit in my jeep and doze or annoy Gooney birds alongside the runway. By now I have given up reading and swimming. Brownie is probably in a psycho ward somewhere in the States. Then suddenly the war is over. An atomic bomb finishes it. Tracer bullets lace the night sky, and salvo after salvo is fired by ships in the harbor. Otherwise there is not much hoopla. One of the PBY crew and I roam the NOB, searching for excitement, bumming drinks, toasting our good fortune. Everybody wants the same thing—to go home.

August 11, 1945, my enlistment ends. All that stands between me and freedom is the deep blue sea. I need what everybody needs, transportation, and there is none. For the rest of August, nothing changes. We have a minor riot when movie star Betty Hutton and her USO troop of jugglers and dancing girls comes ashore. Military Police guard the girls as the Commodore gives them a tour of the atoll. Their show is held in an aircraft hangar. All goes well until one of the dancers does a handstand split, and Betty Hutton points to the girl's crotch, saying, "Boys, that's what you're fighting for." A roar goes up as horny guys rush the stage. For a moment chaos ensues as squealing girls are pursued out the exits, there to be rescued and flown back to Honolulu. Later that week, the Commodore is booed at a boxing match. Thus the war ends with a whimper, when someone cuts the throat of the Commodore's albino Albatross, nesting in his backyard.

Paul C. Mims, born in San Francisco, California, October 4, 1923, grew up in Beaumont, Texas. He enlisted in the Marines in 1941, serving for 4 years. He earned a BA (English) from University of Wisconsin and an MA (English) from University of Pennsylvania. After working as a police reporter for the Chicago City News Bureau, Mims became a career secondary school English teacher in the Philadelphia area. He has a novel and a memoir currently in manuscript.

Jarrod L. Taylor

Sadr City

In the spring of 2008, Iraqi insurgents began firing improvised rockets from Sadr City into the Green Zone in the heart of Baghdad. I was an infantry squad leader assigned to the 25th Infantry Division's 2nd Stryker Brigade Combat Team based at Schofield Barracks, Hawaii. We were deployed and operating in an area about 45 minutes north of Baghdad when our patrol was directed to report to Camp Taji so that we could prepare for a move to Sadr City. Bravo Company, 1st Battalion, 14th Infantry Regiment was about to head into combat. Only three platoons from my battalion would be making the trip to Sadr City, as the rest of the unit had to maintain a presence in our assigned area of operations.

It was my fourth deployment to the Middle East. Deployments can usually be summed up as a year or more of boredom punctuated by brief bursts of intense excitement, aggression, and violence. Four months into this 15-month tour in Iraq, it seemed that this deployment would be no different. This call to Sadr City would change things.

We returned to Camp Taji after destroying an Improvised Explosive Device (IED) in our company sector and began loading our Stryker vehicles with all of the ammunition, explosives, and supplies that we could carry. It was unclear just what we would be heading into or how long we would be gone. The Strykers were loaded down with extra uniforms, lots of Meals Ready-To-Eat (MREs), explosives, hand grenades, trip flares, fuel, and anything else that might prove useful. Some of us managed to make quick calls home to let our families know that they may not hear from us for a while. When my wife asked what was happening, I told her that I couldn't explain but to keep an eye on the news. She was really upset when we got off the phone, but it wasn't long at all before she knew exactly where I was and why I couldn't call. Later that evening, we got word to move out toward Baghdad.

Complacency and boredom had set in over the previous four months. Our Area of Operations (AO) had been relatively quiet. This was to be the first taste of combat for our Lieutenant, some of our younger sergeants, and all of our privates. The newest guys in my platoon had just arrived in country a week or two earlier, and were fresh out of basic training. One soldier from my already undermanned squad, who we called Bobby Gene, was at home on R&R. The rest of the company was in a similar state; we had soldiers who were home on leave or who had been assigned light duty for random medical reasons. We were about to roll into an unfamiliar area that was filled with enemy insurgents, and we were understrength.

The convoy from Camp Taji to Baghdad was uneventful, with the exception of crossing a bridge that was too narrow for our vehicles. Our Strykers crossed with only a few inches clearance on each side of the slat armor. Bravo Company's sector was mostly rural villages and farm-land north of Baghdad, so it was an interesting change of scenery as we rolled into the city. We left behind tall cane fields, groves of date palms, and mud huts. They were replaced with tall buildings, street lights, and divided highways that were several lanes wide. It could have been the interstate system heading into any major American city. As we moved through the city I couldn't help but be reminded of some of the poorer neighborhoods in St. Louis or Chicago. There were store fronts with closed gates over the windows and doors; cars parked down both sides of every side-street, traffic signals, street lights, and signs advertising products and services all over the place. It reminded me of times when I have made a wrong turn and ended up somewhere that I didn't want to be. The big difference between being lost in a big city and being on my first convoy through Baghdad was the amount of firepower I had at my disposal. In my own Stryker vehicle alone, we had enough weapons, ammunition, and explosives to challenge a small army.

At around 2 AM we arrived at our initial staging area. We were told it was called Old MOD. It turned out that it had been the Ministry of Defense under Saddam's regime. Now it housed American troops who regularly patrolled this particular part of Baghdad. We napped for about 45 minutes or so while the platoon leaders and senior noncommissioned officers were briefed on the company's mission in Sadr City.

Our initial objective was to move into Sadr City, conduct raids on buildings near suspected rocket firing sites, and then observe them. These POO sites, or Point of Origin sites were bare patches of land that were likely firing points for the rockets which were still streaking into the Green Zone. My platoon, the "Maggots," was ordered to take control of two separate three-story homes where we could observe from the rooftops. My squad would take one building, while my friend Leo's squad would secure the other. The other squad leader in our platoon was at home on R&R. Just before sunrise, my undermanned squad of six men hit our objective. We literally hit the brick wall that surrounded the property. My driver, Specialist Carpenter, who we affectionately referred to as "Crapenter," misjudged the distance through the Stryker's thermal camera system. His error created an opening in the wall that was about

10 feet wide. It worked to our advantage because we later found that all of the gates were locked from the inside. We busted through a door and flowed into the home. My two team leaders directed their men, and quickly cleared and secured the house. We immediately separated the residents and started questioning them. The homeowner was cooperative, and we didn't find anything in a search of the home. After we had crashed through their wall, broken their kitchen door, and dragged them all out of bed, he actually offered us breakfast and hot tea. We declined, but thanked him. I posted men on the rooftop and instructed the family to remain in certain areas of the house. Then we started waiting. We waited for hours without any word of what would come next. From the rooftop we could hear automatic weapons, zips and pops from stray bullets as they passed overhead, and the occasional scream of a rocket being launched toward the Green Zone. We were only a few blocks from the action, and my men were disappointed. There were fire fights just up the street, and we were sitting here babysitting an empty playground.

It was around 3 PM when we received a call that 2nd Platoon was in contact and their Strykers were running low on fuel. We were going to move up and conduct a relief in place. Now it was our turn to get in on the action. When we arrived, 2nd Platoon had established a perimeter around a disabled Bradley Fighting Vehicle. It had been damaged by an IED and was waiting for a recovery vehicle. The crew was okay, and they were still shooting. They just couldn't move. We parked our four Strykers around the Bradley and waited. Things were quiet for about 15 minutes. Then we heard shots. We started hearing rounds striking the side of our vehicle. My gunner saw a single gunman firing an AK-47 from behind the shell of a white sedan. It was almost completely stripped. The only thing left was the unibody. The trunk lid, hood, windows, engine, tires, and the entire interior had been stripped. It sat about 50 meters down a side street that we had turned onto. Sergeant "T", my gunner, tried to engage with our mounted M2 .50 caliber machine gun. We had never had an opportunity to test fire this machine gun, and it malfunctioned. He tried several times, but only managed to fire a few single rounds. Finally, he got a short burst of rounds put through the gunman's cover. We never found out if he was hit or if he fled. There were plenty of holes in the car, though. At the same time, my alpha team leader "Frolo" called out contact to our left. My bravo team leader Jimmy called out contact from the rear, and our lieutenant's vehicle began shooting to our right. It was our first contact, and we were taking fire from four directions. It was coming from rooftops, windows, and the streets.

The NCOs were all calling out contacts to our Lieutenant, who was in vehicle Bravo 1-1. My friend Leo and our platoon sergeant, Sergeant First Class "AB," were all calling out different distances and directions to enemy combatants who were firing on us. After a few minutes of this, I got a call from our lieutenant, call-sign Maggot 6. "Maggot 2, Maggot 2, this is Maggot 6, over." "This is 2, send it," I said. "Maggot 2, I'm going to need you to dismount your squad and try to find a way to get onto one of these rooftops. We need to get to high ground, so we can get an advantage over these guys, over." I slipped down into my hatch and told my squad that we would be getting out of our armored vehicle under fire. To my surprise they were all excited about it. Even the new guy, "Cowboy," who was fresh out of basic training, looked happy. "Cowboy" was actually assigned to first squad, but was working for me while his squad leader was on leave.

Sergeant "T" dropped the ramp on the back of our vehicle, and we ran out into the street. There was smoke in the air, and the streets were filled with trash and sewage. The smell of rotting garbage and gun powder burned our noses. There were two- and three-story buildings with store fronts on the first floor on both sides of the street. They were bullet riddled from past battles. There were more stripped out cars and even a dead donkey that had been caught in the crossfire earlier in the day. It was what war is supposed to look like. It seemed like a scene from a movie. "Frolo" began moving up the street looking for a way into any one of the buildings. There were tires burning about 150 meters up the road in front of us. Our lieutenant's Stryker gunner, Specialist "Ike," had his M2 .50 caliber machine gun sights set to thermal. He was taking out insurgents through the thick black smoke from the tires.

Under "Ike's" covering fire, we moved up the entire block. All of the storefronts had metal gates or roll-up overhead doors. "Frolo" tried to shoot the locks off of a couple, but they just wouldn't give. A burst of AK rounds zipped past us, and I turned to look at the men behind me. My two newest soldiers looked at each other, then at me, and smiled. They were loving every minute of the action. "Cowboy" called out some people who were running down an alley. I asked if they were armed and he said no. I sarcastically asked what he would be doing right now if he didn't have a weapon. He got my point, and the civilians disappeared out of sight. When we reached the end of the block, there was still no entrance. I called "Crapenter" on the radio and told him I needed a door. He came to our rescue and crashed our Stryker vehicle straight through the front wall of the building. It made a tank-sized hole in it and should have given us room to get in out of the gunfire. Unfortunately, this particular shop was filled with tires in stacks from floor to ceiling. We couldn't get in out of the gunfire on the street.

I moved my squad further up the street, and we rounded a corner into an alley. "Frolo" ran up to a metal door and kicked it open. Inside we found an old woman in a panic. She was frantically trying to get us to look at the identification cards that were hanging from lanyards around her children's necks. We pushed her and the kids into an interior room and pulled the door shut. My two teams quickly searched the home. There was nothing to be concerned about, but one room that I checked was filled with young women and some very small children. They were huddled in the back of a dark room. I jerked the door open and checked the room with the tactical flashlight mounted on my M4. Again, it seemed like a scene from a war movie. I put my finger to my lips and made the "shhh" sound. I motioned for them to stay low. As I pulled the door shut and turned around, Jimmy and I both saw cement steps leading from a courtyard to the roof. Unfortunately, we were looking through a narrow gap between two walls. We could see a door at the base of the steps and realized that it opened into the alley that we had come in from. It was barred from the inside. Iraqi buildings, especially in the overcrowded blocks of Sadr City, are nothing like those found in the United States. The homes are connected like townhouses, but sometimes there are doors connecting upper floors, and the flat rooftops are connected. City blocks have homes that open to the streets, but there are others that are completely within the interior of the block. Those interior homes have street access through small courtyards or narrow passages. It can make a city block seem like a maze when trying to search a certain area or find a specific home. There was no way to break through that door from the alley, so I had to figure out how to get someone through this narrow gap between the walls. I had to get that door open so that we could get shooters on the rooftop. "Frolo" suggested we make one of the terrified kids squeeze through and open the door. I had a three-year-old son at home, and there was no way that I was going to send a child to open a door when there was a fire fight taking place right outside. I dropped my helmet and unfastened my body armor. I pulled it off over my head and laid it on the ground in the courtyard. I placed my M4 on top of my gear. Jimmy looked at me like I was crazy and said, "Are you at least going to take your pistol?" I grabbed the 9mm from my holster and sucked in my stomach to squeeze through the space between the walls. I was barely able to fit through, but I did. As I headed for the door, I passed by a small window overlooking the courtyard. I paused at the edge of the window, and then turned quickly with my pistol ready to fire. I made the turn and thankfully hesitated. "Frolo" was standing in the room on the other side of the open window. His M4 was pointed at my chest, and my pistol at his face. We each let out a sigh of relief, and I moved to the door. I called Leo to dismount his vehicle and enter the building with our company snipers.

As Leo's squad came around the corner, I pulled the latch on the door and let them in. Once 3rd Squad and our snipers were inside, I directed my squad to exit the building, and enter the now open door to the steps. I squeezed back through the space between the walls and grabbed my gear. Jimmy was there waiting for me. After throwing all of my stuff back on, we ran out into the alley to catch up to the rest of our guys. Just as we reached the bottom of the steps, a burst of AK rounds zipped over our heads into the courtyard. We threw ourselves down onto the steps and hauled ass as soon as the firing stopped. We were completely in the open on those steps, and I have no idea how neither of us were hit.

Leo and the snipers crawled up into a firing position on the rooftop and immediately began taking fire. Leo called "Maggot 6" and reported that there was not enough cover to hold the rooftop. About that time, some colonel from another unit called and told us that we were a block further north than we were supposed to be. We were ordered to pull back one block and leave the area that we had just secured.

At the end of the day, we established a patrol base in an empty building. Our lieutenant looked dazed, and I asked if he was okay. He was young and naïve. A graduate of the United States Military Academy at West Point, he seemed to believe that our platoon was going to Iraq to bring justice and democracy to people who had suffered at the hands of Saddam Hussein. Before this first fire fight, he didn't seem to understand that infantrymen are not diplomats. He looked at me and shook his head. He said, "I just don't know how I'll ever explain this to my wife. I mean, there are machine guns firing, people dying all around in the streets . . . but it's so much fucking fun!" He was a different person, and certainly a different lieutenant after that day. We all tried to make a positive impact when we were able to, but he understood that we were all fighting to make it back home again.

We found the streets of Sadr City in a state of chaos when we first arrived. Businesses were closed and services had halted completely. For forty-four more days we fought in the streets of Sadr City. IEDs destroyed a number of our vehicles. We had close calls with Molotov cocktails, grenades, RPGs, snipers, and rifle fire. We kicked in doors, leveled buildings, captured high-value targets, provided medical aid to civilians, built a wall around the city, and kicked soccer balls with the kids. The situation in Sadr City improved, and the rockets stopped. When we left the city, businesses were open, children were playing in the streets, and the garbage and waste had been cleared. More than a dozen soldiers in our company had been wounded, and one young man in our platoon had lost his life. Even those of us who had seen combat before left Sadr City as different men. Our time in Sadr City brought us closer together than any of the other units I have ever served in. Five of us in the Maggot platoon alone received Bronze Star Medals only weeks into our time in Sadr City. More would follow.

Over the past few years I have maintained close contact with a number of the men from Bravo Company. We each remember that forty-five day period fondly, and wish that we could go back to that experience. Throughout the rest of our deployment we regretted having returned to our own area of operations. It was amazing to see such a great difference in the city in such a short amount of time. It was great to see such a difference in the soldiers in such a short amount of time. They grew up, matured, and understood what serving in the Army during war was really about. It wasn't about sitting in guard towers, cleaning weapons, or even shaking hands with village leaders. It was about fighting alongside one another and trying to get everyone back home. Many of the men who fought there have moved on. Even those men who have seen combat since spring 2008 agree that there was something special about the Maggot platoon and the time we spent in Sadr City. It was what war was supposed to be, what we hoped for and imagined before ever leaving home. We fought next to one another and dealt some serious blows to our enemy. They got their licks in too, but we came out on top. The city changed right in front of our eyes, and we knew that we made a difference. I'll never forget those days or those men who served with me in combat.

Jarrod L. Taylor was born on October 19, 1979, in Mattoon, Illinois. He served as an infantryman in the United States Army from 2000 until 2009. Jarrod deployed to Uzbekistan and Afghanistan in 2001–2002, Horn of Africa in 2003, Afghanistan in 2004–2005, and Iraq from 2007–2009. He left the Army in 2009 to pursue a degree in history and a career in education. Today he resides in his hometown with his wife and two children.

Jimmy Castellanos

Desert Snow

Al Anbar Province, Iraq
Spring 2004

One cloudy spring day it snowed in Camp Korean Village. The Marines froze mid-march as flakes drifted over concrete bunkers and through the crowns of date palms before resting on the burlap sandbags above the gunner's nest. It's a miracle, I thought, snow on spring's eve.

But life in Iraq hadn't always been so peaceful, so serene. Following Corporal Brownfield's death three weeks earlier, I had prayed for better days, prayed for a sign of war's end: a letter, a briefing, a pale phosphorus flare—anything to escape the war. His death had begun to consume me; every thought, every daydream, and almost every gesture, it seemed, revolved around his death. If it wasn't for me, Corporal Brownfield would still be alive, I thought, looking at the falling snow—he took my seat on that truck. That shrapnel was gunning for me, not him, I told myself. Three weeks earlier, on a clear night in Al Asad, an air base ninety miles northwest of Baghdad, I watched from a vehicle checkpoint as seven mortars struck our base, killing Corporal Brownfield and wounding three others. Hours before the attack, I had seen Brownfield guarding the same vehicle checkpoint, his rifle loaded and propped against a sandbag ledge where a miniature American flag he had found drooped in the windless afternoon. That evening our platoon was scheduled to make a supply run to Mainside, the northernmost part of the base which housed all the command centers, chow halls, and Iraqi vendors, along with any Third-Country Nationals, mostly Asian contractors that worked as cooks and laborers. Mainside was, by all accounts, bustling with activity, both military and civilian. At the morning briefing, Corporal Brownfield mentioned that I would accompany the platoon on the supply run. You'll be able to get hot chow, he said, and maybe make a phone call home. But when I approached the vehicle checkpoint at 1800 hours, Corporal Brownfield was waiting for me inside the guard post.

"Change of plans, Castellanos," Brownfield said. "You're not going on the supply run."

I nodded in silence. The hot chow and phone call will have to wait, I thought.

"Night guard is a man short," he said, "so you'll have to stay back and guard the bomb dump."

Again I nodded.

"Well, I guess I'll relieve you of guard duties then, Corporal," I said.

"Thank God," Brownfield said, and handed over the radio and security shotgun. "I've be sitting in this shit hole for twelve hours. My ass is killing me."

"Maybe we should order you some hemorrhoid pads," I said, half joking.

"Bitch, it ain't that bad," he said. Brownfield then rubbed his ass the way a collector caresses a porcelain orb.

Corporal Brownfield passed down the orders of the day: patrol reports, night missions, rocket build-ups, and any incoming vehicles that were expected through our checkpoint that evening. By the time he finished, the remaining guard team—six Marines in total—had arrived.

Down the road, Lance Corporal Crosby whistled from a Humvee. The two vehicle convoy was leaving.

"Gotta run," Brownfield said. "You need anything from the PX?"

I thought for a second. "I don't think so. . ."

"Nothing? Toothbrush, food, jerky, headphones—nothing?"

"Get me some chocolate," I muttered. "Like a candy bar or some shit."

"Alright, alright. I'll buy you something good," he said. "See you in the bunker tonight." He sprinted towards the Humvee, but only got a few paces before turning around: "Oh, and I'll give your 'Susie' a holler," he said, and winked before waddling off towards the convoy, his rifle and helmet in hand.

The explosions came early, just as night had fallen. While watching the empty road from the guard post that night, five insurgent rockets struck Al Asad. The first battered the courtyard of a boarded-up mosque, but the second rocket exploded yards away from the transport truck where Corporal Brownfield and Crosby waited for the platoon to finish their phone calls. Three more rockets would follow, all in rapid succession. Blue flashes. Thunderous rattle. A fire in the sky. Within seconds, the attack ceased. On the bed of the truck lay two Marines, one dead and other dying. Corporal Brownfield's face, I was later told, was unrecognizable—swollen, bleeding, thrashed. Killed in action. Lance Corporal Crosby, my bunkmate, took shrapnel to his torso and legs, and although Al Asad, Baghdad, and German hospitals saved his life, he is now paralyzed below the waist. Fleming and Cook, also my platoonmates, both received Purple Hearts, a small consolation for wounds suffered that night. One dead, three wounded, I thought. And now, three weeks later, spring snow. Camp Korean Village. A cool morning breeze. Through the wooden panels of my barricaded window, I watched as the snowflakes swept westward from the bombed-out garage and through the blown-out hole in the perimeter wall before squeezing themselves into the bullet holes on the aft bulkhead. Above us, the flakes drifted like leaflets over the Berlin night, placid and unperturbed. As the Navy Seals in the courtyard brushed away the snowflakes that whirled into their chow, and the controllers dusted the plastic air tower windows, I realized that my sign had come in the form of a spring blizzard. The war will end soon, I thought, and we'll all head home. Even Corporal Piedra, resident pessimist and destroyer of good times, who had twisted his ankle during the mortar attack, paused by the radio tent and in a surge of unusual gusto, lifted both arms skyward, grabbing handfuls of snowflakes as they fell. It was as if he too had forgotten the war.

So many flakes, I thought, but where are they coming from? As I stepped outside, I saw the flakes swirl high above the bulkhead and onto the roof. I stuck out my hand and caught a few. They were dense and slipped between my fingers like grains of jasmine rice. I caught a handful of flakes and threw them at Corporal Piedra, who returned fire. From down the pebbled road came a sound, muffled and faint under the heavy snowfall, almost inaudible:

Born in the U.S.A.
I was . . . born in the U.S.A. . . .

. . . and there at the blown out wall stood a Marine in desert cammie trousers, plastic sandals, and a sleeveless green skivvy shirt. Around his head a red bandana caught droplets of sweat that trickled from his hairline. At his feet burned twelve 50-gallon barrels, the big industrial types of metal construction. In one hand he stirred a man-sized wooden stick that he dipped into each caldron like a witch as he danced and sang to the melody. He had parked his Humvee on the gravel sidewalk with two wheels jammed inside an elevated planter; a black boom box, the retro new-wave type, blared in the bed; in the passenger's seat a filthy mutt wagged its black tail as his master brewed the ashy snow.

"What in hell are you doing?" I asked the private.

"Burnin' shit," he replied, and continued stirring his brew stick in a clockwork motion.

Inside each barrel blazed kilo upon kilo of human excrement mixed with toilet paper and urine and cigarette butts and whatever else had been tossed in. There must have been two weeks worth in every barrel, piled high like swamp muck. From a spare container used to fuel traveling convoys, the private poured a volatile liquid.

"Jus' add a lil' diesel and *voilà!*, shit burns like the best of 'em," he said. The young private pressed his fingers together and kissed them. "The shit paper soaks up the diesel and ain't nothin' stoppin' it then."

I laughed as the young Marine churned the volcanic barrels—shaking and dipping his shit stick in one barrel after another, sometimes using it as a microphone stand. It had been months since I had seen such happiness, such unrestricted bliss in anyone, let alone a Marine. I saluted and smiled at the young devil, but the familiar despair of war impeded any further joy. Corporal Brownfield is dead, I remembered. I could laugh but I could not feel the wonder. I couldn't grab a stick and pretend. The war is still breathing, the rifles still rattling. Brownfield is dead.

My eyes drifted away from the young Marine. I remembered Brownfield's blood dried and caked in the bed of our truck, his helmet frayed from the shrapnel. I remembered the blue lights that ignited the night as the mortars fell. There were seven blasts, a salvo of explosions, and then an eerie silence. Lights out. The next morning I counted over twenty shrapnel holes in the truck bed, but I stopped counting when I saw a staff sergeant washing Brownfield's brains out of his own rifle. Ashes sprouted from the barrels as I walked towards the gunships, clouding the sky and covering the refuelers nearby. And as I looked back at the young Marine, his shit stick now waving in mid-air, I smiled as I realized someone had managed to escape the war.

Jimmy Castellanos is former Marine and veteran of Operation Iraqi Freedom. He holds an MFA in Creative Writing from the University of Arizona and a BA in Biology from Claremont McKenna College. He is currently pursuing an MD and PhD in immunology at Cornell University. His work has appeared in the anthology *Veterans of War, Veterans of Peace*. He is working on his first book.

Gerardo Mena

Baring the Trees

The dead hang
from the dead like leaves
upon an ashen tree—
waiting for their deep autumn
so that they may open
their withering mouths
and fall, but the sad
season never arrives.

There is always a heavy
heat; always bullets
in a rifle; always a young
finger to slap
a trigger; forever
a fresh body to fasten
to a generation.

Gerardo Mena is a decorated Iraqi Freedom veteran. He spent six years in Special Operations with the Reconnaissance Marines. He was awarded a Navy Achievement Medal with a V for Valor for multiple acts of bravery. He has been nominated for a Pushcart, was selected for *Best New Poets 2011*, and has several poems published or forthcoming from several journals. For more information go to www.gerardomena.com.

Carol Alexander

Rewind

A word about this picture: the parents in Bermuda shorts
smile uneasily at the camera, which potentially was held
by the foreign uncle: polyglot, urbane, awaiting reparations.
The subjects look transparently young—he just demobbed,
still military about the hair, the set of shoulders, the parboiled eye.
She hasn't freckled, her legs are white, it wasn't yet the dizzying
June of pregnancy; it might have been the first good morning out.

In the background, children who plainly aren't you or me
scowl at some repulsive thing: a jellyfish or flailing skate
or simply the clotted foam of the clamorous wave, from which
their parents ban them in the absence of the twin lifeguards.

These old photos—yellowed, crackled—leave ample room for reverie;
their people are no longer here to make corrections, to tell us straight
how the landscape lay when droning bombs achieved quietus
in the cratered land, or the wild, corrosive clasp of seas.

Now, this particular snap: it's time to talk of what might not be there.

Say that Uncle tells them of his German war—rooms stripped,
paintings commandeered, cufflinks baldly pocketed, cultured pearls
between the officer's blunt teeth; he fondles them in mother memory,
only months before the bombers carpet Dresden, right before
the old world came crashing down, a city in shambles, mortified.

Say they listened breathlessly on the damp lip of this continent,
gold rings glinting in the fire, sunlight fading them like papers
patterned on boarding-house walls, the shabby palaces
of honeymooners short of cash, children of the late heroic war.

Their smiles, perhaps, hint that Uncle wields the gravitas,
lending some sobriety to the flighty sand, the fickle wave.
On this shore he dines well, in truth has grown rotund and brown,
so that we wouldn't feature him as the gaunt lieutenant wearing
standard-issue boots, threadbare coat, (all since carted off

to be deloused or burned in the ashcans, the implacable fire.)
And here he stands, a courteous émigré, official papers stamped:
the family welcomes him, the knowing survivor, the old new man.
In the café, he orders the *pansette*; on this strip of sand,
he holds forth in immaculate English, one pearl at a time.

A thoughtful picture, rifled from a box that smells of shoes:
the cat has maybe fouled it, found it moldering in the shed,
this embryonic image of mid-century triumphal woe.

See the age of the quick take, the sly leg, the postwar *elan*,
soldier's phantasmal field, a patch of rusted red.

Even the pitted earth between the bombings must have had
its interval, a moment of drawn breath, a measure of repose.
Let's say, with tender smiles, they fed themselves on boiled crab,
mother, father, uncle, drying their buttery hands in linen folds,
tasting the ocean tang with their wine, in that brief lull between wars.

Carol Alexander is a writer and editor in the field of educational publishing. Her poems
have appeared in numerous journals, including *Avocet, Canary, The Commonline, Chiron
Review, Eunoia Review, Mobius, Northwind Magazine, Numinous, Red Fez, Red River
Review, OVS, Poetry Quarterly*, and *Sugar Mule*. New work is scheduled to appear
in *Poetrybay, Poetica, Ilya's Honey*, and the *Mad Hatter's Review*. Her work has also
appeared in the anthologies *Broken Circles, Joy Interrupted, The Storm Is Coming,* and
Surrounded: Living with Islands.

Bill Glose

Desert Moon

Heat of the day. Men hunch over
weapon components spread on ponchos,

fussing like old women at a flea market.
Some nap beneath haloes of buzzing flies.

I lean against my rucksack on the side of a dune
tasting the sweet stillness. Undulating landscape

before me as strange as that of the desert moon,
pockmarked with craters from blows it never

anticipated. Specialist Taylor shows me
laminated photos of his baby girl. She lives

in the webbing of his Kevlar helmet. One day
he hopes to touch her face for real. Tefertiller

is writing home, pen perched in the corner
of his mouth like a swimmer on blocks

waiting for a gun to fire. Rambali shakes
a Tupperware with a scorpion inside. Pincers open,

wait for lid to burp, aching to snap something soft.
Garner offers an MRE ham slice to a stray dog,

thin as a tee shirt on a hanger. It sniffs, skittish,
as if it knows that next week shrapnel will

tattoo its name across Garner's stomach.
His heels will dig tiny graves in sand

while Gomez starts an IV. For now, though,
the dog takes the meat, Garner smiles, and

the desert moon inches across a cerulean sky.

Bill Glose is a former paratrooper, a Gulf War veteran, and author of the poetry collection, *The Human Touch* (San Francisco Bay Press, 2007). In 2011, he was named the *Daily Press* Poet Laureate. His poems have appeared or are forthcoming in such journals and magazines as *Narrative Magazine*, *New York Quarterly*, and *Chiron Review*.

Best Writing from a Missouri Writer

Jay Harden

Between Wives

When my veteran friends, interested ladies, and new introductions ask if I'm married, I drawl I'm "be-tween wives." There is this pause, and they just don't know what to reply back to that. I flash a slow, amusing smile and say no more. And that is where the conversation dies, unless I prolong it with an entertaining explanation. I'm not sure if I am mocking myself or making an attempt to keep conversing. It doesn't matter, really.

Relationships with women are a personal problem and a chronic disease of veterans. I reckon we are unique this way, and I should know. The American public just does not fully comprehend their veterans and those far destinations and events bound up in us. I could write you a book about this misunderstanding, but for now I'll settle for these minor thoughts on one of the unspoken costs of defending what you and I rightfully take for granted. Maybe you will understand us and me and our mutual separateness a little better.

It's been forty years and more since my defining days in Vietnam, and now the highlight of my week, every week, is my group meeting with other vets. We deal with our issues: that legacy from when we were young and naïvely brave half a world away, arriving whole, and returning piecemeal, more or less. My latter days continue defining me: a long, solitary road I never planned on.

I usually sit between Phil and Matt. The three of us have had 10 wives so far. I say "so far" since only one of us is currently married and even that marriage now is weathering a greater storm than combat: the recent death of their 28-year-old daughter. He found her hanging in her room and, being a combat medic, summoned all his skill and courage from long ago, his gained compassion, and great fatherly love to save her, but failed. She lived a few more days until they removed life support and watched her leaving this earth—the earth and the child he fought for in that jungle decades ago. I've lost a child and a wife myself. I don't claim to be an expert in these matters; I just have the sense that his daughter, too, was collateral damage from Vietnam, one of the many costs of war hidden from your view, but not ours.

Matt hurts, too, only differently. He was blown up by a grenade while leading his platoon in Vietnam. Today, he is reconciled to his three children raised by different wives. This is his small and hollow, but grateful, victory, though Matt knows he is forever separated from his living gifts to the world by a chasm of combat consequences so violent, so vast, so beyond their experience, they can never comprehend or even offer forgiveness.

I sit in awe when I contemplate how we humans, in spite of ourselves, have managed to evolve anyway as we stumble though the conflicts of society, geography, and time. Maybe we coped because we didn't hold on to our secrets.

If you think the three of us are unusual matrimonially, you are wrong. The divorce rate for Vietnam veterans exceeds 90%. I can't say what our weekly meetings have done to diminish this, only that Frank across the room is in the middle of a bitter, protracted divorce that is driving him to the edge of self-control as he tries to protect his two boys. It's more damage he does not need.

The fault is not with Vietnam. The fault is war itself.

You the public we fight for; you the public that support us now (and didn't then); you the public need to know the total cost of war. One great cost, the cost in relationships, is unclear, unnoticed, and mostly unmeasured. The quality of our human relationships, I say, distinguishes us from all the other forms of life on earth. That value is beyond price to each of us, to our American life, and to civilization itself wherever it thrives. And every week I see broke and breaking ones litter the floor we circle, writhing into dust like a terminal child in the throes of the Black Plague, in all its horrible, repetitive indifference. There we sit, helpless in a dream, the dream of a cure for our relationships as unlikely as one for our connected combat trauma.

The war in Vietnam changed my relationship with women forever. I, one of the more ignorant uniforms, didn't see it then, it was so subtle. I lost trust in my embrace of my woman, my wife—and other wives, it turned out. I looked the same, but I had killed killers who had killed, and become dark like them, ever vigilant, unable to be vulnerable and tender like before, or accept the same unconditionally from her. That's good enough to make babies, but no good at all for the shining love we knew and I lost. Now I live in my pajamas, a solitary recluse in my house in the company of familiar, buckling depression and a cold computer screen. I startle easily and hate surprises. If I won the lottery, I'd buy one restful night's sleep without nightmares, and then a bucketful more.

The VA does what it can, but declares me not fixable, though positively treatable around the edges. We signed up with our lives for a time, but none of us signed up for this. Yet almost all of us would serve and fight again anywhere if we were asked.

Vietnam was a peak experience that defined us for better—or not. We reached deep and went beyond our presumed limitations because we could and thought we should. For me—and for the rest, I suppose—Vietnam was the most meaningful thing we ever did with our lives, and we cannot ignore that, even as we try to find peace inside it and outside, too.

Maybe my peace will come if I write a low-down country song called "Between Wives." I know the feeling of the song and wail in my mind to its vague thumping; I just don't know the words. Didn't know war then, don't know women now, and can't sing a lick, either. It's just another hope, dead on arrival, from a gray warrior's mind still loose in a strange, shared world—and none of you know. Personally, it would help me feel less alone if you did.

Yes, it's true, not self-mocking, when I say I'm "between wives." I'm not being a calloused veteran; I'm reaching for understanding. Really, I'm reaching for the touch of a good woman; but *between* is where, for now, I think I had better stay.

Mr. Harden is a veteran of the Vietnam War. He came home in 1969 after 63 combat missions as a B-52 navigator with the 4133ʳᵈ Bomb Wing (Provisional). After active duty he served in the Missouri Air National Guard and pursued a science career in the Department of Defense, retiring in 1997. Now he spends his time traveling, researching family history, and learning from five grandchildren. Mr. Harden lives in St. Charles County, Missouri.

53 Alpha

It was June of 2007. Politicians and their parties were vying for the upcoming 2008 Presidential elections. The war had stalled. America seemed to be losing its patience with no immediate end in sight. Democrats played on America's conscience. Republicans, refusing to question their earlier decision to liberate Iraq, sought to implement new strategies in a desperate attempt to gain positive results. Daily, television documentaries and news programs relayed the dangers our soldiers, sailors, and airmen faced. Everyone had a family member or friend who had been, was in, or was about to go to Iraq. Mothers and spouses cried for their deploying and dying loved ones. Iraq had become what many described as our modern day Vietnam.

On the evening of the 23rd, I found myself in the turret of a gun truck preparing for a mission. It wasn't necessarily in my job description, and my previous experiences in both the gunner's seat and in the scout truck had already sparked several critics. I and a fellow Platoon Leader serving in 731st Security Force were repeatedly asked by our commander not to take unnecessary risks. We debated it on several occasions, and only weeks before, I was temporarily thrown out of office when I cited the Infantry motto "Follow Me" as a reason for acting as a Scout Truck Commander, pushing well out in advance of the rest of the team. At that point, not quite midway through our rotation in Iraq, playing it safe was a request and not a direct order.

Major Burns was a barrel-chested, take-charge officer who understood where I was coming from, but he didn't like it. He didn't want or need a dead Platoon Leader and didn't need the heat from our Battalion Commander. I saw it as a necessity. I challenged my soldiers to know, understand, and cross-train in every position. I needed to do the same. My soldiers needed to believe without a doubt that I was willing to assume the same risks they took. Despite their bravery, mission fatigue and combat had taken a mental toll on everyone. A number of my soldiers were growing weary. Violence was climbing and the Iraq Death Toll was near its high. Seeing me in the gunner's hatch set an example for all of my soldiers.

Apart from that, Staff Sergeant Riley, one of my two team commanders, requested that I act as the gunner. We were training a company from the newly arrived 82nd Airborne division. We were tasked to provide them on-the-job training in their newly assigned duties. I'd mandated an extra gun truck to allow for the additional soldiers we were required to train, while still keeping enough experienced Third Platoon soldiers on the mission to ensure our success. If something went wrong, we needed people who knew what they were doing. Rogue 56, strained on personnel, needed another body, and I chose to fill the gap.

I never forced my way into a position and left the duty of assigning tasks to each team leader. I gave each of them the autonomy to make internal decisions. I'd chosen Staff Sergeant Riley for his experience, drive, and tremendous ability. I had two teams to run, and I couldn't be with Rogue 56 on every mission. He was their boss and I was his. If I needed to step in, I would. At the same time, he didn't need a Lieutenant disrupting the team's mojo. Any member of his crew would run purposefully into a hail storm of gunfire at his word, and that's the way it needed to be. Any awkward questions of authority could mean life and death on a mission where seconds counted.

I sat in as a Truck Commander most of the time, but preferred to sit in the gunner's hatch. I counted on Staff Sergeant Riley to make sound decisions and knew that he wouldn't knowingly jeopardize the safety of his crew on my behalf. So when he requested that I act as the gunner that night, it meant that I was trusted and respected. I prodded him, asking if it was his way of getting rid of me, but knew full well the gravity of the job at hand.

The world smells, sounds, and appears different from atop an M1114 gun truck. Inside the truck, the thick windows make vision difficult. Massive equipment bolted to its interior and hanging from nearly every inch of available space add to the sight constraints. At night, perfect sight of the treacherous world outside is nearly impossible. The Driver and Truck Commander are as protected as the engineers could design and still allow them to perform their jobs. With life dependent on finding the enemy and their destructive devices, the crew needs visibility. That is the gunner's job.

The gunner is the nose, ears, and eyes of the crew. The gunner must be focused, have a sharp eye, and possess a trained ability to act quickly. Fiery tanks and devastated gun trucks weighted down with tons of bulky metal are a testament to a need for more than the armor protection. Technology and armor can only do so much to save the inhabitants of a gun truck. Life and death hinges on a split-second decision more than any machine or thick metal. The exposed gunner is perched above the truck. He or she makes a snap decision to halt or continue. They are the tireless watch and the first line of defense.

The dangers of Baghdad and Iraq force the gunner to divide the world into layers. They must constantly filter out what appears to be a threat from what is harmless. In Iraq, Improvised Explosive Devices (IEDs) reign as the king of killers. IEDs are a faceless enemy adding to the death toll at rates far greater than any AK-47 round or Rocket Propelled Grenade (RPG). Piles of trash from lack of sewage controls, pot holes, and previous blast holes line the Iraqi highways and roads. They are everywhere and pose an immediate and potentially perilous threat. The gunner must identify each threat and determine its risk while moving at speeds of 45 mph or greater. Farther out lies the risk of snipers and small ambush teams poised to attack. The enemy hones their skills on an endless supply of convoys and foot soldiers. The surrounding three- and four-story buildings, alleyways, irrigation ditches, corners, coves, and barricades offer limitless opportunities for the enemy force to kill an American soldier.

The gunner's need for line-of-sight supercedes the need for armor. Thin layers of sand-painted metal, broken up by intermittent ballistic glass, make up a turret that semi-surrounds the gunner but offers minimal protection. The gunner's body armor and kevlar add an additional layer, but the gunner's proverbial ass hangs in the wind. Rushing wind and blowing sand blast the face and pierce the kevlar helmet while the gun truck moves full throttle down the war-torn roads, leaving little doubt that IED blasts, sniper rounds, AK-47 fire, and RPG rounds can easily penetrate the loose turret layers. What gives them their advantage perched atop safety, also adds to the likelihood of their demise. It is the most dangerous position in a gun truck. In a combat escort patrol, the position was an honor and a privilege. The soldiers of the Third Platoon, Rogue Security Force didn't volunteer to sit behind a desk. In a world of perverse logic, being a gunner was a bragging right.

This is the world we knew and lived on a daily basis since our arrival in Iraq nearly 4 months before. Day in and day out, we drove down some of the most perilous routes in Iraq, safeguarding supplies, equipment, and sometimes people to locations throughout the gawd-awful country. It was simple, really. We didn't hide from the enemy. We never really changed our tactics, techniques, or our procedures. We simply drove from one site to another. I often pictured it in mind as a duck moving back and forth at a carnival game, just waiting for the enemy to pick up a gun and claim their prize. Only this wasn't a game, and we weren't going to just let them shoot at us without putting up a fight. We shot back. In what felt like a purely defensive and reactionary effort, the gunner was the closest thing to savior and redeemer we had in this hell.

I was in gun truck 363, the fifth of seven gun trucks. We left Taji, a northern suburb of Baghdad near Sadir City, at about ten in the evening.

We were on the outskirts of the mammoth Baghdad within an hour. Night had fallen and the air was thick. The usual mixed smell of trash, decay, and gun powder overloaded my senses. It wasn't my first rodeo, and I was fairly comfortable in the gunner's hatch. But traveling through the notorious Baghdad always left a burning pit in my stomach. The gravity of our location was enough to unease the strongest stomach.

Baghdad was much like Batman's Gotham City. Blown out buildings shadowed by hazy streetlights formed a comic-book skyline. Dust and debris blanketed the streets. Mammoth concrete piles lay on all sides of our path. Street signs dangled from overhead passes and swayed back and forth in the slow moving wind. Concrete chunks ripped from the road every 10 to 20 feet from thousands of IEDs. The city shadows could send chills down your spine if your mind wandered.

At night, we were left to our own. Lighted windows were the only sign of civilian life in the hellish city. An imposed curfew mandated that inhabitants stay indoors past dark. Headlights meant either a coalition force, Iraqi Police, Iraqi Army, or the enemy. Any suspicious movement meant an insurgent and attracted an itchy trigger finger. We waited with bated breath for the slightest sign of danger, ready to kill whatever stood in our path.

I made a home out of my turret. Every necessary survival tool pertinent to our mission success was within reach. I knew exactly where everything was and could grab it blindfolded.

To my front, I had a M240B machine gun. The M240B fires a 5.56 mm round, the same round as the M4 Carbine, standard issue for every soldier in our company. The M240B has a lesser punch than its counterpart, the M2 machine gun with its monsterous .50 caliber round. We had both weapon types on our gun trucks, but the M240B was my preferred weapon of choice. The M240B is easier to wield and maintain. I was comfortable with it. It was an extension of my body and carried enough of a punch to cut a body in two. That's all I really needed.

The M240B was locked and loaded. A belt of ammunition fed into the machine gun from the left and rested delicately inside an ammo can tied to a mounted carrier alongside the turret. Only a depressed safety button need be pressed before I could unleash the havoc of my weapon on any waiting insurgent. Spare ammunition cans rested at my feet inside the gun truck belly. They were my reserve in case of a prolonged fire fight. Most attacks were hit and run, and the chance of needing reserve ammunition was minimal.

To my immediate right, dangling from a cord and placed on the floor of the turret about mid-body, were my night vision googles and thermal sights. Both devices aided with IED detection and worked well for spotting gunmen attempting to use darkness to their advantage. I used the devices intermittently throughout the mission, when I needed to confirm something suspicious or when the vehicle was moving slow or halted. At faster speeds, they could be as annoying as they were helpful.

To the slight rear and right, my M4 was tightly placed inside two spring-loaded fasteners. The fasteners were tight enough to keep the locked and loaded weapon inside its grasp, while making it easy enough to snatch and fire in the event my M240B jammed. I could also utilize the M4 to fire a well-placed warning shot or, God forbid, during close quarters combat. Just below my M4, I had illumination flares for lighting up the sky and searching for the enemy.

To my front and left, I carried a small bag that held my gloves when not in use, cigarettes, lighter, and odds and ends that made life a little more comfortable. Beside the bag, I had a Diet Pepsi. The caffeine kept me awake when conversation turned slow.

On my body, I wore a thick and heavy vest already stained from months of wear and tear. Two ballistic plates, placed inside pouches on the front over my chest and in the back, protected my internal organs. Attached to the vest with snaps and lacing were protective pieces that guarded my thoat, sides, and upper arms. I wore a kevlar helmet and ballistic eyewear to protect my head and eyes from a wide range of dangers. While offering little physical protection, I also carried a folded American flag inside the rear flap of my vest with a piece of paper citing the Lord's Prayer tucked inside it. The flag and prayer went with me on every mission. They served as my mental and spiritual protection.

Burrowed inside the vehicle were Sergeant Jesse Thomas, Truck Commander, and Private Christopher Craig, Driver. Sergeant Thomas was a jack of all trades, filling in on Rogue 56 mission when needed. Private Craig was from the famed 82nd Airborne. He was young, excitable, and anxious to learn. Together, the three of us joked around as much as possible to keep our minds fresh and to maintain alertness on our long and tiresome mission. Keeping a positive energy inside the truck was important to our livelihood, but needed to be evenly balanced with attention directed at the mission ahead.

As we moved deeper into Baghdad, it looked like it would be a peaceful evening. I tried my best not to let the calm create a fool out of me though. I made constant and continuous sweeps of the area directly in front of our gun truck with a high-powered, hand-held flashlight searching for IEDs: occasionally lifting the light up into the rooftops and windows of surrounding buildings. My sweeps were fast paced and systematic in an attempt to see everything and miss nothing. Enemy fire could come from anywhere. On earlier missions, my soldiers had taken RPG rounds from a popular mosque not too far ahead of us. In the case of IEDs, the attack could come from seemingly nowhere. Insurgents had become experts at disguising rudimentery explosives. What looked like a rock or the curb of a road could just as easily be a roadside bomb with the potential of killing or disabling an entire crew.

We approached Check Point 53 Alpha, a long bridge guarded on both sides by the Iraqi Police, otherwise known as IPs. My job should have been a little easier. Houses on either side of the bridge still posed some risk, but in theory, the bridge should be free of IEDs. Unfortunately, that was rarely the case. Past experiences taught us many times there was little or no difference between the Iraqi Army and the enemy. Corruption ran amuck. If they weren't the enemy, they had brothers or cousins who were. If it wasn't a family affair, someone always had enough money to buy them off. If they couldn't be bought, the potential death of a loved one worked well.

On the evening of the 23rd, the top of the bridge had the additional protection of an Iraqi Police patrol car. As our gun truck passed the medium-sized SUV, we peered inside the parked patrol vehicle on our left with its hazard lights on. Three police officers dressed in blue uniforms peered back at us. My eyes locked with two of them as we slowly passed. Something was wrong. Their eyes were large and their expressions peculiar. Their faces seemed a mixture of fear and excitement. It wasn't just me, as my mind processed the situation, Private Craig mentioned over his microphone that they looked odd.

A thunderous blast from just behind us pounded my eardrums and rocked our truck. The flash enveloped me and lit the sky. The concussion shoved me across the two-foot opening of the turret and slammed the left side of my head against the metal. The IED, exploding only a few feet behind our truck, blew shards of homemade explosive, concrete, and gravel in all directions. A piece of explosive burnt my face, while likely a piece of concrete smacked my head and gouged my kevlar helmet. The shock wave brought instant chaos to my body. I ducked into the gun truck and yelled at Private Craig to haul ass out of the kill zone.

Gun trucks on both sides of bridge as far away as a mile heard the blast and felt the concussion. The radio erupted with chatter. Everyone was trying to determine what the hell was going on, to gain situational awareness. Sergeant Thomas began attempts to push information but couldn't get through the chatter. The gun truck just behind us reported that the IP was moving past him. Before any of us could analyze the situation, it was too late and the IP was gone. Staff Sergeant Riley shut all the unnecessary traffic up with a jab on the radio to calm the hell down. Thomas began relaying our status and providing our Battle Damage Assessment. The rear vehicle began pushing information to Rogue Tactical Operations Center over a hundred miles away via a system very similar to an instant message. Gun Truck Two began relaying information to an operations center in our immediate area, over a separate radio frequency. All trucks began searching for secondary devices as we pushed through the area. In a fraction of a second, death came upon us, and the three lives inside our truck were nearly lost. Seconds later, the madness of the moment had passed and order was restored. Each soldier and team member instinctively performed the battle drills ingrained from both practice and experience. Our part of the city had returned to peace as quickly as it had turned to hell.

I was left with an adrenaline overload and a mental numbness. According to the gun truck behind us, the IED was hidden inside a concrete barrier alongside the road. The explosion had ripped a hole through the bridge. My ears rang and all other odors were replaced with the powerful and distinct smell of gunpowder. I thought little of the burning sensation on my face at first and focused on feeding Thomas the information he needed to report our status. However inappropriate, I reached for a cigarette to calm my nerves. I couldn't manage to strike the lighter though. The cigarette dangled unlit for a few minutes on the tips of my dry lips before I finally gave up and let it drop down to the bottom of the turret.

As much as I wanted the mission to end, we still had a long way to go. I had to refocus. The possibility of another attack was no less likely than it had been moments before, and was all that more probable. Secondary devices are common. I was disappointed that I missed the IED. I had failed in my job. I thanked God no one had gotten hurt. As shaken as I was, I didn't want it to happen twice.

I was just as disappointed we hadn't gotten the Iraqi Police Officers responsible for the bomb. I am as sure today as I was that evening that they triggered the IED. I didn't need a judge, jury, or any evidence. In Iraq, guilt was often decided at the lowest level. When someone attacked, we didn't haul them away in handcuffs. Sentencing was decided in the mind of a soldier and issued by his own hands. In many cases, it was the death penalty. I didn't care what their motives were. I didn't care about winning hearts and minds. I wanted revenge. I wanted restitution for the life they tried to take from me and from my family. Iraq was a lawless place. My moral strength was weak. For the next few hours, I cursed them and every IP Patrol we came across.

As we moved on through Baghdad, my senses slowly came back to life and the burning sensation a few inches below my right eye grew more painful.

"Looks pretty red and raw," Sergeant Thomas exclaimed after shining the beam of his flashlight up into the crack of the hatch and onto my face. As we drove further and further, I could feel the wound inflaming. I took my gloves off and wiped away the droplets of blood forming along a 3 inch gash just below my eye. I'd look at it when we stopped to refuel in Scania, a Forward Operating Base a few hours away.

The odds of another attack grew less and less likely as we drifted out of city and passed through the southern suburbs of Baghdad. Less trash made it easier to find IEDs. Fewer houses made it easier to target the enemy. My mind was free to focus on what had taken place. Reality gradually replaced the insanity of my situation. By the time we hit the gates of Scania, the burning sensation on my face began to worry me.

We parked our gun truck on the inside of the outer walls of Scania in an assembly area that housed coalition forces moving north and south through Iraq along Main Supply Route Tampa. Scania was a small compound that served mostly as a way point and truck stop for convoys along the supply route. We routinely stopped there to fill up on fuel, grab some food, and take a short break from the dangers of our mission before heading back out. The process generally took a few hours. Behind the sand-filled blocked walls of Operating Base Scania, I ripped off the 35 pounds of body armor that had weighted me down for the past several hours. Sweat soaked my body and uniform. I took off my kevlar and inspected the small chunk ripped out of it. I jumped down from the top of the gun truck to grab a quick bite to eat with the rest of Rogue 56. After dinner, I'd grab some tylenol from another soldier to ease the pounding headache begining to form on the frontside of my head and quickly working its way to the back. I'd already warned Staff Sergeant Riley I wouldn't be seeing the medics at Scania. I wanted to finish my mission and told him I'd go to the aid station at Camp Adder, our home, as soon as we got back.

Sergeant McGlothlin, known affectionately as "Glock," jumped down from the scout truck parked right beside us. Glock strode up to me. He was his normal cocky self, a prerequisite for all scout truck crew members. Glock was the Scout Truck Commander, adding a characteristically high blend of testosterone and arrogance. The two of us got along well. I tried to return his cocky comments as fast as he issued them. Not only was it the Army way, but he wouldn't have expected anything less. He instinctively began to rub it in with a joke about me burning my face with a cigarette. Before he could finish his joke, he blurted out, "Oh, sh**," completely interupting himself."Dude . . . I'm sorry. I was going to give you a hard time, but that looks fu**ed up!" His comments didn't help my mental confidence much.

Three wash tubs stood outside the tin chow hall so soldiers could clean up before grabbing a greasy cheeseburger and even greasier fries. Cheap mirrors were propped up on the makeshift sinks as an added gesture of civility. The reflection was like a circus mirror with grime and desert dust splattered about. I could see only a raw red streak crossing my cheek with small droplets of blood consistently forming all through-out the wound, no matter how many times I wiped them away. It hurt, but I knew I'd be alive. I guessed it would scar, but not bad. At worst, it would serve as an interesting story for my grandchildren, years to come.

My injury was of course a side show in the chow hall and the high-light of conversation for Rogue 56 as we all stood back at our trucks. Staff Sergeant Riley, even cockier than Glock, gave me a hard time for bringing down his Find-to-Detonation Ratio, a competitive statistic that Battalion used to gauge our effectiveness in finding IEDs as opposed to hitting them. Team Leaders used the ratio as bragging rights and Com-manders used them to reward the good and beat up on those with poor ratios. Rogue 56 had a strong reputation for finding IEDs. They were one of the best teams in the business.

I felt pretty bad that their ratio dropped a little that night. On the way home, over the radio, I apologized to Rogue 56 for missing the IED. The gun trucks in front of me apologized for not catching it before me, and the gun trucks behind me thanked me for clearing it before they got to it. There were no hard feelings, but the ribbing I'd take lasted for the remainder of our tour.

The blast hole at Check Point 53 Alpha was pointed out each time we passed it. It quickly become the butt of many jokes and was named the "LT's Hole." Check Point 53 Alpha, from that night forward, was like a trivial tourist trap alongside the highway back home. The soldiers of Third Platoon would point it out much like a father might point out that the family was passing the home of the largest ball of yarn. Our trucks hit more than a few IEDs in Iraq. Somehow, mine became the most notable. It's funny how little outward thought went into such a grave situation.

The remainder of our mission that night was slow and unevent-ful. The last leg of our journey south of Scania and through the central southern sands of Iraq was about as safe as you could get. The stretch of road could produce an IED, and every once in a while insurgents struck up a small arms attack, but we rarely had problems in the early morning hours. It was around three in the morning when we left and I was tired. My face and head where beginning to hurt like hell. I just wanted to get home and get to bed.

The time and open desert gave me a chance to think about the events. I had escaped serious injury and possibly death by only a fraction of a second and inches. Too many soldiers under the same circumstances were far less fortunate. I had a young son, a future wife, and a family at home waiting for me. I didn't want to die. Not yet. But who did? How many sacrificed much more than I had? In the few months I'd spent in Iraq, I'd already attended more memorial services than I'd cared to count. Death always loomed somewhere in the back of my mind. It was now at the forefront.

Oddly, another part of my brain twisted the truth and told me that all this was normal. Even as I hid my burning face from the blazing Iraqi sun showing itself on an early morning horizon, as we finally pulled up to the gates of Camp Adder, sitting in the gunner's hatch that morning felt as routine as punching in at Eagle Iron Works, a factory job I held years before. Perhaps my mind had succumbed to simplicity, and anything beyond that was too surreal for me to cope with. How could all of this be anything close to normal?

The wound itself would prove very minor. Doctors told me I'd received a concussion, and cleaned what they described as gunpowder and gravel from a patch of skin roughly two inches in diameter from just below my eye. The turret, my Kevlar, my goggles, and body armor had all done their job and protected me.

In the course of weeks the burns would scab and fade, but never really disappear. To most, the mark is barely visible. I can still see it when I look in the mirror, there on the surface. Perhaps it isn't much different than the mental scars from that night, along with others, that were burnt into my mind and more deeply into my soul. Most will never see the effects Iraq left on me, aside from what is distinguishable on the surface, yet they will always be there. They have become a part of who I am.

Captain Jonah E. Krause lives in Des Moines, Iowa, with his wife and three children. He is a graduate of William Penn University where he earned a Bachelor's Degree in Business Management. He has deployed to Iraq three times and once to Kosovo. He's earned two Bronze Stars, the Purple Heart, two Joint Service Commendation Medals, two Army Commendation Medals, and the Combat Action Badge, while serving overseas.

Lauren K. Johnson

The Soldier's Two-Step

Barely five feet tall, she does not hunch under sixty pounds of body
  armor and supplies.
The girls in rags run up to her, tell her she is strong. "No," she says, "*You*
  are strong." And she is
right. And so are they.

She cries into a pink pillowcase she brought from home. For a son's
  broken heart, a daughter's
birthday, an anniversary, missed. Dancing between two worlds; her
  partner the cold barrel of a
gun, music the hollow tones of war and hollow, cheerful voices on
  the phone. This is the melody of loneliness.

The women ask why. Why the risk, the sacrifice? Why do you care? "All
  mothers are the same,"
she tells them, "It doesn't matter what language you cry in."

The men don't ask, they demand: more buildings, more money, more
  time. She carries the
promise on her small shoulders; sharp-edged expectations of two
  countries. This is the burden of
hope.

In her absence, the broken heart mended, birthdays and anniversaries
  were celebrated. She is
haunted by all that she missed and all that she left, unfinished, behind.
  The little girls' faces in
her little girl, the purse where armor should be.

From boots to high heels, from gun to spatula, from Humvee to minivan,
  she keeps dancing.
Because they need her to. And because she is strong.

Lauren K. Johnson

A Rock Called Afghanistan

I first saw Lady Gaga in the summer of 2010. She was staring at me from a photo teaser on a magazine cover; I don't remember her out-fit, only that it was shocking. I wouldn't have been shocked had I seen Gaga's bedazzled performance with Elton John at the 2009 Grammy Awards; or her Stanley Kubric-esque "Bad Romance" music video, which had recently attained the status of most viewed YouTube video in history; or had I seen any of her videos or appearances on major award shows or photos in popular magazines in newsstands across the globe.

But I hadn't. And I was shocked.

Around the same time, I was introduced to a teenage phenom who had also been storming the music world. I don't remember if I heard one of his songs, or if it was a morning radio show announcement that he was threatening to dethrone Lady Gaga herself on the all-time YouTube po-dium that first alerted me of his prominence. I just remember feeling that I must be the last person in the universe to learn the name Justin Bieber.

Somehow, I had missed the fan-screaming, media-barraged, gossip-infused, multi-platinum rise of two of my generation's most iconic performers. Obviously, I had been living under a rock. A rock called Afghanistan.

I had lived under it, or around it, in a secluded training environment for 349 days. As I emerged, my body adjusted faster than my mind. Within a few days, my internal clock registered the 12-hour time change. My feet settled on solid, paved roads they knew well. I gulped long, fresh breaths of American air and tuned my ears to a chorus of car horns, birds, sirens, and ocean waves. It looked like home. It sounded like home. It even smelled like home. But it was different.

The radio stations, previously stuck in a familiar top 40 loop, blasted music I'd never heard by artists I'd never heard of. Everyone could sing along. Everyone but me. The local string of Blockbuster video stores had been abandoned—I was redirected to a vending machine-type kiosk that was so simple and so brilliant I couldn't figure out how it operated. My cell phone was declared archaic. (So was my iPod. So was my laptop.) My brother could wiggle his finger across the touchscreen of his new Android phone and a coherent text message would magically appear. He laughed when, eyes widening in amazement, I asked, innocently, "How does it know what you want to say?"

I had had access to movies in Afghanistan, at least the grainy, bootlegged variety, but in America it seemed visual entertainment was no longer acceptable in two dimensions. From the Pakistan border I had attempted, through halting, unreliable internet, to maintain my connection to the world via the most modern medium I knew: Facebook. But suddenly, my homepage news feed wasn't sufficient. I didn't Tweet and wasn't LinkedIn. Did that make me unimportant or just uninformed?

I had tried to remain informed. I kept the pulse of everything concerning Afghanistan; I monitored the politics, social issues, and agricultural outlook, tracked counterinsurgency efforts through news reports in English and in the local Pashtu language with the help of our unit's interpreters. In my year-long obsession with war, however, I had missed news of other battles: against an earthquake in Haiti, a shooter at Fort Hood, Michael Jackson's doctor, swine flu, high gas prices, a new health care bill. Gaga versus Bieber.

My sister, whose barely pregnant belly I had kissed before deploying, was mother to six-month-old twins.

My high school best friend was a wife.

My grandfather was on his deathbed.

There were physical changes, too. A multi-million dollar construction project had transformed the downtown area into a boardwalk of restaurants and souvenir shops that I wandered through aimlessly, not quite blending in as a tourist. I was a tourist in my own "home"; first as a guest in a friend's spare room, then in a corporate apartment, then finally housesitting in a condo, where I unloaded my belongings from a storage unit into the garage, dodging cockroaches and spiders to dig out a favorite blanket or pair of shoes. The items never quite lived up to the memory.

On the Air Force base where I worked, my office had been relocated and re-staffed with a fresh crop of young Airmen. Perhaps they had heard of me—the enthusiastic lieutenant who loved to write, loved to run, and was usually the last to leave the office. Perhaps they hadn't. Perhaps they struggled to reconcile that image with the new me, the one who passed on journalism assignments, who stayed at the gym while they ran during morning workouts, or sometimes walked slowly behind, favoring a knee strained by 60-pounds of body armor. I still stayed late, staring at my computer, trying to figure out how to care about retirement ceremonies and community briefings instead of direct security threats, convoy missions, and counterinsurgency operations. No rush to leave when all that waited off base was a transient home and talk of other things I couldn't make myself care about.

I was a year older, returning to a world that had also aged a year. But we had grown up separately. We no longer recognized each other.

Lauren K. Johnson, an Afghanistan veteran and former military public affairs officer, has won regional and national-level Department of Defense journalism awards. Her work has been featured in *Special Operations Technology*, *Tip of the Spear*, and *Mason's Road*. Lauren is pursuing an MFA in nonfiction writing at Emerson College in Boston, where she is completing a memoir about the experience of female soldiers during and after war. She blogs at uncamouflaged.blogspot.com.

Ana as'fi

The old man, his wife, and two daughters, roused by the 0200 door
kick knew nothing of rockets. *La*, said the old man. "No." He
spoke for himself and for his family. We challenged again. Again:
La. Through our interpreter, the old man began to offer us *chai* and
honey-dipped dates rolled in white sugar. *Hadeea, Hadeea*, he
repeated. "Gifts," said the interpreter. "He wants to give you gifts.
It is cust-" But the Sergeant stopped the interpreter with a finger.
"Tell him the only gift I want is *that* daughter and her tight pussy
on my face." His finger aimed at the older girl, maybe seventeen,
her nipples beading through the white slip cooled by the desert air.
She looked down from the eyes of peering men. The interpreter
didn't translate. The old man did not understand, and he motioned
the women inside the clay-brick house to prepare tea. But the wife?
She leaned and spit *ali baba* tough into the sand at our boots.
"Criminal." Yes. She understood. The old man turned, slapped her
hard to the head, yelled in Arabic. We laughed. The old man,
relieved, laughed too. He shoved his wife and the daughters back
toward the house. *Rouh*, he demanded. "Go." The women walked
away. Turning to us: *Hadeea, yes?* "No," the Sergeant said. Cupping his
hands, the Sergeant shouted "Third squad . . . move out!"
And we did.

Ana as'fi (*ana asif* for male) means "I am sorry" in Arabic.

Christopher P. Collins

On Leaving for Iraq a Second Time
—for Patrick

It
was like
the last time:

a high school band, American flags, families uncertain;

except my son, his hug
concentrated and arms
two years stronger—

tougher to break free.

Christopher P. Collins is an MFA poetry candidate through Murray State's low-residency program and will graduate in December 2012. He is also a former captain and veteran of both Afghanistan and Iraq. Collins currently teaches high school English and is married with two children.

Nicholas Watts-Fernandez

Bunker Sonnet

Hunkered down in bunkers—concrete; dark, damp
smelling of piss, despair, and ancient dust
Waiting for rockets to drop, pop, and bust
through sandbag shell tops, our minds are high amp

expecting clamorous death with each breath
suppressing creeping fear with short burst fire;
a Marine weapon, heavenly choir
calms my exploding heart in heaving chest

Five minutes . . . Dantean eternity
Final silence. The last blast does not come
Wipe sweat from brow; breathe, and think of my young
sitting quiet at home—praying for me?

Divine intervention reigns one more night
Live to return and continue the fight

Nicholas Watts-Fernandez joined the Navy in 2007, gaining commission through Officer Candidate School. He served on *USS Hué City* (CG 66), and *USS Rodney M. Davis* (FFG 60). He is currently stationed in Kabul, Afghanistan, and will transfer to Millington, TN, upon the conclusion of his tour. He plans on living with his wife Claudia and sons Sebastian and Ivan upon his return. He studied Philosophy (BA) and English (MA) at Southeast Missouri State University.

Jan Morrill

Hyphenated Americans

A far away war
Angry words pelt like bullets
The battle brought home

Imagine risking your life for a country that put your family behind barbed wire because they look like the enemy. My mother's oldest brother, Yoshio Sasaki, a Japanese-American, served in the United States Army *while* his family was interned. For heroic achievement while in action in Italy, he was awarded the Bronze Star.

After the bombing of Pearl Harbor, the Sasakis, as well as all Japanese-Americans on the west coast, were classified as enemy aliens and were forced to sell or give away their belongings in preparation for relocation. Approximately 120,000 Japanese-Americans were relocated to internment camps in California, Arizona, Utah, Idaho, Wyoming, and Arkansas. The Sasaki family was sent to Tule Lake Relocation Center in California. Later, they were moved again, this time to Topaz Relocation Camp in Utah.

Still, my uncle enlisted in the Army and served honorably. Following is an excerpt from the Recommendation for Award written to Uncle Yoshio's Commanding Officer on June 19, 1945:

To: Commanding Officer, 442nd Regimental Combat Team
1. Under the provisions of Army Regulations 600-45, as amended, it is recommended that Yoshio Sasaki, Sgt., Co E, 442nd Regimental Combat Team, Infantry be awarded the Bronze Star Medal.
2. Detailed description of action:
    On 23 April 1945, the third platoon of Company E was the leading element of the attack on San Terenzo, Italy. Although they received some enemy fire, the platoon entered the lower sector of the town and made an encircling movement around the hill to engage the enemy from the rear.
    As the leading elements of the platoon reached a point directly behind the town, they were pinned down by withering fire from enemy machine guns and rifles from the front and the left front. The men took what cover and concealment the terrain afforded and returned fire. During the engagement, one of the men was wounded and lay exposed to enemy observation and further fire.

"Yoshio Sasaki," U.S. Army
Courtesy of Jan Morrill

Sgt. Sasaki left his position of comparative safety and ran 25 yards in the face of intense enemy fire to aid the wounded man. Despite bullets whizzing by him constantly, Sgt. Sasaki administered first aid and dragged his wounded comrade to covered position. After making the wounded man as comfortable as possible, Sgt. Sasaki resumed firing at the enemy.

Because of his courage and fearless action with disregard for his personal safety, the wounded man was spared much suffering and later safely evacuated to an aid station.

Sgt. Sasaki's gallant action is exemplary of the best traditions of the Armed Forces of the United States.

In an excerpt from Uncle Yoshio's journal, he wrote about five Japanese-Americans from his platoon who were killed in action on that day, April 23, 1945. These men fought, even sacrificed their lives, for the United States of America, regardless of the fact their government considered their families enemy aliens.

Recently, I visited the Japanese-American Museum in Los Angeles, location of a monument titled, "Go for Broke," the motto of the 442nd. Engraved on the front of the large, black, curved tribute is a quote by President Truman, taken from a speech given to Japanese-American veterans upon their return from war:

"You not only fought the enemy—you fought prejudice and won."

Sunshine from the cloudless day warmed me as I strolled the circular walk to the back of the monument, where engraved are the names of over 16,000 Japanese-Americans who served in the 442nd Regimental Combat Team, the 100th Infantry Battalion, and the lesser-known Military Intelligence Service.

I'd already searched the site's computer database for the location of my uncle's name. Still, I walked along the wall, scanning through the thousands of names, wondering about the stories of each of the men. When I found my uncle's name, I stared at it, then closed my eyes. Like the 8mm movies he used to film, memories of my kind, gentle, and honorable uncle flashed like a motion picture in my mind. I pressed my hand against his name, surprised at the contrast of coolness to the warm day.

Yoshio Sasaki.

What thoughts must have gone through his head as he fought for a country that "relocated" his family to internment camps? How did it feel to return from battle and have to be issued a pass by armed guards before going into the camps to visit the internees? Most of all, how did it feel for an interned family to learn they'd lost a loved one in battle?

My grandparents were from Japan—*Issei*, first generation. Due to the Naturalization Act of 1790, they were not allowed to become American citizens. My mother and her siblings—*Nissei*, second generation—were born American citizens. However, during my childhood, neither my mother nor her family spoke about internment or the war, perhaps because they, like many Japanese-Americans, were too ashamed. Or perhaps it was too painful a period to re-live. Maybe it was simply their attitude of *shikata ga nai*—resigned acceptance.

As *Sansei*, third generation, I feel a responsibility to remember this history and to remind others that approximately 14,000 Japanese-American men who enlisted and served with the 442nd were Americans, too. The 442nd Regimental Combat Team became the most decorated unit in United States military history for its size and length of service, with more than 9,000 Purple Hearts and more than 4,000 Bronze Stars awarded.

They, like all American veterans, hyphenated or not, deserve to be remembered, honored, and respected.

Jan Morrill's debut novel, *The Red Kimono*, will be published by the University of Arkansas Press, Spring 2013. Her award-winning short stories and memoir essays have been published in Chicken Soup for the Soul books and several anthologies. Her short story "Xs and Os" was nominated for the Pushcart Prize. She is currently working on the sequel to *The Red Kimono*. For more information, please visit her website at www.janmorrill.com or her blog, TheRedKimono.com.

Little World
Baghdad, Iraq
7 May 2007

We were on Route Mercedes in the Ghazaliyah district, next to the abandoned school. Our lead truck got hit by what the Army calls an "Explosively Formed Penetrator," or EFP. No one in the platoon saw the EFP in the dark; even in daytime, I doubt anyone would have. The enemy's ability to conceal these particularly lethal devices inside cement curbs or rocks exceeds our ability to detect them, and before last night there hadn't been any EFP activity in Ghazaliyah anyway. I guess the S2 was actually right for once: Jaysh al-Mahdi and the other Shia insurgent groups are expanding their operations further and further outside Sadr City. But the 2 was still wrong about one thing: this EFP strike was not accompanied by any small-arms or RPG fire. It was not a "complex attack"; it was merely a simple attack. One man died—Staff Sergeant Martinez—and it was over before he knew it. The fucking slug came in through the passenger window, took off most of Martinez's head, spun around and spit out shrapnel that tore up the other three passengers, then exited through the rear driver-side window.

The boom was loud and close enough that I immediately knew someone had been killed. Then came the frantic radio calls, a hundred voices on different nets stepping all over each other. My thoughts turned off. I cleared the platoon frequency, halted the convoy to set up a cordon around the damaged vehicle. I directed the dismount teams from trucks 2 and 3 to pull out all the wounded and what remained of Martinez. I called in a Medevac. None of the other injuries were life-threatening. I heard McGinnis might lose his arm, and apparently Sparks took some shrapnel in the balls and was cursing at the top of his lungs all the way back to the FOB, but they'll live.

Amazingly, Martinez's truck was still driveable. The tires and engine block were untouched. All we had to do was clean his brains off the headrest.

It was a miracle I got any sleep last night. When we finally got back to the FOB at three in the morning, Major Philbin forced me to write a fucking publication-ready novel for a patrol debrief. It didn't matter that my platoon had just finished a grueling six-hour patrol or that we had to be up again at 0900 for vehicle maintenance; it was crucial to Major Philbin that my debrief didn't contain a single typo or incorrectly cased letter. (For the record, it's Soldier when you're talking about Americans, soldier if they're Iraqi.) Joe "Regis" Philbin: a real American hero. He plays World of Warcraft and jerks off in his CHU all day and only comes out for a cigarette break, or when a Soldier's head gets blown off. I hope Philbin's town throws him a big parade when he gets home.

It wasn't dark anymore by the time I staggered into my CHU. I stripped off my sweat-logged body armor vest and heaved it in the corner with the little energy I had left. I didn't bother with my boots or with the bloody, sweaty uniform still plastered to my skin. *My bed. Oh, my bed.* I took two last steps and collapsed into it. I turned onto my back and lay very still, arms at my sides, looking at the ceiling.

The room was loud. The thin aluminum walls and wooden desk vibrated from mortar explosions, some distant, some not nearly distant enough. A helicopter swooped past overhead, perhaps on its way to pick up the most recently dead and disfigured soldiers. The morning Call to Prayer echoed through it all from Baghdad's downtown loudspeakers. The prayer seemed a tortured cry for help that no one would ever answer: *Allahu Akbar, Ash-hadu al-la ilaha illa llah, Ash-hadu anna Muhammadu Rasulullah . . .*

My truck had ridden lead the night before. I was sitting in the passenger seat.

Suddenly my heart was pounding and I was having trouble breathing. The hot, stuffy air closed around me like a wool sack. The air stank of mud and dried blood and body odor. I cupped my hands over my nose and mouth. *Oh God, don't let me die in this place. Don't let me die.*

I didn't know Martinez as well as I knew the other squad leaders. He wasn't shy—and when he spoke he had a loud, rough voice—but he didn't say much. He was short and stocky; his small paunch was only visible when he wasn't wearing his ACU top. His coarse black hair was buzzed down almost to his scalp, and his mustache was flecked with gray. He was from some little town in Utah, but he was Mexican, not Mormon. Martinez was a capable, middle-of-the-pack NCO. Did his job, never stood out. Didn't complain much either. He believed in the war, believed we were making Iraq a better place.

I had this one conversation with him I know I'll never forget. It was during the threat update brief I give to my four squad leaders every morning. I report to them all the enemy activity in our AO over the last twenty-four hours, keep them apprised of the enemy's constantly changing tactics and weapons. A month ago I reported an EFP strike that killed five soldiers from a neighboring battalion. Five men in the Humvee, all five killed.

Martinez quickly raised his hand. "Sir, what's an EFP?"

"I was about to get to that," I said. "It's a new type of shape charge that fires out the slug at a much higher velocity. Supposedly it can pierce the steel on an Abrams. Think of it as an IED on steroids."

"Oh shit, is that like them shits they say they got coming over from Iran?" His eyes got big.

"Yeah. Supposedly they are produced in Iran. Shia groups are the only ones using them right now. Al Qaeda doesn't know how to make them yet."

"What do they look like?" Martinez asked.

"The 2's got the pictures. They're in the battalion TOC. I'll make sure you guys see them soon. Usually the firing cylinder's embedded in a cement curb or brick, or in a fake rock. So if you see a stray brick or rock lying right next to the road, that could be one."

"Sir, there are stray bricks and rocks all over the place." One of my other squad leaders pointed out the obvious truth and shrugged.

"I know. Look, if you cross paths with one of these things, it's probably just your time." I tried to be realistic with my men, and with myself. Death was always a possibility.

Martinez nodded solemnly. "Roger, sir."

One other memory of Martinez lurked menacingly in my mind, but I was mostly able to hold it at bay: he'd proudly shown me a picture of his daughter once. She looked to be about six. She was smiling and her front teeth were missing. I forget her name, thank God.

Hayya 'ala s-salah, Hayya 'ala 'l-falah, Allahu akbar, La ilaha illal-lah . . .

I fell asleep with my face pressed into the pillow. My eyes burned.

When the world returned to me, the sun was just above the horizon, though it was now approaching dusk instead of dawn. The air was pleasantly cool. A slight breeze carried the scent of fresh-raked leaves. There was no sound except for the steady whoosh of traffic on Route 17.

I was standing on the cracked sidewalk at 183 Bergen Avenue, Waldwick, New Jersey, looking at the two-story faded blue-and-white house in which I'd lived 'til I was nine. It was autumn of 1987—the year I turned six. None of this struck me as the slightest bit incongruent. R&R had simply come much earlier in the deployment than I'd expected. The Army hadn't just sent me home—they'd sent me *all* the way home. I was elated and tremendously nervous. I hoped my family would recognize me and not freak out or do anything crazy.

I paused for a few moments, arrested by the sight of this utterly plain-looking house, marveling at trees and foliage, at oranges and purples and any colors besides dirt-brown. Then I crossed our scraggly, sloping front lawn—it seemed so tiny, like a toy model of an actual front lawn—and stepped over a black plastic pistol lying in the grass. The pistol was an imitation Beretta, the model most U.S. officers in Iraq carried as a sidearm. I found myself at the porch steps and saw that the front door was wide open.

I had to stop on the porch. My heart was ripping through my chest and my hands were shaking. I almost wanted the trip to end right there. I took deep breaths to settle myself and became aware of a cool, tingly sensation on my chest. I looked down. To my great relief, I saw no uniform and no blood. I was wearing jeans and a t-shirt, my typical civilian clothing. I rubbed my chest and was surprised to feel the edges of a pair of dog tags that hung from around my neck. This was unusual. I never wore dog tags when I wasn't in uniform. Even in uniform, I always tied them to a belt loop; I never wore them around my neck. I'd always hated the feel of the metal against my skin. I removed the dog tags and stuffed them in my front pocket. Once my heartbeat had slowed and I felt calmer, I entered the house.

Mom was in the kitchen, vigorously chopping dinner ingredients on a cutting board with her back to me. She looked thinner and tidier than I'd ever seen her. Her hair was longer, darker, and fuller; it covered the entire back of her neck. She wore a red sweatshirt with the sleeves rolled up and blue jeans. It occurred to me that she was only a few years older than I was now, but the relationship between us felt exactly the same. She was still my mom; I was her son. She could've been younger than me, a teenager, and I would have looked up to her with the same respect I've always felt.

She scooped up a handful of whatever she was cutting and tossed it into the large pot boiling on the stove. The kitchen was warm from the steam and smelled of herbs and spices. Ventilation fans above the stove whirred loudly.

I didn't know how to start talking to her. I was terrified that anything I said would trigger some sort of chaos. Why would she recognize me? I was twenty-five. She'd never seen me older than six. As far as she was concerned, I was a strange man who'd walked straight into her kitchen while she was cooking dinner. *And* she had a knife. Still, beneath this near-paralyzing anxiety, I knew I had to try. "Hello?"

She kept chopping.

I cleared my throat. "Excuse me," I said.

Mom's shoulders relaxed. She set the knife on the countertop and turned around. Her jarringly youthful face was flushed and sweaty. She looked slightly agitated. "Yes?"

Her lack of surprise caught me so off-guard that I could only stand there stupidly for a few seconds, wondering how to proceed. I decided that telling the truth was the best option. "Look, I'm sorry to just barge in here on you. I don't know how to put this. It's going to sound like the craziest thing you've ever heard, but I swear I'm not a stranger, and I'm harmless. I'm Chris—your son." I put my hands up in a gesture of innocence, made my voice soft and reassuring.

Mom arched her eyebrows arched a little, but she didn't look all that impressed.

"Uh, so, I know this is probably hard to believe, but you have to trust me. I'm Chris from the future. I'm twenty-five now. I just wanted to stop in and say hello, see how things are going. This has actually been a fantasy of mine for a long time."

Mom broke into her familiar bright, genuine smile. Still, I could sense that she was slightly impatient. It was as if she knew everything I was going to say before I said it. "Wow, twenty-five. So what's that like? Is it what you wanted?"

I shook my head. It was so bizarre I had to just go with it. "Yeah, it's good. Everything's good. I'm happy. My life is good. I just—"

"And how's the Army?" Her smile dropped.

"What? The Army?" Did she know I was in the Army?

Mom narrowed her eyes. "Chris, come on."

My gaze fell to the flower-patterned linoleum floor. I remembered the pattern from when I'd played with my toys under the kitchen table while Mom cooked dinner.

"I never wanted you to join, you know." She didn't sound angry or even disappointed, just concerned. "I never wanted you to go to West Point."

"I know," I said in almost a whisper.

"Are you safe, Chris? Tell me the truth."

I looked up to see her suddenly desperate, pleading expression. "I'm very safe," I said. "I never leave the base. The worst thing I have to deal with is boredom." I wanted to stamp the words into her, over and over.

Mom nodded. I knew she didn't believe me.

"Mom?"

"Hmm?"

"I just don't understand. Why are you acting as though any of this is normal?"

She grabbed a rag off the counter to wipe her hands. "I'm sorry," she said, her voice shifting gears. "I'm in the middle of making dinner right now." She flashed an apologetic smile, turned around, and resumed chopping. "If you want to help you can set the table. There's four of us. Five, if you want a plate."

I gaped at her. How in the world did she not find this fascinating? Someone had actually managed to travel back in time. Not just any someone, *her son*. And she was worried about making dinner? Jesus. At least she'd given me a task. I felt ridiculous, standing there like a big dumb ape in that little squeezed-in kitchen.

"Wait—before you do that, could you put the garlic back for me? Up there." Mom opened a cabinet next to the refrigerator and pointed at a spice rack above her reach.

I took the garlic and put it back. "What are you making?"

"Sausage and peppers. Are you hungry?"

"No, not really. It smells good though."

"I know why you're here," Mom said.

I froze.

"Christopher is upstairs playing in his room. You know how he is, he goes into his own little world sometimes, keeps himself busy for hours. After you set the table, go say hi. I'm sure he'll be glad to see you."

My heart started pounding again; I had to take deep, slow breaths. Why Mom knew my purpose and acted as though a visit from Future Man was part of her nightly routine instantly ceased to matter. I was standing right there next to her but she was talking about *me*, another me. Christopher. Her words, her description of Christopher, this encounter that I now realized was going to happen: all of it overwhelmed me. I closed my eyes, placed my hands on either side of my head. My temples throbbed. *Breathe. Stay with it. Stay. Don't leave.*

For years I'd had a recurring dream in which I'd traveled back to my early childhood. In the dream, however, I'd always been an ageless, invisible presence that could only observe from a distance. I'd enter my old house and spy on the 1980s versions of my parents and younger brother. As much as I wanted to, I could never observe myself; it was as if even the dream had to abide by the universal law that one person cannot exist in two places at once. Yet whatever was happening to me now was no dream, I was sure. I had a body now. I could talk, take part in conversations. The sensations, smells, and images were incredibly vivid. It was all real. And my younger self was upstairs, waiting for me.

The certainty that I wasn't dreaming, that I'd managed to defy reality, filled me with a sense of power and confidence. "Are you sure I can go? It's ok with you? I don't want to scare him or anything."

Mom stopped chopping and turned around. She looked amused. "Chris, you're not gonna scare him. Just go and say hi."

I finished setting the table and walked into the living room. Everything was as I remembered it—the brown-and-white brick fireplace with Mom's winged angel statue on the mantel, the convex, multi-paned window overlooking the front yard, the "Monique Valdeneige" painting of cats perched on a windowsill. The antique wooden chair and coat rack beside the front door. The cream-colored walls, the dark brown carpet, the lighter brown sofas, the bookshelves filled with Mom's books were all . . . beautiful. I was home.

My younger brother Eric was standing on the middle cushion of the large sofa. He was two. A diaper bulged inside his gray sweatpants. He pointed at me and began squealing and bouncing on the cushion when I walked into the room.

"Hi, Eric."

He raised his arms to his sides for balance and stepped cautiously from the sofa onto the adjacent coffee table. Then, crouching first, he leapt off. His stumpy legs buckled when he landed, and he face-planted on the carpet. I thought he might cry, but he rolled onto his back and began giggling, his small chest heaving.

"Are you ok?"

"Yes!" His voice was shrill as a whistle blast.

I had no idea how to interact with a toddler. I felt even more awkward than I had in the kitchen. "Are you having fun?"

"Yes!" He rocked himself into a sitting position, then rolled back and kicked his legs over his head, as if he were attempting a reverse somersault. He didn't have the strength, and his legs collapsed in front of him. He lay spread-eagled on the floor, shrieking in delight. I couldn't wait to tell present-day Eric that I'd gone back and seen him when he was two. I knew he'd get a kick out of it. I missed my brother.

Suddenly I got the feeling that I was being watched. I turned toward the staircase and saw a young boy peering between the wooden handrail supports. He wore a red plastic pair of prank eyeglasses with big blue eyeballs covering his eyes. He was smirking mischievously.

For a moment the entire room seemed to shake and my vision blurred. It was similar to the disorienting feeling I'd had when IEDs exploded near my Humvee. My consciousness felt stretched to its limit. I nearly blacked out.

"There you are," he said. "It's about time."

The initial shock passed, but my head was still churning. I couldn't move. I was afraid that if I so much as flexed a muscle or spoke a single syllable, I'd somehow lose all this. It was too good to be true. It *couldn't* be true. And yet it was. It felt as true and real as anything I'd ever felt. I was standing there in my jeans and t-shirt and dog tags, looking at myself from twenty years ago. *He was right there in front of me.*

"Aren't you gonna say anything?" The boy's hands were curled around the handrail supports.

My throat felt tight and parched, as if I hadn't used my voice in years. What could I say? The moment seemed far too precious to spoil with mundane words. Besides, what if I said the wrong thing? What if who I'd become scared him?

I remembered the confidence I'd felt in the kitchen at having defied reality. It dawned on me that none of this was an accident or a game or a cute dream. This was a mission. I had been ordered to come back to my childhood, and I was here with a very specific objective. I didn't know what that objective was, but I had to push forward, at all costs.

I gulped, squeezed my eyes shut. "Hi."

"Hi." A squeaky, high-pitched version of my voice responded.

I kept my eyes closed in the hope that it would somehow both preserve the moment and make me appear less threatening. "Uh, you know who I am?"

"Mmm hmm. You're Chris."

I opened my eyes. He was still there, still wearing the prank eyeglasses. Still smirking. He had a mound of thick brown hair with an Alfalfa cowlick and bangs down to his eyebrows. His smile, my smile, revealed a pair of missing front teeth. God, it was weird.

I hesitated, worried that a step toward him would be too much, yet nothing about my visit thus far had seemed at all disruptive. My fascination overpowered any unease, and I walked to the foot of the staircase.

Christopher sat on one of the middle stairs. He wore my all-time favorite piece of clothing—my purple t-shirt with the blue gorilla. Mom still had to dress me in the mornings before school; if left on my own, I'd have worn that t-shirt every single day. Christopher also wore red Adidas running shorts with a white stripe down each side and white tube socks pulled up to just below his knobby knees. Neighborhood friends had teased me for wearing my socks pulled up, once it became fashionable to push them down. I'd kept pulling them up anyway, 'til the lonely day the taunts broke through and I realized I had to conform.

"So . . . how's it going?" I said, ashamed of how absurd it sounded.

Rather than answer, Christopher snapped his head forward. The blue eyeballs fell down his cheeks, hanging on thin plastic springs below his chin. He shook his head side to side and the eyeballs flung about like swings on an amusement park ride. My initial stab at conversation apparently hadn't interested him. This didn't surprise me. I'd never liked vague, small-talky questions.

"I'm sorry," I said, rubbing my forehead. "I'm a little confused right now. You recognize me? Have we met before?"

Christopher removed the eyeglasses. His real eyes seemed closer together compared to my current face, perhaps because his face was smaller. He shrugged. "You're my friend."

I had no idea what to make of this. Clearly, he knew more about what was happening than I did. I felt enormously humbled. He trusted me completely. I was no stranger. I had an odd urge to fall to my knees and shower him with gratitude.

"Wanna see my toys? I got some new Transformers."

Uh oh. I felt dangerously close to crying. I swallowed, pushed it back down. "Yeah, ok." My voice barely registered.

Christopher slapped his hands on his thighs. "Well, what are you waiting for? Let's go!" He stood and ran to the top of the stairs. "Come on! Don't just stand there."

"I'm coming, I'm coming."

He led me into my old room. I was relieved at how familiar it felt, as if I'd only left it behind a few months ago. I was also greatly amused to see a blocky wooden end table that I still use in my present-day bedroom in my family's new house. Some things just don't change.

I'd interrupted Christopher in the midst of quite a battle. Bucket loads of colorful action figures were sprawled over the fuzzy beige carpet. Some were standing, others had fallen. Many were intertwined in ongoing combat. A plastic green and gray castle with a red-eyed skull above its portcullis sat directly in the middle of the carnage.

"Ok, here's what's happening," Christopher said, eager to brief me so he could return to the action. "He-Man and the other good guys are trying to protect Castle Greyskull against Skeletor and the bad guys. Skeletor is very bad and evil." He held up Skeletor. The figure's sharply-chiseled features reminded me of the characters from the movie *300,* which I'd just seen on Hajji bootleg. "I'm He-Man, but you can be whoever you want from the good guys. There's Battle Cat, Optimus Prime, Hot Rod— he's one of my new ones, Sergeant Slaughter, Deep Six, Ultra Magnus. . ." He held up each figure as he said their names.

"I remember," I said.

"Make sure you kill all the bad guys at the end, but don't make it too easy for them. Some of the good guys have to die too. I usually let Battle

Cat die since I don't like him as much." He held up Battle Cat again. "So who do you want to be?"

He-Man was always my top choice, and his unabashed corniness made him seem the coolest pick now. Since he was taken, I went with my second favorite character, Optimus Prime.

Christopher passed him over to me. The talking part out of the way, he plopped to his stomach and resumed his defense of the castle. His enthusiasm and focus were palpable. I knew he spent hours carefully setting up the figures, waging these epic room-sized battles, then fighting with Dad about cleaning them up. The tip of his tongue was visible at the corner of his mouth, my habit whenever I'm concentrating on something important.

I studied Christopher's technique for a minute or two, remembering. It wasn't simply how you maneuvered the combatants against one another; you had to make the appropriate sound effects: audible punches and kicks and head-butts, grunts and screams, occasional cheers. Once I got on my stomach and joined in, I was pleased with how quickly it all came back. The main trick was to keep the outcome of each duel in doubt as long as possible; this both heightened the suspense and made the bad guy believe he had a chance.

As successive waves of attacking enemy met their fate, I caught myself continually zoning out to watch Christopher. He seemed like a natural at directing this full-scale, intricately-detailed battle. He always seemed to know exactly who to make die and who to make live. It was all part of a plan that existed only in his head. What I found particularly mesmerizing was that Christopher had truly entered into his own little world. I'd somehow lost touch with what it was like to exist in that way, folded up into yourself, the larger, complex world left far behind. If only for a short time, the larger world doesn't matter. It's just you.

The battle had ended. Skeletor was dead. Christopher and I were sitting on the lower bunk of my bunk bed. We'd been talking for a while, I don't know how long. Mostly, he'd been talking. He'd been telling me about first grade and Ms. Criqui and the different boys and girls in his class.

Suddenly I got very fidgety. There was something outside I needed to see. I stood. "Hey, come over here a minute." I led Christopher to the large window overlooking the neighborhood.

A Bravo Company Humvee was parked in the street directly in front of my house. Though the Humvee was intact, the passenger window looked like it had been bashed in with a baseball bat. Sergeant Martinez was in the front passenger seat, slumped over and motionless. Christopher and I couldn't see anything else from where we stood.

"Look." I pointed at Sergeant Martinez.

"Who's that?"

"That's Sergeant Martinez."

"Is he ok?"

I swallowed over a hard lump in my throat. "Yeah, he's—he's fine. He's just tired so he's taking a nap. He had a long day." My voice cracked and my eyes began to sting.

Christopher turned to me. "Why are you crying?"

I rubbed my eyes, tried to laugh. "I'm not, I'm not."

Christopher placed his hand on my arm. "Yes, you are, Chris. You're crying."

This broke me. It was sudden and complete. I lost all control.

I felt Christopher's arms around me. He hugged me close to his small body. "It's ok, Chris, it's ok. Please don't cry. You're going to be ok."

I cried harder. "Oh God, I couldn't . . . I'm sorry. I'm so sorry. Please. . ."

He kept his arms around me until I was finished. Then he stepped back. "Better now?"

A final sob shuddered through me. I wiped away the tears. "Better."

"Wanna go outside and play guns before dinner?"

I managed a smile. "Sure, that sounds fun."

"Well, don't just stand there. Let's go!" He grabbed my hand and pulled me out the door.

My eyes opened. I was looking at a white, dirt-smudged ceiling, instantly aware that I was awake and that I'd been dreaming. I picked my head up off the pillow. My body armor vest, with my name on one breast pocket and US ARMY on the other, stood against the wall. An M-4 rifle lay against the vest. *Yep, a dream. I'm back now.* The air was hot and still.

I looked at my wristwatch: 0822. Though I'd been asleep for less than three hours, I felt completely replenished. I felt happy. Not overjoyed, just . . . reassured. Strengthened.

This feeling has propelled me through another long, difficult day. After vehicle maintenance, we got called on an unexpected mission to pull security around a Bradley that caught on fire on Route Michigan. I watched the flames engulf the abandoned vehicle and thought of Sergeant Martinez, of the letter I have to write his family explaining that he didn't die in vain, that it was for a good cause. I kept imagining his daughter reading this letter one day. I wondered whether she'd save it, perhaps even pass it along to her children when she grew old. How long will it be until Sergeant Martinez's sacrifice is forgotten? How long until all the sacrifices from this war are forgotten?

I think about sleep, and I want so badly to revisit the world I entered last night. I want to finish playing guns with Christopher, to sit down to dinner with my 1987 family. I want to see Dad this time, when he was young and vital. I can't even begin to express how deeply I want these things.

Yet something tells me I will never have the dream again, not as I felt it last night. If I return again, it will be as the invisible, distant presence. Last night was a one-time gift. It gave me what I needed, and now I must push forward.

Chris Whitehead is a recent graduate of the Rutgers-Newark MFA in Creative Writing Program and an Army veteran of two tours to Iraq. He currently resides in Wall, New Jersey.

Gerardo Mena

Ode to the Enemy Sniper

Searching for your defining
moment, you've come to dance
in our little war. Life is nothing
more than a turn

of the windage knob, a slight
adjustment for distance, a tight
lungful of breath, a sight
bearing black reticle,

that crosshair etched into your lens
like a crucifix, reaching for the edges
of your omniscient circle, a transfer
of kinetic energy from man,

to machine, to man. The word
Dragunov strikes fear into your enemies,
but in you it triggers
a yearning for combustion, a need for heavy

recoil running deep throughout the recesses
of the body; and so you aim steady, you squeeze
slowly, propelling your projectile towards
the plexus that turns off the world.

You are an artist, casting ballistic
beauty onto your canvas,
a surgeon—your bullet,
a magnificent scalpel.

Gerardo Mena is a decorated Iraqi Freedom veteran. He spent six years in Special Operations with the Reconnaissance Marines. He was awarded a Navy Achievement Medal with a V for Valor for multiple acts of bravery. He has been nominated for a Pushcart, was selected for *Best New Poets 2011*, and has several poems published or forthcoming from several journals. For more information go to www.gerardomena.com.

Christopher Lee Miles

War Is Steel

War is steel,

        and steel: the antithesis to bone.
Unconcerned, steel floats in slopping Arabian water
and never caresses land. The bones remember land
and the land remembers steel, the pit where it once
belonged, or the strip where it bedded down

        with the roots now tapping
        the foreheads of sailors. The wind-swept
        teal-blue surface of the Gulf does not mirror

the sleek destroyer's hull. Signal flags unfurl,
the mast sways like a metronome, red lights swivel
in their jars: general quarters, fire-suits on,
man battle-stations, launch tomahawks:

        not a system,
        but the effect of the system, the equanimity
        of pushing buttons, the man-shame of death-fear
        within a gas-mask's face-grip. The void
        of reflections filled by orders. Orders we must

follow the way steel must hold the keel taut, the way each rib
rocks in the sea's body: *a roll and a pitch and a heave
and a pitch*, a tongueless mouth

        eating the steel plates we strike from.

Christopher Lee Miles's work appears in *Connecticut Review*, *Cortland Review*, *Atlanta Review*, and is forthcoming in *Sugarhouse Review*, *Salamander*, and *War, Literature, and the Arts*. A veteran of Operation Iraqi Freedom and Operation Enduring Freedom, he lives in Fairbanks, Alaska.

In Less Than a Minute

"Know what this is all about?" I asked Ben Fischer, 1ˢᵗ class boson's mate, as he joined Rico and me on deck.

"No idea," he said.

"Maybe they're gonna send us home," Rico said. "You know, an early out for good behavior, like when you're in prison." Rico was the gunner's mate on our boat crew.

"Don't know much about prison, Rico," I said. "Why don't you fill us in?"

"Oh, they'd like your fresh little ass, Murph."

I gave him a good-natured shove. It was 1966, and our ship, the LST *USS Sussex County*, had been on station in the Mekong River for three months. I was a 3ʳᵈ class radioman. Aside from our regular jobs on the ship, Ben, Rico, and I made up the boat crew for the number two LCVP. Ben was the coxswain and skippered the boat, except in obvious combat situations, when Lieutenant, JG (junior grade) Henry took charge.

"Attention on deck!" Ben shouted as Mr. Henry and another officer came through the hatch. The three of us, in blue ball caps, white t-shirts, and dungaree work pants, snapped to attention. Mr. Henry, a lanky, coffee-colored six-footer, was wearing a new set of gold Lieutenant's bars on the collar of his crisp khaki uniform.

"As you were," he said.

"You got promoted," Ben said. "Way to go, sir." We all congratulated him and shook his hand.

"Thanks. I want to introduce you guys to someone. This is Ensign Douglas Piercy." Piercy was baby-faced but solidly built, with light brown hair and a fair complexion. He stood about five-two. "Ensign Piercy will be replacing me as communications officer. He'll also be taking command of the number two boat."

Everyone had been wondering about Piercy. He had come aboard yesterday and spent most of his time sequestered in the officer's quarters. This morning the XO had given him a tour of the ship.

"What are *you* gonna do, Mr. Henry?" Rico asked.

"I've been transferred to the *Wexford County*. I'm leaving tomorrow."

"Aw, man." Rico verbalized what we were all thinking. It would be tough losing Mr. Henry. Our first day on station, we were unloading Marines up a narrow tributary when the boats came under small-arms and mortar fire. It was loud and crazy and everyone was ready to shit themselves. Mr. Henry had been a rock and somehow got us focused. We returned fire, got the guys off the boat, and everyone made it through okay. He'd been with us on some other tough assignments, and we had really come together as a team. Thanks to him, we believed there was nothing the number two boat couldn't do.

Mr. Henry introduced us to Ensign Piercy one by one, and we shook hands. He had an eager smile, a strong handshake, and seemed genuinely pleased to meet us. It was a good start, I thought.

"Ensign Piercy, anything you'd like to say to the men?" Mr. Henry said.

Piercy seemed startled at first, then gathered himself up as if he were about to make an important political speech. He clenched his right hand into a fist and drove it into his left palm after every few sentences, to emphasize points. "I'm really glad to be here in *Nam*," he said.

Mr. Henry started to roll his eyes but caught himself.

"I know a lot of guys would fight to stay away, but it's all I could think about since I got out of OCS. Going to Nam, that's all I've wanted to do. And four months later, here I am." He smiled, smacked his fist into his hand. "I'm really happy to be assigned as your boat skipper. We're going to have fun."

Mr. Henry winced.

"I've been on a lot of boats," Piercy said, "so I know a few things there. My uncle had a twenty-eight foot Thompson, and I used to take it out in the Chesapeake all the time."

"Doug." Mr. Henry looked at his watch. "The Captain wants to spend some one-on-one, time with you and these guys need to get back to work. Why don't you finish up later."

"Oh. Okay."

"Good to meet you, sir," Ben said and saluted. We all saluted and the officers saluted back and took their leave. It looked like Mr. Henry was chewing Piercy out as they went through the entrance hatch.

"Couldn't wait to get to *Nam*," I said.

"We'll see how long that lasts," Ben said.

"He's gonna have some pointers for you, Mr. Coxswain," Rico said to Ben. "After driving his uncle's Thompson, I bet he knows a thing or two about seamanship." Rico clenched his fist and theatrically smacked it into his palm. "He'll have your boat-coxswain ass squared away, post haste."

Ben grinned and we all laughed, but I wondered—what were we going to be in for with Ensign Douglas Piercy?

Aside from being over-the-top gung-ho, Piercy turned out to be a decent guy. As communications officer he was in and out of the radio shack, so I saw him a lot. He was curious, eager to learn and rarely exercised his authority, which was refreshing compared to other young jerk officers I had worked for. He was the same way in the boat, wanting to learn as much as he could from Ben. We went out on a few training runs, and he basically sat back and watched. There was no doubt he loved every minute of it though. You could see it when he put on the helmet and flack-jacket, his mouth spread into a wide grin, and he seemed to get a little taller than his diminutive five-two. Maybe it was the baby face, but he reminded me of when I was a kid, carrying a toy gun and wearing my dad's old army jacket, fighting Germans and Japs with my buddies.

On one of our training runs, Piercy brought a camera and took pictures of the crew and the number one boat doing a landing. At one point he handed me the camera. "Get a couple shots of me," he said. I got him standing next to Ben, then with Rico and the 30 caliber machine gun, then one of just Piercy, his arm resting on the gun as he looked into the distance. I handed the camera back. "Did you get the jungle in the background?" he asked.

"Yes, sir. Got it."

"Okay, good," he said. He snapped the leather case over the lens. Rico was standing behind him. He made a wild face, clenched his fist, and pantomimed driving it into his palm. I turned away to keep from laughing.

While on station, the *Sussex County* served as a hub for all military boats operating in the southern part of the Delta. Boats came and went every day: Navy PBRs (river patrol boats), Army LCMs (mike boats), South Vietnamese craft of every variety, Aussie and other allied boats, all heavily armed and many showing signs of a scrape or two. At night we frequently had boats rafted alongside. When Ensign Piercy wasn't on duty, he was talking with the boat crews and enthusiastically observing everything.

A few weeks after he arrived, the sound of automatic weapons and sporadic explosions brought everyone up to the deck. To the north, black smoke rose slowly over the jungle in two wide towers, its lazy rise incongruous with the frantic pops and splattering of gunfire beneath. Someone pointed down river and we all turned to see two Navy A-1 Skyraiders, heavily loaded with ordinance, rapidly approaching at low altitude. We could see the pilots as they passed over the ship and then veered toward the smoke. Within seconds, a series of loud explosions rocked the nearby jungle, the blast concussions eerily visible.

The ships loud speaker blared, "Prepare for aircraft arrival."

Boson-mates scrambled to the main deck and pulled on their life-jackets as the thumping sounds of a helicopter approached. Seconds later, a Huey gunship appeared on the port side, hovered over the deck, and set down. The engine was running, the blade still turning when the pilot pushed open the door and got out. He immediately went underneath the aircraft. Piercy was watching everything from the rail on the 2nd level outside the radio shack. I joined him.

"Sir," I said.

"Hey, Murph."

"What's going on?" I asked.

"He called in and said he'd been hit by small-arms fire."

We watched as the pilot ran his hands along the body of the helicopter feeling for leaks, checking for structural damage, moving fast as if he had somewhere he needed to go. He finally waved at the ship's bridge, got back in the helicopter, and lifted off.

"Those guys do it all, don't they?" Piercy said. "They're into it hot and heavy every day. God, what I wouldn't give." He shook his head. We listened to the pounding of the engine and watched the Huey head out over the jungle toward the smoke. The gunfire had stopped.

"So you guys have been under fire, huh?" Piercy said. He looked up at me.

"We had a few rounds fired at the ship when we first dropped anchor. They haven't bothered us since."

"No, I mean out on the boats," he said.

I nodded. "A couple times."

"Man, that's gonna be something."

"We're kind of hoping it doesn't happen again, sir."

He thought for a second. "Right. I hear you." He turned back and tried to spot the Huey. We could still hear the engine in the distance.

Several days later, around four in the afternoon, a troop transport helicopter set down on the deck and twelve heavily armed men, two officers and ten enlisted, got off. The way they carried themselves and their compact weaponry said right away these weren't the normal Army and Marine troops we had been dealing with up until now. They assembled in a loose group as the officers talked to our XO. Then there was a spontaneous cheer, and the men dropped their equipment on the cargo-hatch cover and hustled down to the galley as if they were about to have their first real meal in a long time.

Twenty minutes later the boat crews got the call.

Ben, Rico, and I went to the armory and checked out our weapons. We were readying the LCVP for launch when Ensign Piercy climbed aboard with a Thompson sub-machine gun. "Okay. Listen up, guys," he said. He was trying to be all business, but he was bubbling with excitement. "We're taking a Navy SEAL team about three miles inland."

I glanced at Ben and nodded. He had guessed they were SEALs.

"The number one boat's got the lead, so Lieutenant Powers will call the shots," Piercy said. "I've been told it's all familiar territory until the last mile." He unfolded a small chart made from an aerial photo of the Delta and handed it to Ben. We looked over Ben's shoulder as Piercy pointed at the spot. It was in a small tributary, maybe a hundred feet wide at the most, and very close to the bombardment we had watched a few days ago.

That could be a good thing or a bad thing, I thought. I glanced at Rico. He looked at me for a moment, then turned around and started stowing ammo boxes in the compartment next to his machinegun.

Six of the SEALs came on board along with two more of our guys, Spin, a gunner's mate, and Marty, a boson. Spin and Marty were best friends and often joined our boat-crew when there was a need for more hands. They were both carrying M1s, relics from the Korean War that still filled out the LST's armory.

The davits swung out, and the deck crew winched the LCVP down to the water. Ben fired up the engine as Rico and I released the cables. Ensign Piercy had us move forward fifty feet off the starboard side of the ship. We went to idle and waited for Lieutenant Power's boat. Piercy sat with the butt of the Thompson resting on his leg, his arm encircling the gun as he took the wrapper off a long cigar.

He caught my gaze and nodded. "Nice day for a boat ride, eh, Murph?"

I wasn't sure what to say. I think the guy was still playing dress-up. I wondered if he had brought his camera. "Just another cruise on the Chesapeake," I said.

He started to smile, but then realized I wasn't smiling. He turned away and slipped the stogy in his mouth, unlit. He looked ridiculous.

The number one boat came around the bow from the port side, and we fell in behind at about ten knots. Ben kicked the engine down to maintain a safe distance. Diesel fumes from the lead boat swirled at their stern and thickened the hot, humid air. I did a radio check with Lieutenant Powers and then with the ship; everything was working fine.

We left the river and entered a familiar tributary about four hundred feet wide with jungle looming over both sides. This area had been cleared of hostiles several months ago and, as far as we knew, was fairly safe. It would go on that way for about a mile until we came to a stretch of mud flats and tall grasses. After that, all bets were off. The stream would narrow, the jungle would close in again and how we did was the luck of the draw.

The SEALs seemed awfully nonchalant for guys who were about to get dumped off into enemy territory. The five enlisted were still talking about the meal they just had and joking with Spin and Marty, making fun of their old guns. I was sitting in front of Ben with the radio receiver. Rico was in the gun turret behind us. Piercy and the SEAL lieutenant were a few feet away, talking. I couldn't hear them over the drone of the engine, but Piercy, cigar in the corner of his mouth, his back stiff as a rail to gain optimum height, kept his gaze focused up-river and pointed out things to the lieutenant like a tour guide, one who had been here a hundred times before.

We passed through the flats and entered the new tributary. The channel narrowed and the jungle closed in. The radio crackled with a call from Lieutenant Powers to "look alive."

"Roger that," Piercy answered.

The SEAL lieutenant spread his men out to cover both sides of the boat. Rico chambered a round in the thirty. Piercy moved next to Ben and held the butt of the Thompson on his hip. We reduced speed and motored slowly up-river, the diesel engine now a soft burble.

After a few minutes, we went around a bend and found the water strewn with huge limbs and broken trees, many stuck in the mud in awkward positions, some with roots still attached. On the eastern side of the stream, what remained of the jungle was blackened and twisted. The stench of gasoline and cordite still hung in the air from the bombardment three days ago. Hundreds of bare tree trunks stood splintered apart or with their tops completely gone. I wasn't sure we could get by the debris, but the first boat pushed through and we followed close behind, logs and branches clunking underneath, scraping the length of the hull, then twisting and bobbing in our wake.

When we got close to the drop point, the coxswain in the lead boat pointed at something along the edge of the stream. Lieutenant Powers checked it with his binoculars, and then turned and motioned for us to look. It was a body, one of ours, bloated, face down in the mud, legs in the water. As the wake from the number one boat rolled along the shoreline the man's boots surfaced and submerged with each successive wave.

Everyone in the boat stared as we went past. I was reminded of a previous deployment to the delta when we had aided in the recovery of a downed helicopter where twelve guys had been killed. It was nothing I ever wanted to do again. I glanced at Rico, our funnyman, who looked back at me as if he bore the weight of the world on his shoulders.

"Let's stay alert, guys." The lieutenant directed the comment to his team, but all of us, including Ensign Piercy, went back on guard and tried to refocus on the difficult business at hand.

We made the landing without incident, and the SEALs were off the boat and out of sight before we raised the ramps and backed away from the shore. I hadn't realized how comforting their presence had been and suddenly felt very exposed. It would be good to get back to familiar territory, but there was something we had to do first.

When we reached the spot where we had seen the corpse, the lead boat went idle and our radio speaker crackled with a call from Lieutenant Powers. "You guys execute the recovery. We'll stand off and provide cover."

The boats were a hundred feet apart. I could see Powers looking at us, holding the mic, waiting for a response. Ensign Piercy was sitting with his arm hooked over the gunnel staring at the body. He seemed frozen in place.

"Sir?" I said.

He threw the cigar overboard, and then turned and looked at me.

I waited a moment then pressed the mic and responded for him. "Roger that, sir."

Ben motioned for Spin and Marty to join him at the helm. He pointed at a clearing about twenty feet downstream. "I'm going to beach right there and drop the ramp. You guys are going to have to get your feet wet. Leave the guns. Be careful and be as quick as you can." Ben turned to me. "Murph, you need to have things ready when they get back on board."

I nodded.

"I want to be off the beach in less than a minute." Ben waited for this to sink in. "Okay, let's do it."

Spin and Marty went forward and lay their rifles on the deck. I opened the main storage compartment and got a body-bag. Ben turned the boat and headed toward the bank. The stench of rotting flesh wafted over the bow.

I unfolded the heavy bag and watched the bloated corpse at the edge of the jungle grow larger and more real. I wondered about the guy, how he ended up all alone here in the river. Ben jammed the motor in reverse and revved the engine. The boat drifted to the bank and stopped in the mud.

Rico stood ready on the thirty as Ben dropped the bow-ramp. Spin and Marty scrambled ashore. Ensign Piercy looked away and took a deep breath.

The sailors approached the corpse and, one on each side, grasped its belt and the neck of its flack-jacket and hustled it toward the boat. Foul bugs and entrails dropped and splattered into the shallow water. Both arms were gone; one at the shoulder, the other just above the elbow. A lot of facial flesh had been cleaned to the bone.

The three of us slipped the rubberized plastic around the body, tucked things in as best we could and zippered it shut. Ensign Piercy leaned over the side and vomited into the river.

Ben lifted the ramp, revved the engine hard in reverse, and the boat slowly backed away from shore. He gave Powers a thumbs-up.

Piercy wiped his face and sat down on a rusted toolbox. He looked up at Ben, Rico, and me. He was shaking.

"Sorry," he said.

He shifted his gaze to the bag, removed his helmet, and held it in both hands. "Sorry."

We fell in behind the number one boat. Rico lit a cigarette and took a long drag.

Russell Reece is a Vietnam vet who served in the Navy from 1963–1966. He has had stories and essays published in *Memoir(and)*, *Crimespree Magazine*, *Delaware Beach Life*, *Delmarva Quarterly*, *Sliver of Stone*, *EarthSpeak*, *The Fox Chase Review*, and other online and print journals. Russ is a University of Delaware alumnus and a board member of the Delaware Literary Connection, a non-profit championing the literary arts in Delaware. He lives in Bethel, Delaware, along the beautiful Broad Creek.

Levi Bollinger

Distant Seitz

We sit in lawn chairs and listen,
Kevlar helmets pressed on our skulls,
flak vests snapped to guard our souls,
and still we gaze above, into that starry
chasm, where we know mortars fly.

And again the silence, and again jarred
by an invisible shove to the chest
and burst to the ears from the impact.

> *Log Base Seitz.* someone says
> *Of course it's Seitz, dumbass.*
> *Poor bastards are gettin' it again.*
> *You boys are damn lucky*
> *   you don't have anything*
> *   to do with logistics.*

Silence again,
punctuated by another body shove
and another eardrum blast.

> *Anderson was hit the other day.*
> *No kiddin'?*
> *Yep, shrapnel right in his ass-cheek.*
> *Purple heart an' a trip back stateside, huh?*
> *Yeah. Blood gushin' everywhere, though, they said,*
> *   and he was screamin' and floppin' everywhere.*

Still, we gaze into the ethereal mess,
where unseen mortars sail,
whistle through the steamy
atmosphere, plunge down,
down, into a wild fray of
splayed camo-netting and
sandbag-shelled tents, rip
themselves apart amid
grids of connex boxes,

burst and slash,
shred and mangle.
Soldiers there hunker
in bunkers below,
probably smoking,
probably cursing,
probably wanting
to sleep.

But we, under the arc of those trajectories,
stare above at the same smattering of
heavenly beauties in divine parade
that has smiled lightly down on millennia
of Mesopotamian bloodshed.

We say they're stunning, seen in their collective splendor,
seen in the marshaled glory of their gathered masses,
seen from an impossible distance that fails
to account for the raging self-combustion
and churning fusion boiling in the core
of each celestial heart—each pinprick
of majesty housing its hellish
conflagration in seas of cold
and lonely distance so
remote from any other
speck of light that
it may well be
your best option
to torch a roaring
inferno of self-
fired destruction
and let the
enormity of
the universe
see that
by God I do exist. . .

But oh so tranquil seen from here,
down here under my sweaty Kevlar,
looking up and knowing invisible
missiles float overhead even now.

How much longer you think this will last?
At least another hour, I bet.
Hell, 'til we get home.
Probably even then. We just won't hear it there.

So we sit and stare as more mortars explode,
worry that home seems as far as these stars.

Levi Bollinger

Blind

The sun sings his last warbling orange
and yellow rays to the approaching night.

LT and O'Fallon echo in giggles
as they toss bits of gravel into the
purpling sky, into the river of
bats flitting from light to darkness,
watch bat after bat
dart, strike, crack
its blind head into
a stone its sonar
mistook for a meal.

Behind them, in the distance, squats the wall:
perimeter, the lone row of stone shutting
sun from view and us from a field
of fledgling cane, a ramshackle farmhouse,
and beyond that, unseen Iraq.

Tossing rocks into the stream of flailing
bats, they fail to see how in nine months
the stones of that wall will haunt them,
fail to see, in nine months' time, on an
Easter Sunday, under heavens the color
of ease and infant laughter, that
the field of waving cane beyond will
erupt into a hammering of AK-47's,
assailants unseen among slender
streaks of green pocked with yellow-orange
flames of muzzle flashes. The stone wall will
ping and scream under the barrage.

O'Fallon doesn't see that he is
the machine-gunner on watch that day,
doesn't see his hands bolt to action,
train the muzzle on any movement in the reeds,
smatter controlled bursts to pin down

enemy advances, hold assailants in place for
riflemen to pick off, for the armor to
roll in and snuff out:
his conduct a meet offering to
the Rule that trained his hands to act.

LT likewise blind, he
leads his victorious watch to
search the dead for intelligence
and to recover weapons, blind
when O'Fallon stops at the twitching
boy of twelve facedown in the crumpled
cane, riddled with seeping pools of blood,
pools possible only from an automatic rifle—
O'Fallon's the sole
such rifle on watch.

Tall in the cane,
O'Fallon is able
to see the boy rattle
and gag into afterlife.

LT will tell him it's a clean kill,
that black light reveals gunpowder
on those stiffening fingers:
running ammo to the others—
certain an enemy combatant.
We will all mouth the same
muted words to his deaf ears.

Still, the twitching boy of twelve pierced
by O'Fallon's rounds pierces
his nights' silence until
sleep stops and
O'Fallon roams,
marked
by black rims and bloodshot,
to visit the watches of each night,
a ghost groping for atonement:
blood calls from the cane.

But here in this falling dusk, all we know
is that he and LT get their kicks
by smacking bats' heads with
bits of gravel as the summer
suns melt into the sprouting
cane beyond the stone wall.

Levi Bollinger

SPC Browning Speaks

I still can't stop my hands from shakin. Ole Lentz
is tellin me that it's because of what
I done. It's true he seen it all, but we
just don't see all this shit the same.
                                        We ate
our chow at sunup and drove to checkpoint four—
you know the one, it's past the gate and out
in central shitville—the one where all they do
is search the hajjis needin on the post.
The hajjis' trucks is strung all up and down
the road just like a rusty caterpillar,
all rolled in dust and baked in sandy grit.
Them hajjis loaf around, and squat down on
their haunches, some even light a fire
and boil each other tea—I never seen
a guy so stinkin crazy for a tea.
So anyway, they're everywhere around,
they squat, they smoke, they sip their tea. They stand
out there in them weird dresses that they like
to wear so much, without a thing to do
until we get on down the line and search
each one to let 'em come inside and dump
his rock or sand or what he's got and get
back out again. Who knows how long they wait
on us to freakin check 'em out and check
'em in again? But they don't seem to mind.
They squat on down in the shade of their trucks,
they boil some tea and jabber craziness
like all this shit is somehow normal.

We pull up and it's scorchin hot already—
I'm soaked all through and coughin in the dust—
and me and Lentz start searchin hajjis while
Ole House and Barker start on all them trucks.
And you know how it goes—we stack 'em in
a line and Lentz stands back a ways and eyes
'em with his rifle. I sling mine and start

119

to pat 'em down—you know, to check for bombs
or guns or whatever. And Lentz just chills,
just lounges with a lazy rifle, burning all
his cigarettes, relaxin, squintin in
the sun. And me I'm up there sweatin bullets,
every second thinkin one of these damn
hajjis is gonna knife my throat or some
bullshit like that. So I'm there in the dust
and sun and sweat's just rolling off my nose—
and no one likes to have to pat them hajjis
down anyway, I mean, there's all them
gay jokes every time, but worse is when
you get a bony one—it's gross to feel
the twitchin bones through all their robes and skirts.

I got through ten or so before it snapped.

Just as I was pattin down this one, just when I got
to his legs it happened. Right below
his knee I felt a metal bar. And that just
ain't supposed to be there. I mean, the sun,
the sweat, ole Lentz back there just gawking on,
and then I feel that metal bar. A gun?
a knife? A bomb? I wasn't gonna wait
around to ask. I mean, survival mode
just kicks your ass to action. I seen myself
lunge, shove him back against the truck and grab
my rifle off my back and smash the stock
into the hajji's teeth. His head slammed back
against the bed and blood was squirtin all
around and I didn't even know I done it.
I didn't even know 'til later that
he slumped right down and I was there on top
of him, just poundin the piss all out
of his mangled face and all that I could think
about is if I'm ever gonna get
to lie again on my daughter's princess bed
and whisper one more goodnight fairy tale.
I guess I kept on poundin him 'til all
my knuckles busted on his broken teeth,
until I heard how Lentz was screamin at

the others. All around us hajjis waved
their crazy hands and screamed like demons
and Lentz was there with his rifle wild—
he jerked it back and forth and screamed right back
and no one understood just what the hell
had happened. I saw it then in Lentz's eyes,
his coolness gone and him a thinkin,
"So this is it. I can't believe I'm gonna kill
someone today. I'm gonna hafta do it."
I stopped and grabbed my rifle, raised the skirts
of the groanin hajji and saw the weapon. Except
that it was not a weapon. It was just
his metal leg. He didn't have a foot
below his knee. A fuckin fake leg is all.

I backed away and raised my rifle, saw
the man in the midst of all that screamin.
He slowly reached and touched his dripping face
and stared at all the blood now running down
his hands. He turned and spat out more. They sat
him up again and brought a cup of tea.
They all kept pointin to the leg and shoutin.

Lentz said later on that it was bad
to be so tight. He says I ought to be
more chilled. He says to me that type
of thinkin is what sent us over here.
The shoot-first mind-set, he says, ain't right.
I told him if this one-legged guy would
'a lifted up his damn skirt from the start,
we wouldn't have this problem. He knew what
we was doin. He knew that we was huntin
for weapons. By the way, if Saddam would
'a lifted up his freakin skirts way back
in March then we would all still be at home
and readin fairy tales to daughters.
But Lentz responds we got no rights to wave
our rifles everywhere and tell them all
to lift their skirts and let us look around.
I ain't so thick I don't see what he's sayin',
but hell, no matter how it happened,

I'm here right now and right now hafta do
whatever a man can do to get his self
back safe to whisper goodnight kisses
to his sleepy little princess.

                              But still,
and maybe it's the knuckles that I sliced
on his split teeth—or maybe the memory
of seeing all them screamin hajjis crowd
around me there—or maybe it was when
I seen him wake back up and touch his shredded
mouth and moan, fake leg bare in the sun,
but I can't stop shaking, and I don't know why.

Levi Bollinger is a resident of Southeast Missouri where he is happily married and teaching high school English courses. In the spring of 2003, his Army Reserve unit was called to active duty, and he served a year at the Baghdad International Airport and surrounding area.

Jesse Goolsby

Be Polite But Have a Plan to Kill Everyone You Meet

The Afghanistan pasture floor feels like a fairway under their boots, soft and tended. A mangy group of goats huddle off to the side as Wintric, newly arrived, removes his camouflage blouse and stands in a line next to Big Dax and Nettles, plunging syringes into children in the narrow valley. The dirty and hungry kids come forward with growths, bulges of skin on their necks, temples, hips. Wintric asks what day it is, and when Nettles says Wednesday, Wintric questions why the kids aren't in school, but everyone ignores him. Big Dax, who towers over everyone, can sense Wintric's nervousness and tells him to touch the kids, to hold their hands, to sing, anything, as he presses the needle into their shoulders. Nettles glances at the naked mountain peaks and says they're as safe as they'll ever be because no one ever shoots when the Army inoculates and clothes.

"Still," he says, "stay close to the children, especially the boys."

Big Dax says some of the kids risk having their arms cut off to get the shots, that's why they only see the worst. This seems like an exaggeration to Wintric, who nods and lifts a little boy's sleeve up to the nub of the boy's shoulder joint and fumbles with, then drops the cheap syringe.

"You from San Francisco?" Big Dax asks Wintric, hoping to help.

"Four hours north."

"Oregon?"

"No. California. The good part."

"Ocean?" Nettles chimes in.

"Mountains. Logging. Two thousand people. A lake. Some cows. Think Montana, but with San Francisco assholes in the summer."

Wintric takes a drink of water and motions to the next in line.

"You like Barry Bonds? 'Cause he's a prick," says Big Dax. "Probably got the nuts the size of gnats."

"You'd love him on your team."

"Yankees don't need him."

"Oh, Jesus."

"Maybe that's what we're giving these kids, some nice steroids," Nettles says as he rips another rubbing alcohol pad from its wrapper. "Creating a super-race of Afghanis that can hit a baseball a mile."

"Nettles, you dumb shit, these are victims," Big Dax says while tending to a girl with a neck goiter.

"Us or them?" Nettles asks.

"Don't piss me off, Nettles. We got first-world problems."

"Not here."

Wintric sees Big Dax's left boot tap the ground.

"Are you ticked because you don't get your daily Burger King, Wal-Mart fix?"

"These aren't fast food issues, man," Nettles says. "We got staying alive problems. I worry about one of these kids blowing us up. I worry about the dirt road exploding on our way back. I don't worry about these things in Colorado. So shut the fuck up about your first-world problems."

"You know the life expectancy of these kids?" Dax asks, straightening his six-foot eight-inch body. He pauses and watches Nettles scratch his neck. "It's low thirties, you whiny bitch."

Nettles inhales. He's too tired to argue, but he says, "I must've checked the Doctors without Borders block instead of the US Army. My mistake."

There isn't a single child that looks well fed, and as Nettles feels their arms and hair, and holds their hands, he thinks of his two daughters. His mind goes to Shannon, his oldest and the prettier one, who refuses to eat anything unless she has a dollop of crunchy peanut butter on her plate. She didn't cry at his base send-off, and while first proud of her strength, he now fears her indifferent look as he walked away.

Nettles would sing the ABCs to his girls every night while he tucked them in, so this is what he sings in the gorge, and after a while he leaves out the letters and just hums. The melody calms him.

Wintric says, "Do you know any Metallica?"

But Nettles ignores him. He thinks of the minuscule amount his daughters are growing each day, how Shannon will be old enough to play catch when he returns, how they might want to tuck themselves in.

After the shots, the three men wait around with some amputees and play cards. The wind has picked up, and the injured look up in reverence and wait for their limbs to fall from the cloudy sky.

"Jim Abbott had one arm," Big Dax says, as the men sit and pick at the ground.

"Who?" Wintric asks.

"He had an arm," Nettles says. "Was missing a hand."

"Threw a no-hitter," says Big Dax. "For the Yankees, Wintric."

"Did he use?"

"He had one arm," says Big Dax, "Why would you use if you have one arm?"

"One hand," says Nettles.

"Jesus Nettles, who cares if it's an arm or a hand?"

"It's a big difference."

"He didn't use, Wintric. Not like your boy Bonds."

"They'll never prove it," says Wintric.

"Nuts the size of gnats."

"You've seen 'em yourself?"

When it's time to pray, an old man floats down a red and brown prayer rug as the children join the limbless adults, their voices echoing off the valley walls.

"They know not what they say," Big Dax says. Wintric guesses he means the children, most likely illiterate, repeating the chant placed before them since birth. But maybe he directs the jab at the entire group, kneeling and bowing and rising in unison.

Before too long, a C-130 lumbers overhead and dips its wings as the parachute opens on the crate of arms and legs floating down to them. Nettles wonders out loud if the Afghans think Allah is a C-130 pilot or the plane itself.

"Rain down the healing."

Big Dax says it's all about will and raises his thick arms to the sky.

"Do they thank Allah for bombs?" he asks.

Wintric is quiet. Nettles's comment on the possibility of the dirt road exploding on their way back still rattles in his mind. He considers how his body is assembled, piece by piece. He stares at the crease between his forearm and bicep, then fingers the space, wondering what exactly a ligament is. At home station he's seen soldiers with new carbon legs and arms. They're usually silent and alone. He studies the up-armored Humvee they'll ride back to base. The hulking vehicle seems invincible, but he's seen videos of convoy ambushes, the dark cloud, pressure shock, and weightless Humvees coming back to earth as mangled coffins. Wintric already longs for his 1985 Ford Bronco. He'd installed a six-inch lift, a tow kit, and oversized, gnarly mud tires. The dull tire-tread hum on the highway drove his girlfriends mad, but he'd take them mudding, or deeper still into the forest to fool around. Sometimes, he'd bring his revolver and throw lead at squirrels, paper plates, or posters of basketball players he used to hang in his room. But now, his weapon has the safety on, and he doesn't know when he'll need it, so he looks at the menacing but helpless Humvee and hopes that when they're done today, the dirt road will just be a dirt road.

Once the body pieces are organized, the three men help fit everyone, but most of the arms are too long or the wrong shade of skin, but the armless don't seem to mind. They have a few legs left over, so they send the confused citizenry home with extras. As they climb into the Humvee they confirm emergency plans, coordinate with the other vehicles in their convoy, and start the engine up. It's getting dark, so the men do one final look around before heading out. And as they drive away, Big Dax rolls his window down and points to the line of people, the newly healed limping away, grappling plastic legs piled high like firewood.

"Vote for us," he yells.

Vibrant yellow and red kites fly above a hot August afternoon when a bomb explodes on a brown building in Kabul. Someone whistles at the three men just before a crazed pulse unfolds the air around them. Nettles throws up on his boots and Wintric comes to with Big Dax dumping water into his eyes, cursing. Bodies and flames litter the street, shit and screams everywhere. A few people run, some stumble as though learning to walk with missing knees. Nettles picks out a scrap of metal from his bicep, then reaches down to drag a silent boy away and feels the boy's shoulder detach and his arm slide smooth from his body. Overhead, entrails hang from electrical wires. Big Dax almost shoots a man running in to help. A bearded man in white linen snaps photos, as he steps over slithering bodies. Wintric tries to yell at him to help, but nothing comes out, and Wintric goes to walk, but nothing happens, and he feels wet inside and sees in textured waves. He watches the man cover a charred corpse's genitals with a blue cloth before clicking away at the carcass. The man kicks the corpse before hurriedly walking away, and Wintric screams but hears nothing, just now aware that he's somehow trapped within his body. So he closes his eyes, but he sees waves of smoke and people, someone firing a rifle into the air, then Big Dax, running nearby, waving at him, saying something, nodding, thumbs up, then reaching far down for him.

Soon, ambulances arrive at the scene then leave, people with various flags on their uniforms fill out paperwork then depart, Afghan men and women shriek in the streets then go, and although debris covers a once busy intersection, workers already tend to the mess.

That evening Nettles listens to the calls to prayer. Wintric dozes off in the corner without a blanket, dried blood mixed with dirt blacken his throat and the back of his hands. Nettles's limbs and mind ache, and he sifts through anger and despair. He touches the bandage on his bicep and thinks about the size of the future scar. He monitors his fingers and wills them to stop fluttering, but his digits refuse. Emotion pools within him and he finds himself on his knees, hoping to tap into some communal source of faith and belief. He tries to focus, but soon his mind drifts to the millions of people praying against him and his country. He pictures a vast field, a massive crowd of white-robed men and women slowly bowing together, the haunting force and beauty of mass synchronization.

Nettles considers the problem if Allah or God or some other cloud of justice places spiritual devotion into the equation, because surely America will lose. He thinks of how he's taught his daughters to pray, and what to pray for: safety, food, recovery. His youngest daughter, Fallynne, is old enough now to speak a simple offering. Nettles's wife sent an e-mail of what Fallynne recited every night, said she always finished with "thank you." Nettles can see his wife and Fallynne at the side of Fallynne's bed, kneeling, with her elbows on her purple Rapunzel comforter. His wife said they were working on "Amen," but she thought that "thank you" was just as good. For the first time, Nettles considers the purpose of "Amen," and after saying it softly four times, realizes he has no idea what it means. He thinks of waking Wintric, but he won't know. So he says it one more time as the melody from the minarets filters through the window. No matter what Big Dax says, Nettles knows his aren't first-world problems. In Afghanistan, everything he knows about the world has a different name, and worse, he doesn't know the meanings of the English words he uses for salvation.

Big Dax smokes outside, feeling his dirty dry skin and picturing all the swimming pools he's swam in. He's heard that the Army is helping to build a new public pool nearby. What he wouldn't give for a few laps without his Kevlar vest and helmet and heavy boots—to purge the unsettled dust of the Shamal winds from his ear, mouth, and chest. He's not that strong of a swimmer, but to coat himself in chlorinated water would be to return home. He misses the cool water and the chemicals, the tanned female lifeguards, community pools, base pools, a resort pool he once visited in Vegas shaped like a banana. He recalls his neighbor's pool in Rutherford, New Jersey, where he grew up. The pool had an eight-foot-tall diving board, way too high for the normal-sized backyard in-ground, but Dax and the neighbor kids would cannonball and jack-knife off the board and float in the summer air and bet each other to do belly flops, although no one did. But before he can dwell in his comforting memory, he imagines a dark man there, in his neighbor's backyard, strapped down with explosives in a slow motion diving board jump: the board fully flexes before snapping, launching the man high into the air where eleven-year-old Dax and a couple local kids watch the terrorist click the hand-held detonator, again and again, but nothing happens, only a violent fall into a too shallow pool.

Big Dax wasn't in Rutherford the day the towers fell. He was up visiting his grandmother in Watertown before heading to basic training, but he watched the news for two days straight in disbelief. Dax pictured himself in camouflage, taking aim at people, missing, and he felt the nerves in his body ping. He would have to kill now, something he'd hoped to avoid when he signed up for the GI bill and travel. And really, in his small world, this is why he despised the terrorists. People dying, diving from the towers, it was dismal business to be sure, but now, after joining the Army in times of relative peace, he would be asked to shoot, and probably be shot at.

After returning home to tens of funerals, Dax stayed up late replaying television clips of people jumping from the trade center. The news had stopped showing them, and he couldn't understand why. Without these clips, the whole thing was like any other demolition of steel and concrete. But these scenes showed men and women falling through the air, barely alive. This is where the pain lived, in impossible choices on a clear autumn morning. Dax never considered choosing between flame and gravity, but watching the people fall to their deaths, weighing which way to die, he knew he would pick gravity.

One night, when his father spied him watching the clips, his father shook his head, although Dax wasn't sure why.

"It's our biggest mistake, son. People think we're more important than we are. Remember this, you can love God, but God doesn't give a shit. You want to celebrate births and winning the lottery and graduations? You give credit to the heavens? Fine, but you better celebrate this shit as well."

Dax hadn't thought much about God, about intervention or justice, so he sat there in his living room and stared at his sober father pointing at the television.

"It's okay to feel good when you make them pay."

Tonight, in Afghanistan, Big Dax smokes his third cigarette down and, without licking his fingers, pinches the burning end flat. As he enters the room he sees Nettles on his knees. Big Dax considers "No one's listening" or "Only people should be on their knees are hot women," but he swallows both down easily and walks to his bunk, lies back, and lets the nicotine do its work.

While on patrol in a quiet mud village, an elderly man they've seen a couple times offers what the men think is his daughter to Wintric. This is the opposite of what they'd been briefed, that Afghan men would purposely disfigure—often with fire—the faces and bodies of adulterous women. It takes Wintric a moment to understand. The daughter smiles with her green eyes when her father taps her leg with his cane. She is tall and smells like lavender. Her age is hard to tell, but Wintric forces his mind to flash eighteen. She offers her hand to Wintric in the narrow alley. He steps close and nervously takes back the girl's hijab to reveal her dark hair. It's hot in their gear, but the shade of the alley helps.

Big Dax says, "Don't do anything. There I said it."

"Second that," says Nettles, and strokes his rifle, so adjusted that it feels a part of his body. "But seriously, don't do anything. You have five minutes to check that house for weapons." The father stays quiet, then moves down the street. Nettles follows. After Wintric enters the shabby dwelling with the girl, Big Dax leans on the thick mud walls of the building, waiting, thinking about the shade and smell; then, after catching a few harmless kids staring him down from a house nearby, he considers the result if he'd been born in that very alley.

Later, as they walk in the storming afternoon, the men pass a quail fight inside a small hall. Dozens of men circle a small mat and cheer the frantic, bobbing birds.

"My state bird," Wintric says. "Little bastards are easy picking where I'm from, and good eats."

"Jersey doesn't have a state bird," says Big Dax.

"I thought every state had one."

"Yes," says Nettles. "Isn't Jersey's the shit bird?"

"Funny. But we do have a horse and two ugly bitches on our flag. That much I know."

"We got a grizzly bear, but no grizzlies," says Wintric. "And we got brown bears that are red and blonde. One ate the dog I grew up with."

"Nettles," Dax says, "I think we found us a true California hick."

Undeterred, Wintric seizes the opportunity and talks of his rural hometown in Northern California, of playing football on a losing team that carried fourteen guys total, of what it means to get out of the small town and escape past the lumber mill and county signs that trapped most of the kids. Big Dax and Nettles let him carry on. They don't ask any questions about the quick girl encounter, but later, after drinking enough mouthwash to feel something, Wintric tells them that he began to undress the girl, but stopped himself. She had grabbed his hands and placed them on her bare shoulders, and he left his hands there for a moment, feeling her body heat and fear before walking out. He says he wouldn't be able to live with himself. There's a girl waiting back home.

"No one's ever waiting, my friend" says Big Dax. "They're living and moving on. And don't get mad. It sucks, but it's true."

"That's bullshit," says Nettles. "If you had someone at home you'd know. I'm no punk. I know we're not in some damn movie, but sometimes things end up okay. I feel sorry that this is all you have. You have right now, then, when that's gone, you have the next moment, then that's it. What do you look forward to, man? If all it is is surviving, that's shit."

"Easy," says Big Dax, sorry he'd opened his mouth but not willing to admit it.

"Her name is Kristen," says Wintric. "The girl at home."

"One day, the people we're trying to kill will be in charge again," says Nettles. "One day soon, we'll negotiate with these fucks, even though they've killed us and tortured us and today we're trying to kill them. So yes, I think about who's waiting for me, because if I think about all of this, I'm done."

"You guys believe what you want to."

So Nettles does. He lives his return home in advance. He feels the departure out of Afghanistan, out of Kyrgyzstan, out of Germany, the squiggly coastline of Maryland and Delaware, landing at Baltimore, out of Baltimore, across farmland into Colorado Springs. He sees his family running to him across the tarmac, his daughters jumping into his arms, walking into the home his wife bought while he was away, and after his girls are tucked in, his wife's skin and weight pressed against him, her hands and mouth on him, on top of him, under him, the pressure build and release, home.

So Wintric does. He sees Kristen naked on the shore of Lake Almanor late at night, standing in the low beams of his Bronco, waving her arms, urging him out of the water, to come to her and this place, his home, again.

Big Dax sees the child in the far distance, but he doesn't yet know it's a girl. While the checkpoint he mans is set-up for car inspections, there hasn't been any for an hour. Behind a half hive of sandbags, Nettles listens to early Pearl Jam and writes in his journal while Wintric spits tobacco into an empty Dr. Pepper bottle and plays hearts with a Lieutenant who they all like. Wintric has won three games in a row after the Lieutenant told him the Giants suck.

"Call this payback," Wintric says, as he shuffles the cards.

Big Dax has watch, but there's just this kid, a wide open dirt plain, wind, and boredom. It's been four hours since his last cigarette, and he feels it in his skin. A mongoose darts across the road, surprising him, and he thinks about the little non-descript mammal tearing up snake after snake. Do they ever lose? Then: his back tattoo. It was supposed to be a boa, but for thirty-three dollars outside Fort Jackson, you get what you get, so he sports a green creature along his vertebrae that appears more eel than snake. He's nicknamed it snake.

And again, the child, now walking toward them.

"We got any candy left?" Big Dax says to no one in particular, but nobody answers.

Big Dax thinks he sees the kid wave, but no, just a white shawl, pink pants, no shoes, twelve, maybe ten years old, walking, alone? singing to herself and holding something, books? and a shawl, a wave, and holding something, be nice to me honey, "guys, where's our candy?" scope up and focus this walking girl, no shoes, pink pants, a soccer ball in hand, a quick game and a high five? another heart and mind, and a gust lifts her white shawl, and silver there, a gust, a silver vest flash, metallic? and another gust and yes, a silver vest, and a surge inside him, an electric yell to Nettles, LT, "scope her, scope the girl," distance, three hundred yards, "call it in, Wintric," such a slow pace but sweating, walking with bright pink pants, focus on her face, quiet now then singing, a prayer? and lobbing this spotted ball to herself, this afternoon, flip safety off and heartbeat and heartbeat and LT on loudspeaker, "Estaad sho yaa saret fayr meykunam," (stop, or I'll shoot) a shawled girl, a little fucking girl with her soccer ball, black and white hexagons turning in her hands, stepping closer and no cars, all alone, look past, scope past, nothing, but flat earth, forgotten land, "Estaad sho yaa saret fayr meykunam," (stop, or I'll shoot) you girl, two hundred out, LT, mother fuck why, "shoot at one hundred," he says, the white chest and her moving lips and brown mole on her forehead, singing, a singer, grow, then she stops and shakes her head no, and shakes her head no and walks again and Nettles with his gun up too, and she stops again and feels at her chest, a skin and bones chest? a wired chest? silver strung explosives? but a soccer ball, an athlete, young muscle and no shoes, bare feet on the road, sweating, how far have you walked child? a wave, waving, coming, "Estaad sho yaa saret fayr meykunam," (stop or I'll shoot) this girl, two hundred out, loudspeaker, "Turn it up, LT, max it, max it," Estaad sho yaa saret fayr meykunam, (stop, or I'll shoot) this child, already haunting Big Dax, Wintric frantic miming, opening his blouse over and over, Nettles's voice, "Dax, your shot," one seventy-five, "your shot," stop now, stop now, "your shot," a singer, her pink pants on the road, today, where's the wind? scoping her dead chest, the guts inside, little bitch stop now, away now, don't force this, one hundred fifty yards, heartbeat in hands, singing now, praying? and dropping the ball, lunging, then running here, arms open, dead chest hunting, bitch stop now, bitch stop now, my God, get this dead chest scoped, "Estaad sho yaa saret fayr meykunam," (stop, or

I'll shoot), "your fucking shot,Dax," I'll shoot, I'll shoot, this girl, this
time, somehow I'm here, right now, Nettles's gun bursts and the girl still
long strides, uninjured, this athlete bitch, white shawl pressed, a vest
underneath, this center chest heartbeat, crosshairs clean, hunting this
singer, quick breath, then hold this afternoon, this shit, this white shawl,
pink pants, bare feet, now pull, this trigger pull collision sound, puncture
down, down, bare feet down, jolt there and quiet, the soles and heartbeat
quiet then jolt, her legs, the wind, this girl, my girl, so still, near calm,
still down, never calm, quiet.

Jesse Goolsby is the recipient of the Richard Bausch Fiction Prize and the John Gardner
Memorial Award in Fiction. His stories and essays have appeared in a variety of journals
to include *Epoch*, *Alaska Quarterly Review*, *The Literary Review*, *Harpur Palate*, *The
Journal*, *The Greensboro Review*, *Blue Mesa Review*, and *War, Literature & the Arts*. His
fiction has been noted as a "distinguished story" in the 2010 Best American Short Stories,
and selected for the 2012 Best American Mystery Stories. He is an active-duty US Air
Force officer and lives in Alexandria, Virginia.

Walter Baker

In the Military Garden of Remembrance

The roses along the gray stone fence are soft as old vellum
Faintly perfuming the ether breathed by those still breathing.
And inside are no thorns, nor harm to stop and smell them.
No, only springtime on the greening earth, a humid pleasing
Of the senses, a cant of sunlight lights velvet grass, so trim.
New-opened buds vie with colored plastic flowers, teasing
The poor bee between real and unreal, sham and Seraphim.
Fresh-leaved trees leak yellow seeds of new life conceiving.

But the sprinklers that wet the little iron flags do so in vain.
The once-life beneath, that lived for those above, was aware
When time was and now isn't, his like could never be again.
Still, it was worth all, what he lost and they could only bear,
A father gone, a brother stepped into mist, friends here lain,
If only his sacrifice, given with a ragged last minute prayer,
Helped keep our land from the grasp of an enemy's domain,
Well, then the loss of springtimes—and roses—holds no pain.

Walter Baker was a USAF captain, 1963–1968. He has a Master of English Literature degree from long ago and not much used in his middlin' career as an FBI agent. Walt's prose and poetry have appeared in *Flashquake*, *Poetry Renewal*, and *Raphael's Village* (first prize, Independence Day Contest). He has had a yellow toenail for thirty years after his son dropped an Etch-A-Sketch on it.

Colin D. Halloran

No Hero

Recently I marched in a parade. It wasn't Memorial Day or Veterans' Day. It wasn't even the 4th of July. The parade wasn't in my hometown, a small, good ole American farm town. It wasn't in the city I live in now, the largest in New England, the 10th largest in the country. Hell, it wasn't even in my state. No, I marched in a parade held in town I'd never been to in a state I've never lived in.

It was Twitter that informed me of this parade in which recently returned veterans from Afghanistan and Iraq were to be honored. I searched in vain for some similar event in a major city, including my newly established home of Boston, but there was nothing of the sort. So on a Sunday afternoon of no historic significance, my girlfriend (also an OEF vet) and I made the drive up to Portsmouth, NH, a small city on the border with Maine, where once there was an Air Force base. But not since 1991.

We went because we don't know too many other young vets in the area. We went because I have a book of poetry about my Afghanistan experiences coming out, and this was an opportunity to schmooze with a concentration of my target market. We went to network. We went because it was a beautiful Sunday afternoon and we had nothing else to do. And there was a discount liquor store on the way.

We went because we hadn't been honored yet. She marched in the Veterans' Day parade in New York City in 2010, the year she got back, but that's it. I hadn't marched at all, maybe because of my injured leg, maybe because I didn't want to don a uniform again. Maybe because it took me so long to accept "veteran" as a part of my identity.

It was one of those preconceived notions that I wasn't even aware I had. How could I, at 20 years of age, be in the same category as all those venerable old men of The Greatest Generation and the crotchety Vietnam Vets on the bus? The prospect of marching, or even identifying myself, as a veteran just didn't seem right to me. When I read accounts of World War II, talked to the people who served in it, watched *Band of Brothers* or *Saving Private Ryan*, I found myself grateful I hadn't been in their war, and wondering how people could possibly be calling us "the next greatest generation."

I went to this parade in hopes of finding some like-minded individuals, some sense of community that I lost when I separated from the military, some sense that these crazy thoughts, ideas, and feelings I have maybe aren't so crazy after all.

What I found was a group of nine other Gulf War II vets, including the one I'd driven up with. That's right, in the only such parade in New England, there were ten of us, along with the elder Shriners and loads of Vietnam vets. Yet even with such a small group of peers there, I still felt those familiar pangs of self-doubt and guilt.

There was a Navy corpsman who served three tours, the first two in Nasiriyah and Fallujah for two of the biggest battles of these wars. There was a fellow Army infantryman who had also done multiple tours. A former Marine who enlisted in the Army after 9/11 and served a combat tour each in Iraq and Afghanistan. And then there was me. One tour in Afghanistan that I couldn't even complete. Regardless of the fact I had no choice, I'd broken the cardinal rule: I left my men behind.

And as we marched through 1.2 of Portsmouth's 16.8 square miles, these were the thoughts going through my head. As the people cheered, clapped, yelled, "Thank you!" and waved flags, I kept my eyes downcast, my mouth taut in contemplation. As older veterans saluted and children waved, I kept my hands by my side. My girlfriend the public affairs officer was much better, waving, smiling, thanking the folks for coming out and supporting us—whether they'd planned to or not (many seemed surprised to find a parade, but stopped and watched, because that's what you do).

But I avoided eye contact. Didn't accept the crayon-drawn cards or the smiles that echoed those of the boy I'd seen die in the desert.

And all I could think was *I'm no fucking hero.*

Colin D. Halloran is a former enlisted infantryman who served in Afghanistan with the US Army. He has since earned two degrees, most recently with an MFA in Poetry from Fairfield University. He is an internationally published poet and photographer, and the winner of the 2012 Main Street Rag Poetry Book Award for *Shortly Thereafter*, a collection of poems about his service in Afghanistan and the impact it had on him upon returning to the civilian world.

Randy Brown

what sacrifice has been

in airports, well-traveled souls
confuse boots with heroes
and buy us sandwiches
while flat-talking boxes buzz

with bullet-lists and mug-shots of the fallen:
3-second shrines
to soldiers they will never know
like you

this war is on us,
they want to say,
thanks for your service
have a nice day

they elevate our routine dead
with casual regard and separate
us from them
with unsustaining praise

they do not grasp our names are found
on medals and on stones
and on the lips of friends who've seen
what sacrifice has been

In 2010, Randy Brown was preparing for deployment to Eastern Afghanistan as a member of the Iowa Army National Guard's 2nd Brigade Combat Team, 34th Infantry "Red Bull" Division. After he dropped off the deployment list, he retired with 20 years of military service. He then went to Afghanistan anyway, embedding with Iowa's Red Bull units as a civilian journalist in May–June 2011. A freelance writer in central Iowa, Brown blogs at: www.redbullrising.com.

Steven Croft

The John Wayne Hills

The hot air comes in with
little dust through my tan, nylon
neck gaiter, pulled up like an outlaw.
The heat of the Mojave penetrating
the iron of the armored carrier,
two pull levers to steer, a
series of switches to start
the engine, are hot like
the desert. The olive-green,
low scrub bushes contrast
with the tan dirt and rocks
they imperfectly cover. The hills
are picturesque—not mountains, but
reaching for some geologist's
name-deciding dividing line where
the blue sky takes over.

As we convoy on we are
like the horse-borne cavalry
of two centuries ago, or,
more like a cavalry flanked
by movie cameras, fifty years ago.
But this time we scan the hills
for Islamic "insurgents." This time
the make-believe is the men
in the hills have RPGs, may have
set IEDs. The rabbits, the foxes,
the snakes wait for our disturbance
to pass. Their struggle for survival
is now—they have no interest
in games—our real struggle
is still half a world away.

Steven Croft is a member of the 1st Battalion, 118th Field Artillery Regiment, 48th Infantry Brigade Combat Team, Georgia Army National Guard, with whom he deployed to Iraq in '05–'06 and Afghanistan in '09–'10. They are currently scheduled for a JRTC rotation at Fort Polk, LA, in 2013, after which they have been informed they may return to Afghanistan. He is the author of a chapbook of poems titled *Coastal Scenes* (The Saltmarsh Press, 2002).

David Lawrence

All Fun and Games, Until

A few days ago the headquarters band put on a "concert." They papered advertisements all over doors and conference rooms and break-rooms and bathrooms throughout the compound. Actually, this group was a subset of the larger headquarters division band. These guys specialized in "rock-n-roll," with "a little bit country" thrown in for variety. Kind of like Donny and Marie, I guess. The band's name was Avalanche.

The band went on at 11:45 in a dingy little alley between two aluminum relocatable buildings on the west side of the headquarters area. Their opening number was Boston's "More Than a Feeling." I guess they were trying to reclaim the song after having been persecuted by the techno version of the seventies classic that frequently plays in the NATO gym on base. Damn those Slovenians and their godawful music playlists.

Alas, the rendition Avalanche performed did their countrymen no favors. When the female vocalist delivered the power line, *"I close my eyes and I slipped awayyyyy,"* so did about half of the ten or so curious onlookers who'd prairie-dogged from their desks when they heard the amplified racket outside.

But the disaster that was Avalanche wasn't fazed by a few wrinkled noses and headshaking. They bravely soldiered on, military rockers that they are, through their "hit-all-the-genres" prom band set list. Next up was Michael Jackson's "Beat It." *This is a brave bunch*, I thought to myself: launching into a cover of one of the King of Pop's all time smash hits, a song which also features one of the world's most recognizable, face-melting Eddie Van Halen guitar solos. It just isn't the same when the singer has to self-induce the echo fade of the signature line.

Just Beat It (beatitbeatitbeat badump bump badump bump)

You almost get the sense that this was her admonition to the few people sticking around, marveling at the Twilight Zone-esque experience they were witnessing: in a war zone, listening to a U.S. Army division band at midday on a Wednesday cover Michael Jackson's "Beat It."

Behold!

Through the thin walls of my building I heard the band continue: Carrie Underwood's "Last Name," Lynyrd Skynyrd's "Simple Man," a Toby Keith number I immediately forgot since it didn't mention a boot-in-the-ass or beer for my horses. Then it was time to switch genres again, something a bit more emo: The Muse's "We Will Be Victorious." A little something to give hope to us despairing, FOBbit-dwelling PowerPoint rangers, evidently. The band got through the first verse of this march-of-the-automatons anthem when blessed Providence intervened: the blissful two-part harmony of the chorus suddenly found itself upstaged.

"ATTENTION FROM THE OPERATIONS CENTER," boomed the disembodied Orwellian voice over the emergency loudspeaker. "THIS IS A TEST OF THE BASE ALARM SYSTEM." A near deafening sine wave of sound poured out of the alarm towers just a hundred yards from my building. The band wasn't going to give in without a fight. *They will not control us,* they continued to sing. "ROCKET ATTACK. ROCKET ATTACK." Another wailing siren. *Never be afraid to die.* "MASS CASUALTY. MASS CASUALTY." *We will be victorious!* More blaring sirens. "GROUND ATTACK. GROUND ATTACK. GROUND ATTACK."

Mercifully, the band's set and the alarm test ended together. Giant Voice Emergency Alarm System 1, Avalanche 0.

I think of the popular Reagan-era antidrug ad: "This is your brain. This is your brain on drugs." Maybe it's time for a new campaign: "This is war. This is your brain on war."

I was at a concept of operations briefing the other night. One unit was briefing an op that involved three key efforts: Objective Pabst, Objective Miller, and Objective Miller Lite. I quickly scanned the room, assuming I'd see some of the younger staffers tittering. Surely this is a joke, I said to myself. It wasn't. Had ten years of endless war so beggared the English language that we're left only with the names of poor-quality, watered-down domestic beer to give to our operations? That's a grim indictment on a number of levels.

The meeting was chaired by a heavy-browed one-star general who kept his salt-and-pepper hair closely cropped and whose ruddy face bore all the hallmarks of being maintained by a seventies-era Remington electric. His chin looked like it could take the burrs off the end of a hastily hewn piece of aluminum pipe. His close-set eyes and gruff, monosyllabic locutions bespoke of a profound lack of inquisitiveness. I called him General Keyrock, after Phil Hartman's memorable unfrozen caveman lawyer character on *Saturday Night Live*. My general's development was arrested at the "real" Keyrock's only-recently-unfrozen days.

Objectives Pabst, Miller, and Miller Lite were briefed in detail, and all appeared to be "wired tight," as they say.

"Well," General Keyrock finally drawled, "Ah s'pose this looks pretty good. But I got one problem: I don't like these names." For a flash I felt guilty. Maybe the guy's brighter than I thought. I figured he'd talk about the incongruity of having objectives named after alcoholic beverages here in our teetotaling region. This is the birthplace of the Taliban, after all. Perhaps a brief reminder of cultural sensitivities being instrumental to counter insurgency. I would even have given him credit for castigating the planners who'd code-named these objectives after such rot-gut.

The general's next statement brought me back to reality. "I'm a little worried," he said, "that these two things are too similar. I mean, if things go pear-shaped on y'all out there, are we sure we're gonna be able to tell the difference between Miller and Miller Lite?"

Stifled laughter thinly disguised as throat-clearing, sniffling, and other tics began sweeping through the room. The briefer, a young special forces captain sitting just a few feet from General Keyrock, remarkably kept his composure. From the back of the room, a senior NCO finally said it.

"One tastes great, the other's less filling, sir." The room roared. The general, expressionless, turned slowly in his chair to face the mirthful crowd seated behind him. A hush fell over the room. A constipated grin slowly broke over the general's face, and the room exhaled. The laughter came easier. The general turned in his chair again.

"Gimme that fucker," he said to the captain who'd briefed the operation. The captain dutifully slid him a single piece of paper, and General Keyrock scratched out his signature.

Operation Low Brow Adult Carbonated Beverage will proceed as planned.

We're about a week into "Mustache March." Since deployers can't get in on the zany fun that is bracketology and round-the-clock college basketball mayhem, they create their own contest. But this tourney doesn't involve fast breaks and slam dunks. The only demonstrable skill in this competition is the growing of facial hair. These people just won't listen to me. Thankfully, as I'd made my facial hair feelings known long before I was even aware there was such a thing as Mustache March, no one bothered to subject me to a mustache full court press.

The rules governing Mustache March aren't many, and what rules do exist are spelled out clearly on the accompanying (you guessed it) PowerPoint slide which heralds this foolish competition. The only hard-and-fast rule is that you must shave on March 1. No hairy running starts. You must stay within military grooming standards, which are notoriously stingy. There's a Tom Selleck Award for the guy crowned overall champ. There's The Creep Award given to the wearer of the worst mustache. And there's the Baby Stache category, the winner of which receives the I-Haven't-Hit-Puberty-Yet Award.

"I'm surprised there isn't an award for 'Now-I-Look-Unprofessional,'" my Marine buddy said to me over dinner, his disapproval of Mustache March apparent. Man, Marines can be so straight-laced.

In my own twisted mind I imagine a different version of the tease for the Masters that CBS puts into heavy rotation during the NCAA tournament. A harp or flamenco guitar plays a lazy, bucolic tune over a soft-focus montage of tired, red-eyed, and weakly mustachioed staff officers hunched over their computers, nugging PowerPoint slides. Jim Nantz's silky baritone floats in effortlessly halfway through the montage: *A deployment tradition unlike any other . . . Mustache March.*

Mustache March gets a lot of buy-in. And since there's actually an award for the pre-pubescent look, there are a lot of guys who throw discretion—and self-respect—out the window in order to get in on the action. Young and old alike, officer and enlisted participate. Mustache March is an equal opportunity offender.

Not everyone is pleased, however, and I don't just mean my Marine buddy and me. I was walking to work when I saw a middle-aged man in civvies approaching. Before he got to me, he stopped a soldier about twenty feet in front of me who was likewise walking towards him.

"Hey specialist, you have a boss?" the man angrily asked the young soldier. I couldn't hear the soldier's reply from my position behind him, but I deduced the question flummoxed him.

"Yeah, *a boss*," the man sneered. "You know, someone you work for. A supervisor?"

Evidently the soldier answered in the affirmative. "He ever call you out for only shaving part of your face?" he asked the tongue-tied trooper as I walked past. I would have loved to hang around to hear the young stubble-lipped specialist explain the finer points of Mustache March to someone I assume is a retired sergeant major. But I couldn't think of an inconspicuous way of doing so. Maybe if he could have convinced his accuser he was an odds-on favorite for running away with the Baby Stache title, he could have brought him around. Not likely, I would guess.

Ah, the band keeps playing my tune, so to speak. This morning I received the following e-mail:

> Our Band Company is planning their trips to other regions. While waiting for approval, they want to conduct threat analysis and evaluation therein. Will you push this request to your intel shop in support of an upcoming band tasking?

The message came from a U.S. Army major. I sat at my computer, staring at the screen, blinking in disbelief. *Where do I begin with this one?* I asked myself as I regained a measure of composure. The *band* asking for an *intel* report? Maybe the pseudo-operational flavor of the *"threat analysis and evaluation therein"*? The redundancy of "analysis" and "evaluation"? That their projected tour stops regularly accommodate USO shows, congressional delegations, and other ministerial-level VIPs? They may as well be asking for "threat analysis and evaluation" of Myrtle Beach. Therein.

But then I realized I'd overlooked the coup de grâce of this e-mail in my first four or five breathless readings. Tucked away in the sender's signature block was this timeless, priceless nugget of warfighting wisdom:

Keep your enemy close, but your friend closer.

My paroxysms of laughter began anew. A few people seated in the rows nearby doubtless thought I'd had a psychotic break. George Costanza might have diagnosed a full-body dry heave.

I couldn't resist; I forwarded the e-mail to my sister and to my Marine buddy. They both replied immediately.

"I think I just shit my pants," the marine answered. "Doesn't he have that adage backwards? And what's up with the singular 'friend'?"

"Sun Tzu is crying in his Tsingtao," was my sister's philosophical response.

Then I replied to the request for the band's threat assessment.

"Sorry, but no," I said. I must not have been the only one to push back, as I didn't get another e-mail asking for an explanation for refusing the request. Truth was, I figured I was doing the well-meaning major a favor by letting this thing die on the vine, though I spared him of this sentiment in my reply.

"NINE LINE J-CHAT, ONE CAT ALPHA. STRIKE!" the army specialist called out loudly from his workstation on the front row. J-chat is the software program the tactical controllers use to communicate significant events taking place on the battlefield, and the nine lines which comprise the report succinctly capture all the relevant information of the incident: who's involved, where, when, the nature of the violence—IED, small arms fire, indirect fire, etc. From the radio report of the patrol to the tactical operations center to the division, where I work, the process can take a matter of seconds. Once it hits the joint operations center at division, the Medevac desk officer begins making arrangements for airlift. Reports of the wounded are divided into three categories: A, B, and C. Cat-A wounds are potentially life-threatening: amputations, arterial bleeds, patient unconscious. NMC. Non-mission capable. "Strike" is the brigade task force whose member suffered the injury. It's commanded by a colonel from the 101st Airborne Division from Fort Campbell, Kentucky. At least for another week—until the task force led by a brigade from the 10th Mountain Division takes over. The 10th Mountain guys have already begun RIPing in. Reinforcing in place.

"ACK. Thank you!" a major calls out from the back row at her Medevac desk. Acknowledge. Thank you for alerting me to another tragedy.

I'd just finished an e-mail to my buddy Tim in Bagram. Last night we received one of those bureaucratic plums via e-mail attachment: a PowerPoint etiquette slide not-so-pithily stated in . . . a PowerPoint slide. PowerPoint has gone meta. This particular line on the slide made me laugh: "No maps in your PowerPoint slide. If you need a map, use a map. PowerPoint replaced butcher paper, not maps."

"I had no idea butcher paper was in such copious supply in World War Two," Tim had e-mailed me. "Did PowerPoint replace winning wars, too?"

I was in the throes of this clever exchange on the pros and cons of PowerPoint when the nine-liner came in, and nothing was going to keep me from manufacturing yet another witty rejoinder. Or so I thought.

"Attention in the operations center," the shift director, a U.S. army major, announced from the back of the room. "Just so everyone's tracking, we have a Medevac in Strike's AO"—Task Force Strike's area of operations. He removed the laser pointer from his sleeve pocket and circled the vicinity of the incident on the projection screen's map. "Single round gunshot wound, suspected sniper fire. 4/4 Cav. It's not looking good. Let's keep it down in here so the folks working this can give it their undivided attention. Thanks."

4/4 Cav. They arrived in Kandahar about a week ago. They've probably been patrolling all of about seventy-two hours. I suddenly recalled the numbness I felt watching an Army nurse write the names and ranks of soldiers and airmen on a dry-erase board in the surgeon cell at the division headquarters building, Bagram, about four hours after I'd arrive in country. That board contained the names of U.S. service members killed and wounded by a suicide bomber moments earlier at a bazaar just inside the gate at a medium-sized forward operating base. One minute you're fingering near-worthless Afghan trinkets, fake Oakley sunglasses, or pirated copies of movies currently playing in theaters in the U.S. Next minute you're dead. I thought about the families of the people just written on that board, who had no idea their loved ones were hurt or gone.

Pneumothorax.

TBI. Traumatic brain injury.

DOW. Died of wounds.

And now here I am, a safe, well-fed, jokester REMF e-mailing back and forth about stupid PowerPoint rules while some poor kid is fighting for his life with a rifle round lodged in his head. And the shame and guilt washed over me. And fear. Fear that I was becoming desensitized, inured to the insanity, and fearful of what that portends for my family life after this deployment. There's no question I've changed, that I'm changing, that I'll continue to change. I can't be the same person I once was, the man I was before going to war.

I remember bunking with a guy at Manas Transit Center in Kyrgyzstan on my way to Afghanistan. He had just completed his deployment and was headed home. I'm not sure I've met a more unpleasant person, who struck me immediately as such, in all the time I've been deployed. He was just a nasty sonofabitch, and I only roomed with the guy for about thirty-six hours. I commented on this guy's irascibility to my wife Julie.

"Let's get something straight right now," she told me. "Don't even think about coming back to me acting like that guy." We laughed together, and I assured her that wouldn't be me. "I'm going to be hungry for *you.* That's who I said goodbye to, that's who I want to throw my arms around when you get back, you understand me?"

I do. And she wasn't laying down the law. She was seeking reassurance. We both knew that the odds were very much in my favor that I would survive this deployment without being killed or suffering physical injuries. But the emotional tolls are always the great unknown. "The mind is a place unto itself," we read in Milton's *Paradise Lost,* "and can make a heav'n of hell and a hell of heav'n." Not for nothing, these are the words of Satan. I write these notes, I pray, I seek wisdom and solace in the timeless strength and beauty of scripture and other literature, all in an effort to fulfill the promise I made my wife to return whole—in body and mind. But God, I hate this place. Never mind that my war, as a FOBbit-dwelling staff officer, is a joke, a farce.

That's not deep or profound or shocking. It's elementary. Inevitable. And it sucks.

The soldier from 4/4 Cav didn't make it. He never had a chance, despite being Medevaced in twenty-three minutes.

"God's own country becomes stranger and stranger," Albert Einstein wrote when describing America to his son Hans, then an engineering professor at Berkeley. "But somehow they manage to return to normality. Everything, even lunacy, is mass-produced here. But everything goes out of fashion very quickly." I took considerable comfort from this line when I encountered it in Walter Isaacson's wonderful biography of the famous physicist. While Einstein's theories endure, perhaps his observation on craziness in the U.S. *has* become obsolete. Maybe it was never true in the first place. But at the very least, I'm hoping and praying for something, *anything*, that might help slow-roll lunacy's next production line. I'm ready for some normality.

Dave Lawrence is an Air Force lieutenant colonel who deployed to Afghanistan from 2010–2011. He possesses a deep and abiding respect for those brave men and women who went outside the wire every day to do remarkable things. He wrote over 75,000 words long-hand in green GSA hardback notebooks during his deployment; this essay represents a few. His new "normality" now includes teaching English at the United States Air Force Academy outside Colorado Springs, CO.

Liam Corley

Care Package

Boxes from known names came stuffed
with flavors to hoard, use as currency,
devour as a second childhood.
After rifling through ones marked "any sailor,
airman, soldier, or Marine" for coffee bags
and better razors, we sent
hard candy, deodorant, and all
the other bric-a-brac
to Chaps as aid for the Kabuli poor
who may yet outlive
our being here.

From one I drew a knitted cap and breathed
stale air, wool yarn, and heaves
of a Mankato granny suffering painful joints
for the sake of our shaved and coverless heads.

That night a six-year-old froze,
stretched out by her brother and mom;
a click away I dozed in fatigues
beside a green terry robe on a hook.

This I want America
to see: a gap-toothed child
sucking on a watermelon
Jolly Rancher, a taste foreign
as the clacking of needles in a warm
midwestern home. Why,

she asks.
I don't know. I guess it's just
a way to support
the troops.

Liam Corley

Something Else You Don't Need

Nudged awake by a loud enough
report, I pull near
the armor, helmet, and gun I know
the big mike will call for soon.

The Macedonians at the gate
survive, swaddled in checkpoints
manned by Afghan police, their history
not yet repeated.

Just Tuesday I walked past the Hesco barrier
and ducked around the concrete wall. Unaccountable,
the chicle boy I didn't buy from last week
holds out his hand again,
in it a pack of something
I don't need. Today he tumbled upward
like a leaf blown back to an awestruck
branch, tossed like my girl as she flies confiding
from my arms.

Only Tuesday he plucked a pen from my sleeve,
bold like so many urchins I've met in marketplaces or on
roadsides free of an overseeing eye.

Knowing how this type of news spreads,
I put the dime-store pen in a pocket, saving it
for some form to fill out, some check
in a box,

where it lies still in a bin,
packed between the drop-down
holster and boots that never fit
right, no good even
for this, the story of its life.

Liam Corley has written poetry continuously since his deployment in Afghanistan in 2008. A long-time reader of American poetry, he teaches literature at California State Polytechnic University, Pomona. His work on war and writing can be found in *College English*, *War, Literature, and the Arts*, and *Chautauqua*.

Brian Curran

Cleaning Up our Mess (October 2003)

All we could see in the direction of CP1, heaving and surging across the horizon, were walls of smoke. This was obviously no trash fire or even a burning Humvee. The smoke climbed hundreds of meters and tapered off into the clear cloudless sky. It was so much smoke that we stood in a monstrous shadow as we approached from a kilometer away.

"What the fuck is that? It looks like a fuel truck is on fire," Sgt. Mullins said without hesitating to drive toward the smoke.

Strangely, there were no transmissions on the battalion net about a fire; even as we turned the final corner to the checkpoint, we were staring down a road that led into a wall of black, beyond which nothing was visible. Soldiers were wading like surfers through the hazy mirage, unconcerned, going about business as usual. We crossed the highway, through the narrow parking area, to the incoming side of the checkpoint just before the exit, and stopped on the side of the road.

"What is this fucking smoke?" I screamed over the engine noise at a sergeant standing nearby as we pulled up.

"Sir, they burnin all that dead brush on the road, so da hajis stop hidin in da bushes and shootin at da convoys."

"That's it?" I said, relieved and confused simultaneously.

"Yup, everything's alright, sir, sure enough," he said completely relaxed, turning his palms upwards and shrugging his shoulders. "You shoulda been here an hour ago; these guys came with a huge fucking gas tanker truck, and they hooked up da hoses and just soaked the entire side of da street. It was like shooting fire hoses, only diesel fuel instead of water. I thought they was trippin, then they just lit it up. Shiiit. Threw a fuckin match and WHOOSH!!!"

Mr. Hussein approached from the parking area.

"Hallo, Lieutenant Darren, how are you today," he said with an Arabic accent and extending his hand. We shook hands and we both placed our hands on our chest for a moment. Then he did the same with Sgt. Mullins. Mr. Hussein was a small man, but he looked especially small today. There was a bit of nervousness in his eyes, perhaps from the fires out front, and he trembled just a bit and his handshake felt frail and his button-down shirt was soaked in sweat.

"Okay then, let's go," I said. Mr. Hussein hurriedly got in the back of the truck, anxious to get away from the checkpoint.

"We have a patrol to make right away this morning," I yelled to the back of the truck over the engine. "We are meeting the commander right away at CP5. Then we are going straight out to Al Salaam village."

He strained to hear me, then he nodded without acknowledging if he had understood or not. We wound through the route that we took every day. First we went past OP1, and we looked up through the windshield to see the soldiers for a moment as they sat in their wooden nest perched atop the concrete double wall overlooking Al Salaam village. Then we passed OP2, which we couldn't see because the newly built OP was tucked back into the double wall where it was no longer visible. Finally, we approached CP5, and we turned into the empty compound of buildings and saw four trucks already staging for the patrol.

The commander was standing in front of the first truck with a group of eight soldiers, waiting impatiently for us to arrive, even though we were a bit earlier than expected. Sgt. Mullins stopped. Then Mr. Hussein and I stepped out of the truck, gave a quick wave goodbye, and Sgt. Mullins drove back out of the little compound by himself and turned in the direction of the palace complex.

"You, Lieutenant, you're coming with me," Cpt. Mason said, "You and Mr. Hussein are going to be in the back of my truck, then the tow truck, then the gun truck, then the other Humvee. We are going to go straight to the tractor, hook that shit up, drag it into the city, then come straight back. And I don't give a shit if it makes it in one piece or not. That's it. We are not going to make nice with anybody or fuck around in that fucking town, if anything happens, take orders from me, it's a simple as that, no fucking around. Any questions?"

The group collectively shook their heads with an unconvincing "no sir" and walked to their trucks. Mr. Hussein followed me and got into the back of the commander's Humvee, and I walked around to the other side and got in. Cpt. Mason's driver started the engine. We could hear the other engines starting in the trucks behind us, and we could hear the driver making the radio checks, but we could not make out all of his words over the engine.

"The convoy is good, sir," the driver said to Cpt. Mason.

"Alright, call it into HQ and then go ahead and move."

After calling it in, the truck moved forward out of the abandoned compound to CP5. The soldiers opened the gate and stepped back. Our truck turned onto a gravel road and headed along the other side on the airport double wall, with small farm fields on the right side, toward Al Salaam village. Our convoy moved very slowly because the tow truck was lurching forward little by little on the narrow gravel and rocking back and forth. We didn't drive far until we reached a big empty farm field. Each driver, Cpt. Mason, and Mr. Hussein stayed in the trucks; the passengers all stepped out.

The field had an irrigation ditch through the middle. It cut about two meters into the ground, but there was only a small trace of water at the bottom, as it hadn't rained since we had arrived in Baghdad. The ditch was man-made but probably many decades ago. Standing over the ditch, I could see the remains of the fighting months before, mixed in with the trash. I spotted an old gas mask, covered in mud. It was as if it had been buried under the mud, but when the ditch had filled with water at some point, it had washed the mud off and uncovered it.

"Hey, Sergeant Jackson," I said, "you want an old Iraqi gas mask?"

"Hell, fuckin no, LT," he replied. "You don't know where that thing has been."

While we stood there, the Humvees and the wrecker came around the edge of the wall down a path cutting through the cultivated fields. Those on foot left the edge of the canal to where the path crossed over into the open field. We met the vehicles and drove down the path until it stopped at the airport double wall. Down the wall, we could see OP1 and vaguely make out two little green helmets. Cpt. Mason stepped out of the truck and stood beside it. A look of contempt on his face was meant to create some fear in the soldiers. The soldiers pretended he wasn't there because they wished he wasn't, which only made his contempt grow until he had to yell at somebody.

"Darren, are you just going to stand there? Get the soldiers moving!"

Before I got to the wrecker, it had left the path and headed for the tractor. The field had been plowed several months earlier and the ground had baked in the sun and become hard, creating dried waves as hard as rock. As the wrecker crossed the field, diagonally, it rocked back and forth, thrashing the entire truck from side to side. For a moment it looked as if the axle of the truck might break or the truck might roll on its side, but we knew the truck was built to withstand abuse. Sgt. Lewis had to make a wide circle to back up to the tractor and hook it up. As he backed up to the tractor, Cpt. Mason and I walked over to the wrecker to check on the progress.

"Have you ever recovered a tractor before, Sgt. Lewis?" I asked.

"No, but I've recovered a '78 Dodge out the bottom of a lake once."

"Well, this should be an exciting first for you then."

"No, sir," Sgt. Lewis said bluntly, "I just want to get the fuck outta here."

"Oh, come on, this is fun."

Sgt. Lewis ignored me after a sarcastic look and hooked up the tractor to the back of the wrecker. There was no place to hook up the trailer hitch, and both of the front tires of the tractor had been shot out, so he chained the front fender to the crane of the wrecker and lifted the front off the ground to drag it more easily. With the field dry and hard and uneven, the tractor obviously wouldn't take well to being dragged, but he didn't care. Cpt. Mason didn't care either. They both wanted to get the job done. The rest of the soldiers cared a little. Most of us wanted the tractor to arrive at its destination in one piece, but we didn't care out of altruism or empathy or compassion. We cared because we were embarrassed that the tractor got shot up to begin with, and we didn't want the village that we regularly patrolled to hate us, which they already did. But it could be worse. Cpt. Mason rarely came to the village, and the mechanics were just doing what they were told, jacking a tractor out of a field, so they could go back and fix trucks and watch DVDs.

The front of the tractor was quickly lifted up off the hard ground, and the front of the frame was loosely attached to the towing hitch. Sgt. Lewis got inside the wrecker and started it up. Then, stepping on the throttle, the truck moved forward until the towing chain snapped tight. It briefly stopped, as if it couldn't tow the load, but with a little more throttle, the truck jerked across the field toward the path. By the time the tractor was back on the path, the rear tires had come off the rim, and the tractor was awkwardly floundering behind the wrecker. The wrecker stopped on the path to wait for the soldiers to follow. Cpt. Mason gathered the soldiers from their security positions, and I and Sergeant Jackson got into our vehicles, and all of the trucks moved toward the village that bordered the field.

While the soldiers had been working, some bystanders had shown up. A man and two wives, or maybe a wife and a grown daughter, with their heads covered by scarves but their faces showing. Pretending not to notice the Americans pulling the tractor out of the field, their subtle form of resistance, they continued with their regular work of gathering grass to feed their animals and sticks to burn in their ovens. The women carried bundles on their backs, while the man watched like a slave driver.

The trucks pulled down the path, across the irrigation ditch, and drove the long way around the wall. The normal access to the field was large enough for the typical Humvees that patrolled daily but not large enough for a wrecker pulling a tractor that was shaking back and forth. Cpt. Mason led the three truck convoy down the path and around the end of the wall onto the main road that led to the village.

It was less than a kilometer to the village. The road was narrow, with trash alongside the entire path. There were old buildings, too, that had been looted for anything of value inside and were just skeletons along the side of the road. In the distance behind us, over the cultivated fields, we could still see the wall at edge of the airport, now quite far away—out of range for the OPs to support us if something happened but still reassuring.

Cpt. Mason took his time moving toward the village. He enjoyed the opportunities when he could exert authority, definitely a man that enjoyed power trips. They had to listen; they had no choice. He had convinced himself, in order to rationalize his egoism, that the more frightened that they were, the more respect they would afford him and the less likely they would be to attack our convoys. Normally he didn't participate in the convoys, so he could justify his actions without fear of reciprocation. Most soldiers who actually executed the patrols believed the opposite, which had made the captain increasingly unpopular for some time now.

At the fork in the dirt road, one side led to the main entrance of the village and the other led through the back, through the mud and chicken wire pens where the villagers kept their animals at the southern edge of the village. The lead vehicle veered left to avoid towing the tractor through the small roads of the village. The locals saw the convoy and immediately began to follow it. By the time the convoy arrived in the village, there was already a crowd gathered of dirty children dressed in old American t-shirts (no doubt given to them by some charity), curious farmers, and shy women who stood in the distance with their heads covered in scarves, so only their pretty young faces could be seen.

The soldiers stepped out from the vehicles cautiously and prepared their rifles for possible attackers, while I checked on the mechanics. Dirty, annoying kids, the stench of farm animals, and the trash didn't bother SFC Jackson or myself, but the younger soldiers were uncomfortable and anxious with the attention that they garnered.

Curious children would gather close to the soldiers. They would attempt to be polite to the children while maintaining enough military bearing to please their commander. Nobody liked having the kids that close.

A teenager walked up to me with a soccer ball and asked, in English, "You play football?"

Surprised, I responded, "Yes, uh, I do," but quickly turned my head away so Cpt. Mason would not see me making small talk.

I quietly said to SFC Jackson, "Let the kids crowd us if they want; we probably won't get fired on if the kids are crowded around."

"I don't think anything is going to go down. If they were going to do something, they would have done it by now. I don't know what we are waiting for; the tractor is here; we should dump it and be on our way back already."

Meanwhile, Cpt. Mason asked among the locals where the owner of the tractor lived. A person claiming to be the owner's cousin said that the owner had left the village and that the tractor should be left where it was. The mechanics wasted no time dropping the wreck from the back of the wrecker. All four tires had separated from their rims and the chain from the wrecker had left a large dent in the front fender of the tractor and, as the wrecker dropped it, it looked like an abandoned piece of garbage not even worth fixing.

Cpt. Mason grabbed me and two soldiers, told them to get in his vehicle, and drive it around to pick him up. I did as I was told and soon was moving toward wherever Cpt. Mason had decided he was going. His driver went through the village and was directed to turn and stop at a specific home on the main street of the village. The sheik, dressed in a long white robe with a matching head scarf, came from the doorway. He was an old man with a big smile on his face, carrying his prayer beads in his right hand. It was indiscernible whether the smile was sincere or masking condescension for the American commander. But, nevertheless, the sheik gregariously greeted Cpt. Mason and welcomed him to the village. Cpt. Mason did not smile in return. He shook the sheik's hand and explained to him the previous operation.

He ended the conversation by sternly saying, "I don't want the tractor to ever be used to steal things or do anything illegal again," while Mr. Hussein translated for him.

The sheik responded with a big phony smile, now clearly masking his scorn, eliminating all doubt, reassuring Cpt. Mason, again through Mr. Hussein, that it would never ever happen again. I wondered if Mr. Hussein was even translating correctly or if he was making it sound nice so that nobody would get mad—perhaps many deaths had been prevented by clever translators. Mr. Hussein was my favorite translator. It would have been interesting if he could translate the meaning and the tone of the sheik and not just the words.

I watched, wondering why it was necessary for us to accompany the commander just to stand on the side. The soldiers watched the tops of buildings for possible attackers, oblivious to the conversation only a few feet away. A nervous child approached, explaining something in Arabic and pointing to a nearby building. I told a soldier to pay attention to the rooftop. But the soldiers and I all knew that it was probably nothing and continued to pay close attention, anyways, as it had become our instinct.

Cpt. Mason pulled a box of bottled water from the back of his truck. The particular water, a Greek brand, had recently been recalled for dangerous mineral contents and was only carried in the back of their truck to pour over their fuel-injector-pumps when they overheated. He passed out bottles from the box to children that crowded his truck. Soldiers, determined to remain focused on security, only momentarily turned their heads to watch for a few seconds at a time.

Children swarmed the truck begging for the water until it was gone. Cpt. Mason never smiled at the children. He simply passed out the water robotically, sometimes pushing away an annoying child and focusing on children that begged less aggressively. The children seemed excited and happy.

When the water was gone, the soldiers got into their trucks and drove back to through the village to their starting point. Most of the crowd had dispersed, and the tractor remained where it had been dropped.

"Are you good?" I asked Mr. Hussein.

"Yes, Lieutenant Darren, we can go."

The drive back was uneventful. We moved back along the gravel path that led to CP5. The soldiers recognized us, we had already radioed ahead, and they opened the gate. They didn't dare ask the commander to stop, even though they normally would if it were another captain driving through their checkpoint.

I jumped out of the truck at the checkpoint and went back in the concrete room in the double wall to wait. Eric, the officer in charge of the checkpoint, was sitting on a cot alone in the room, and I sat down next to him.

"What are you doing here?" he asked.

"What the fuck are you doing here, why aren't you outside with your soldiers on the checkpoint?"

"I'm taking a break; we rotate and it was my turn," he stuttered like he was embarrassed.

"The commander wanted to be sure that I came with him on a mission, but he couldn't be bothered to take me out to OP4 and drop me off himself, so I'm waiting here for Sgt. Mullins to pick me up."

"What was this mission that you just had to be on? Why he couldn't just do on his own? Or, for that matter, send you alone with a bunch of soldiers to do it?"

"Cpt. Mason shot up a tractor. The civil affairs people found out about it and complained to the brigade commander. The brigade commander told us we had to take the wrecker out and drag the piece of shit back to the village."

"He just shot up a tractor? Why would he do that?"

"I don't know. I guess there was a context to it, but I can't imagine that he had a justifiable reason. Anyways, I think he only shot out the tires."

"That is fucked up. The commander just shot up a tractor. That is seriously fucked up. Was there an attack or something like that?"

"Using a tractor in an attack? Come on, Eric," I said sarcastically, "don't try to make sense of this, please."

"No, seriously, he's going to get in trouble for this, isn't he? He can't just shoot up a tractor for no good reason."

"We'll see if he gets in trouble. I doubt it. It's not like we get in trouble if we shoot up a bunch of people." I could see that Eric was really concerned, so I wanted to get his mind off of it. "Ya know, the commander fucked his cousin."

"What? Which commander?" Eric replied.

"Cpt. Mason. He told us one night. I was playing UNO with Jake. The commander was there and we wanted to be polite, so we asked him if he wanted to play with us, but we didn't ever think that he would actually play. But he did, he just came over and played UNO with us. We were talking, and he told us that he fucked his cousin at a family reunion. He even said that his wife suspected something because whenever they see the cousin, she is always extra nice to them."

"Why would he tell you that?"

"I think that he thought that he was impressing us. I don't know why he would think that. It's not exactly impressive to fuck a cousin at a family reunion."

Brian Curran served as a lieutenant in the US Army 1st Armored Division from May 2001 to May 2005 and in Baghdad, Iraq, from May 2003 to April 2004. He received a PhD in electrical engineering in 2012 and is currently working as an engineer in Berlin, Germany. His story "Cleaning Up Our Mess" is an excerpt from his yet unpublished novel "One Block Away."

The Ride Home

I was talking to the ground troops, coordinating movement of the bodies from the wreckage to our birds. From the top of the hill, I watched young men marching through long grass. They were sifting through debris to salvage the ammunition and radios from in-between and under the folds of the sharp metal edges of the helicopter. From behind me, and over the whir of the rotor blades, an infantry soldier approached and asked me to talk to one of his troops.

"Can you talk to him? He won't say anything to me. He's just sitting there, and we can't get him to say anything. Just go talk to him and see if he's okay."

He pointed to the soldier kneeling on his haunches at the top of the opposite hill. His hands were gripping his M4, the plastic butt was digging into the soft sand, and his head was heavy against the barrel.

"I really don't think I can. I wouldn't know what to say. I've never lost anyone like that."

"No, you can. Women know what to say. Just go talk to him."

He pushed me gently, and I could feel the pleading in his eyes even though they couldn't be seen behind his goggles. Without saying a word, I sat beside the soldier and looked out for a moment, trying to see what he saw only an hour ago. His brother had been sitting in the back of that helicopter—the one smashed into the ground below us with fourteen bodies spilling from the windows, or piled on top of each other in the cabin section. I thought about which one might be his brother. Not the one underneath the helicopter. I could still read his nametag. Not the pilots, who, despite the limp way their arms hung, and their heads slumped forward, looked as if they were still making that final flight through the desert.

Maybe he was the one whose spine had disengaged from his body, holding a place in the crew seat. Maybe now it didn't matter. He would remember bumping knuckles prior to take off or talking about their first meal when they get home, or maybe they talked about seeing their girlfriends for the first time in over eight months. Maybe he was the one who took baths with him when they were toddler and joined the Army to be like his big brother.

I took his hand, and it felt rough like—like—sandpaper you could say, but it was more than that. I imagined running my hands over the dried up riverbeds that traversed the country. I put my arm around him loosely, like when it's not quite cold enough to wear your jacket all the way. He told me about how he lost his other brother, a Marine, in Fallujah. He told this to me, a stranger, sitting beside him in the dark. I searched myself for the answer to his problem, and then I asked him the only question I could think—if he wanted to fly back with us on the Medevac helicopter.

Inside of our helicopter, the pilots sat helpless, waiting for the bodies of the dead to be loaded in the back. I told our captain that this soldier was going to ride back with us. That he lost his brother in the crash and another in Fallujah. He needed to get away, somewhere to dim the vision. I pointed to the back of the helicopter, at the seat he would be sitting in, facing the bodies stacked up in twos, still armored and helmeted, arms dangling from the litter pans. Their fingertips would extend to his knee-caps. His face would be parallel with their chests. Was that his brother? Or the one below him? Would it matter? When they are camouflaged, body armored, helmets dipping below their eyebrows, feet twisted out. Even with his goggles, he mightn't be able to tell one from the other.

I found my way back to the soldier sitting on the hill to tell him that he couldn't ride with us. To tell him I was sorry. To tell him, as the world undoubtedly would, that there was nothing I could do for him. I hugged him lamely; our body armor clashed.

Our crew returned to the site in the early dawn to pick up the remains of soldiers too enmeshed in metal, too shrouded by night, too mangled to carry up steep hills. Perhaps his brother was one of these bodies, zipped and tagged in a black vinyl bag.

I only saw him once more, the one that survived; his face, which I had never actually seen, was glossy and posed, in a magazine article about parents who lost their children in war.

An army medic for six years, Good spent two of those years deployed in Iraq and Afghanistan, working as a flight medic, treating wounded Soldiers on the battlefield, and learning about the nuances of war.

Jay Harden

For A Future Believed In

I never was in Vietnam;
I just flew over, let loose, and waved.
I never heard
The screams from 35,000 feet.
So I never heard
The cheers, either.
I lived in silence with what I had done
Until 40 years later
When I found my brothers,
Them silent, too.
And we went to war
A second time:
This time, not for our country.
This time, for ourselves.
We spilled our guts again
And no blood flowed,
Only the healing truth.
Which was the greater battle?
For them,
The intense and internal many,
I often wonder;
For me, I know.
My latter-day warrior ways
Are unfolding
And the outcome is
Deliberate, difficult, long,
And yet to be.
I fight uncertain,
As loyal to me now
As I was then
To them.
We brothers,
Battling as always
For a future
Believed in.

Mr. Harden is a veteran of the Vietnam War. He came home in 1969 after 63 combat missions as a B-52 navigator with the 4133rd Bomb Wing (Provisional). After active duty he served in the Missouri Air National Guard and pursued a science career in the Department of Defense, retiring in 1997. Now he spends his time traveling, researching family history, and learning from five grandchildren. Mr. Harden lives in St. Charles County, Missouri.

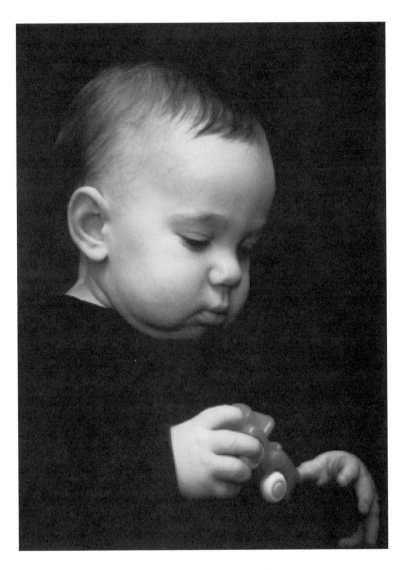

"The Way We Were: Portrait of a Vietnam Veteran's Grandson"
Photo by Jay Harden

Aaron Horrell

Deep and Free

After the rain someone cried.
Someone danced and somebody died.
Someone loved someone deep and free
Because that is how love is supposed to be.

The flowers did not forget to bloom
The day I took my camera and left my room.
I need to talk to the trees.
I need to get down on my knees.
I need to look closer at the little things in life.
I need to learn to live deep and free
Because that is how life is supposed to be.

I walked beside the pond
And took my usual trail into the woods,
But today I was longer gone.
Today I stepped with quieter steps.
Today I looked and listened.
Today I found nature deep and free,
Because that is how it is supposed to be.

Aaron Horrell

Baby I'm Already Back

Don't ask me when I'm coming back.
Baby, I'm already back.
I'm never really ever gone.
You're the rock I'm built upon.
And if I don't make it through the summer,
Don't ever think it was your fault.
The work was hard and good for me.
The rest was more than I could see.
And Baby, there's a lot to see.
So don't ask me when I'm coming back.
Baby, I'm already back.

I'm right beside you in your bed.
You will know every word I said.
And if you don't make it through the winter
It could have been my fault.
The work was hard and good for you.
The rest was more than you could do.
And Baby, there's a lot to do.
So don't ask me when I'm coming back.
Baby, I'm already back.

I've never really gone away
Long as you ask me to stay.
And if we don't make it through together,
It would have been our fault.
The work was hard and good for us.
The rest was more than we could guess.
And Baby, there's a lot to guess.
So please, for God's sake, please don't doubt me.
You don't have to be without me.
And don't ask me when I'm coming back.
Baby, I'm already back.
Baby, I'm already back.
Baby, I'm already back.

Aaron Horrell

All I Ever Wanted

All I ever wanted was for canvasses to talk.
Paint to cry out.
Light to be soft.
Hard lines to be muted.
And for men to stop.
All I ever wanted was for eyes to open up.

I studied nights alone
Applying color with care.
I listened to the music
To see how much was there.
And the paint walked.
The canvas talked.
The light was soft.
And I conquered the world.
All I ever wanted was for paint to cry.
Light to shine.
Butterflies to fly.
For men to open up their eyes.
All I ever wanted was for canvasses to talk.
And behold . . . canvasses talk!

Aaron Horrell joined the US Navy in late 1971 during the time of the Vietnam War. In boot camp he was one of two enlistees from a company of 80 young men chosen to be Sea Bees (Construction Battalion [CB]). He was sent to a training school in Port Huneme, California, where he became a brick/block layer. During the next 3 1/2 years he traveled with Navy Mobile Construction Battalion 74. He is an artist and nature photographer and writes a weekly article for the Southeast Missourian newspaper titled "Through the Woods." As manager of Painted Wren Art Gallery in downtown Cape Girardeau, he exhibits his own paintings and nature photographs and also provides wall space for other local artists. He has a daughter who is a captain in the US Air Force.

Transit

As usual, the only sounds in the hospital tent when I arrived were the rustle of canvas and an occasional cry from one of the mortally wounded insurgents in the POW ward. Such cries were always met with the same bored rebuke of the security policeman tasked to guard the prisoners. "Shad up. . ." he'd say, in an accent I was never able to pin down. "Yer dyin' already so be a man 'bout it. . . ." I think the reason I couldn't place his accent was because it was all accents mixed together—New Yorker, Cajun, Dixie, surfer dude—an untraceable voice that could belong to anyone or no one. That's the way I saw the world during my last week in-country, waiting for the freedom bird to take me away from Iraq in disgrace, back to the world of highways as smooth as ribbons, clean sheets, rain, and a long and loving marriage.

Okay, so the marriage wasn't loving. For that matter, it wasn't even long. Amy and I had only been married six months when the trouble started, almost a year before my Air National Guard unit got its deployment orders. Once in-country, I blamed the war because that was the easy thing to do. "That's so cold," my buddies would say when I informed them of Amy's unfaithfulness, how she had hit the sheets with her boss, probably as soon as the wheels went up on our deployment bird. But the lie, like all things easy, wore out its usefulness. And soon after went my discipline and patience for being somewhere I didn't want to be. Which was the whole reason I was in the hospital tent, busted down a stripe, cast out among my unlucky brothers-in-arms, and not where I should have been which was perched in a sandbagged watch tower, guarding the northeast perimeter of the base.

On this particular night—my third as a transit "volunteer"—I arrived late for my midnight to six shift. The in-processing nurse was a young captain who sat behind a field desk chewing gum and staring at a radio terminal that occasionally burped to life with news of inbound helicopters. She was vaguely attractive—the way all women in a war zone are vaguely attractive, which is to say, discernibly female—but I didn't think much of her because she clearly didn't think much of me. Also, as I signed in for duty, I noticed she smacked her gum like my wife did— each bite a punishing blow upon the dead, flavorless wad. She handed me a clipboard of chores just as she had done the two nights previous, without so much as a hello.

After hanging my helmet and Kevlar vest on a nearby rack, I suited up in a teal hospital scrub then worked my way down the tent's narrow corridor separating the wards—each of them the size of a 2-car garage. The dim utility lights strung through the ceiling braces and modular layout put me in mind of a sci-fi movie about a deserted base camp on an alien world, sterile and endless and brimming with danger. The doctors were gone, either off-duty or asleep in one of the dark rooms that connected to the main corridor. I walked gingerly through the first ward—the one designated for American and British wounded. I emptied the garbage and collected the blood- and shit-stained sheets, marveling at the soldiers who had been choppered in the day before, some missing limbs, some missing faces, all of them sedated to a point that they would not even awaken until they were back in the world.

That night only three wounded occupied the twelve beds, a far cry from the bad old days of '05-'06 when the wounded filled the room and lined the hallways. I hustled up a bag of sheets to run out to the laundry depot. One of patients was awake, a heavy-set American soldier with wide, searching eyes. I pretended not to notice him and went about my business.

"Hey," he said across the room. A soupy red light from the blinking life-support equipment filled the space between us.

"Hey," I said, and turned back to ramming sheets into the cloth sack.

"No, I mean c'mere," he said, insistent. "Seriously, dude, I need you over here."

I shuffled closer, primarily to tell him that I wasn't an orderly and was only there as punishment until they could ship me out. But he waved his hands dramatically, as if anticipating just such an excuse.

"You're not a doctor, are you?" he said, much louder this time.

I shook my head.

"Listen, I need some water. Can you get me some water?"

I took in the whole of him and realized that he wasn't really that heavy-set. His entire mid-section was wrapped in layers of bandages that culminated in a bulge of gauze near the base of his neck. A yellow sheet of legal paper, folded neatly in half, was clipped to the chart at the end of the bed. Across the sheet were scrawled two words: *NO WATER*.

"Yeah, I know what it says, man," the soldier said. "But I'm dying of thirst over here. Seriously."

"I'll get a nurse."

"Screw the nurse! What's she going to say? She's just going to look at the chart and say no, right?"

The wounded man in the next bed stirred and opened his eyes. I could tell from shape of the blanket covering him that he had lost his

164

legs. "Hey, shut up," the legless man said to both of us. "I'm trying to sleep."

"You shut up!" the thirsty soldier said. "You get all the water you want, right?"

Across the aisle, on the other side of tent, the third patient began to groan. I wondered what I had done to deserve this outbreak of awakenings. It was the most I had ever interacted with any of the wounded.

The first patient sighed and adopted a more measured tone. "Seriously, I'm sorry, I didn't mean to yell. My name's Tom. You like the Air Force? The Army sucks. Can you believe one of those Hajis shot me? Went right though my Kevlar. Bullet-proof, my ass. Where you from, man? You married? Got kids?"

Before I could answer he said, "Okay, whatever, I don't really give a shit. I'm honest though, right? That counts for something. Just get me some water, okay?"

"I can't do that. It might kill you."

"Man, you don't know what it'll do. You said you're not a doctor."

The legless soldier was now staring at both of us, his eyes filmed over with drugs and something else—some undruggable pain smoldering just beneath the surface of his skin. A smattering of get-well cards and letters from the States papered the tent wall behind him, most of them addressed to *Dear Soldier or Airman or Marine,* scrawled in crayon by tiny innocent hands. Many depicted crude drawings of stick figures with guns, American flags with not enough stripes or stars, and deformed airplanes propelled by orange flames, things only tiny innocent hands could draw. My wife had child-like handwriting. She had written me once during my tour. Only once and it wasn't to wish me well. It was to ask me why I had left without signing the divorce papers and what the hell was wrong with me.

"Hey, do you hear what I'm saying, man?" the thirsty patient said. "What the hell's wrong with you?"

"I'll get the nurse," I said, turning away.

"I'm not kidding with you, man! Hey!"

But I had already ducked out of the ward, back through the corridor to the nurse's station. Before I said a word to the captain, she held up her hand and shook her head. "Can't do it," she said.

"You can't do what?"

"Extend your detail. Three days is the max for all transits." She licked her lips as if what she were about to say tasted good. "Especially those with disciplinary issues."

"That's not what I wanted," I said. "Believe me, the sooner I get out of this fucking nuthouse, the better."

She released an exaggerated sigh and said, "I am so, so, so sorry you feel that way."

I scoffed and then told her that the new patient wanted something to drink.

"Can't have anything. Doctors orders."

"I know that, but he keeps asking for water."

"He. Can't. Have. Any."

"He's disrupting the other patients."

"Believe me, sergeant, they've got more than enough to worry about."

I turned and listened for the thirsty soldier's shouts, but there was nothing—only the white noise of the desert wind, the distant groan of the Iraqi wounded, and the irritated guard saying, "Oh shad up why don't cha?"

At some point during the next few hours I knew that the sirens would sound, and we'd all have to duck for cover from inbound mortars. The hospital was a favorite target of the insurgents because of the immobile, the helpless, the thirsty. Since I'd been there, the attacks had always missed wide. But maybe tonight would be different and they'd get lucky. Maybe tonight, a round would find its mark and the groaning would stop. Or better yet, one of the attacking insurgents would actually survive our counter-strike from the predators buzzing overhead that stealthily zeroed in on their mortar tube's heat signatures, and maybe that insurgent would be brought to this very same hospital he had targeted, a replacement for those who had died slowly the night before. The God of War was such a cut-up.

When I turned back, the captain was staring up at me, her mouth slightly open as if trying to divine what to say next. She had blue eyes, loose and swimming around in their sockets with an intense and disturbing interest. I hadn't noticed her eyes before because I couldn't remember her ever looking at me. She had, until now, carried herself in a no-nonsense manner—at least when it came to me. *Clean this, pick up that, don't give the patients water.* All between ruthless smacks of her gum. But now the gum was gone, and there with something different about her expression, something well shy of contempt. Pity? And then I thought, pitifully, was it possible for a woman—any woman—to feel pity for me?

"What are you doing here?" she finally said.

"I told you, the guy's going nuts in there. He's—"

She was shaking her head. "I mean, what are you doing *here*, in the hospital? Why did they detail you here?"

I stared back at her and sighed. "My wife left me," I said. "For a dentist."

But then it appeared—that look so familiar to me, a clash of guilt and understanding in her eyes, the sudden need to apologize, to relate, to comfort. "Look, I'm sorry," she said. "It's this place, you know?" And here she made an all-inclusive gesture with her hand, toward the rack of helmets and Kevlar, up at the ceiling braces, out into the vast alien world that surrounded us. "It makes me seem a little insensitive at times." She gave a little laugh. "Okay, maybe most of the time."

I nodded, averting my eyes, setting my bottom lip to quiver. "This war," I said in a trembling voice that decorated my lie. "This damn war."

James Mathews is a Chief Master Sergeant in the D.C. Air National Guard and a graduate of the Johns Hopkins University Master of Arts in Writing program. He is also the author of *Last Known Position*, a short story collection and winner of the 2008 Katherine Anne Porter Prize in Short Fiction. His fiction has appeared in many literary journals. His website is www.jamesmathewsonline.com.

Sonja Pasquantonio

War Wounds

Three months deployed:
He prods, "Skype once a week."
"It's hard" he fumes. *Like I don't know.*
He attacks via email, "Who are you with?"
I reply. Because I have to. Because I have to.

Four months:
He's working extended hours
So am I. So am I.
His relentless emails, "You didn't call. Call me. Why
aren't you calling?"
I call. Because silence triggers a maelstrom, and I'm bone-tired,
emotions stunted.

Six months:
Departure delayed. "It's not MY fault," he storms.
Doggedly. "Why do you need a private email?"
Ava's potty-trained now.
He stalks my Facebook account. "Who's Casey?"
You've come undone. "Just a friend," I t—y—p—e warily.

Home:
We converge at the airport. He's slumped against a wall, muscular arms
crossed tightly over his chest.
Little daughters tumble forward in a whoosh of shimmering
blond hair and chubby arms,
the oldest tottering on impossibly long legs.
Scents of lavender and sunshine in a jumble of innocent tears and
"we missed yous" erases time with hugs.

My eyes scanning, I monitor his lips—held hostage—they, for a moment,
twist into a smile. My eyes target his, but he shifts and instead, unwraps
his arms in a rehearsed motion. He knows reintegration, has seen airport
greetings, but it is I who becomes the enemy.

I'm home.

Sonja Pasquantonio is an active duty Air Force officer and Assistant Professor at the Air Force Academy. She served in Afghanistan, Kosovo, Saudi Arabia, Qatar, and numerous humanitarian missions in South America. Her work has appeared in *Connecticut Review*, *War, Literature, and the Arts*, and *In the Fray*.

Monty Joynes

Don't Tell His Mother

Tom knows it's rough over here.
They mortar his camp every night.
Don't tell his mother.

Don't tell his mother,
And perhaps she won't recognize
That strange named place in the paper.

All fiery hell walks the mortars in.
His salt sweat tears more than equal hers,
But don't tell his mother.

Don't tell his mother
The product of her womb, somewhere flesh hit
Is in pain of leaking his young life.

For God's sake,
Don't tell his mother.
Let the government do it,
As they have the thousands before.
Let him die,
And then tell his mother.

Monty Joynes began a writing career under the mentorship of George Garrett at the University of Virginia. As a graduate student in Sweden, Monty made movies instead of grades and was drafted into the Vietnam War-era Army where he served with the 91st Evacuation Hospital. After a career as an editor and publisher of magazines and books, he began to write novels and non-fiction. Eighteen of his books have been published.

"Army Mom": Terri "Grumpy" Slider and dog, Kalani, cross the nation from Rancho Cucamonga, California to DC each year to honor her son (serving for 12 years) in the Army. The emblems and patches on her jacket and hat tell a story.

Photograph by Sheree Nielsen

A multi-award winning writer and photographer, Sheree writes inspirational essays that interweave family, nature, and travel. Professional credits: *AAA Midwest/Southern Traveler, Abaconian, The Eleutheran, AOL/Patch.com, Missouri Life, Nurturing Paws Anthology, C.H.A.M.P., Cuivre River Anthology IV* and *V, Folly Current, Storyteller,* among others.

Shaun Yankee

Liberation Requiem
Baghdad, Iraq 2003

Dusk is upon me, the sun sees its final hour
The orange halo of heat recedes, shadows of uncertainty revived
Every hair raised, heart racing, pupils dilated; absolute calm and clarity

The suspense heaves, oh, what this night could bring
The night and all that it holds, the stage is set, curtains open

A single spark ignites the cacophony of a chaotic symphony
Fireflies dance spontaneously, ravishing, relishing a mechanical tune
Full of ferocity; attracted by flash patterns, pure instinct

Following the lead, they fight for the front line
Their cry crescendos, shrieking, calling, claiming the unsuspecting
    victim
Pure predators, painfully perfect

Holes burned into flesh and concrete
Bodies bleed, buildings crumble all the same
Lyrics written in blood, etched in stone

Pests scatter and die, an eerie silence is all that remains
Stillness fills the world around, fog covers the stage; the fragrance, a foul
    smell

The curtains close, adrenalin retreats
Focus comes back, I hear their fate

A shameful war, more lives wasted
A twelve-year-old boy, a forty-seven-year-old man, a pregnant woman
All capable, all victim, all liberated
Judgment for all, this is not my rite

Shaun Yankee and his wife, Jennifer, live in Bay City, MI. He attends Saginaw Valley
State University where he is President of the Cardinal Military Association, and is pursu-
ing his Bachelor of Science in Nursing degree. He served five years in the U.S. Army as a
Military Police Officer and participated in the invasion force of Iraq (OIF I).

James A. Moad II

The Poet & The Wounded Warrior's Return

Sing to me of the man, muse, the man of twists and turns
driven time and again off course once he had plundered
the hallowed heights of Troy . . .
—The opening line of *The Odyssey* by Homer

In January of 2011, a fall on an icy incline did enough damage to warrant rotator cuff surgery back in the U.S. I'd just retired from the Air Force and was living in Germany at the time. A single visit to the military hospital nearby made me realize that I wasn't a priority there, nor should I have been. While the Landstuhl Regional Medical Center serves the local military community, it has another mission as well. It's the first stop outside the war zones for many of those wounded in Iraq and Afghanistan.

As I left the hospital, passing by the ER, I watched a crowd of medical personnel gather around a bus that had just arrived. They began offloading stretchers, one after another, filled with the wounded warriors who'd arrived at Ramstein Air Base just a few hours before on C-17s. I examined their faces, and after twenty years of service, many looked like little boys to me. With IVs hovering above blanketed bodies, the stretchers moved briskly past me toward surgeons and doctors waiting to treat the physical wounds of war. After watching the scene unfold before me, returning to the U.S. for surgery seemed like a modest inconvenience.

So, I returned to Colorado Springs for my surgery—my old stomping grounds, where I'd taught War Literature and helped edit the international journal, *War, Literature, and The Arts* (*WLA*). A few weeks later, after a four-hour procedure to piece together my shoulder with seven screws, I spent a dozen days convalescing at a friend's condo in town. It was a perfect setting on the eighth floor overlooking the city and the mountains beyond. There were only two limitations: no Internet access, and the TV's tabletop antennae provided reception to only six local channels. Knowing I wouldn't be inclined to read in the first week or so following the surgery, I'd checked out a stack of DVD's from the library—documentaries on the Greeks and Romans, a biography of Winston Churchill, a few movies, and the Ken Burns' histories of Jazz and World War II. Each of them meant to augment my research for a collection of short fiction I'm writing on the peripheral effects of war on society.

I started with the Greeks, reintroducing myself to the myths and warrior culture depicted in the epic poems of Homer. Like many students of literature, the *Odyssey* has always held a special fascination for me. I was reminded that The Trojan War lasted ten years, but what I'd forgotten was that it took another ten years for Odysseus to find his way back home to Ithaca. Homer's narrative imparts the return of the warrior-king in such a magical way that it's easy to forget the poem is also (metaphorically) about the struggle warriors endure as they assimilate back into society. The trials that Odysseus and his men faced echo the challenges that all warriors endure as they attempt to adjust back into the life they once knew.

In addition to watching DVDs, occasionally I'd surf aimlessly across those six local channels. Mostly for the local and national news, but on one of my last night's there, PBS re-aired an episode of *Frontline*, entitled, "The Wounded Platoon." Tired and low on sleep, I came across it toward the end of the episode and almost skipped over it. Before I could switch the channel, though, the narrator mentioned Fort Carson—the army base on the outskirts of Colorado Springs—grabbing my attention. One scene of the skyline looked exactly like the view outside the condo.

The documentary tells the story of the Third Platoon, Charlie Company of the 1/506 infantry—a forty-two man unit that spent two tours in Iraq. It details their struggles after returning home to Colorado Springs. About the same time, on the north side of town, I was using the Literature of War to highlight the mental challenges soldiers endure after the wars are fought. As future leaders, my colleagues and I considered it imperative that the cadets understand the complexities of those challenges and the need for moral leadership in the conduct of war.

In contrast, "The Wounded Platoon" recounts the disintegration of the unit over a four-year period and a failure of leadership. By 2009, seventeen members of the platoon had "been charged or convicted of murder, manslaughter, or attempted murder." And that was what they did back home. The documentary also highlights (in the words of the soldiers themselves), the murder of innocent Iraqis, the widespread abuse of illegal drugs, and those prescribed by army doctors to help them cope with the pressures of war—many of which have highly suspect side effects that don't warrant their use in a combat zone.

None of this, of course, is new to me or to the cadets I taught in my four years at the Academy. The actions of these soldiers both in the war zones and back at home echo the same experience of veterans from the Civil War to Vietnam. The literature of war—stories, letters, essays, and poetry—reflects this in vivid detail. Within the psychiatric community, Post Traumatic Stress Disorder (PTSD) has been accepted since the 80s as a condition that warrants professional help—one which continues to plague a military culture that stigmatizes the warrior in need of mental help. As for the misuse of legal and illegal drugs on the battlefield, there's no surprise there, either. In World War II, a variety of methamphetamine drugs were used by all participants (the U.S. included) to keep soldiers and airmen focused on the mission. In Vietnam, beer was airdropped to units in the jungle, and amphetamines were issued to soldiers to keep them alert. Not to mention all the illegal drugs used by troops to suppress the horror of what they'd seen and done.

So, while shocked at the level of violence occurring in my own backyard, the rampant drug and alcohol abuse seemed almost a given to me. All of this and more is detailed in and can be seen in the documentary online. It also didn't surprise me that the commander of the 1/506, Colonel David Clark, said that he was unaware of his soldiers' mental status. There are over 200 men in an infantry unit, and there's a necessary distance between a commander and junior soldiers, as well as a distinct difference between what a colonel experiences on the battlefield compared to a young enlisted man. Col. Clark's assessment is that if a soldier seeks solace in alcohol or drugs, he's "wrong minded." He may be correct, but it's as if he doesn't understand the temptation to silence the demons through alcohol and drugs. Odysseus, as the great captain and leader, forced himself to listen to the sweet Siren's call so that he would know the power of temptation on the men he fought beside.

As a commander, there's no question that Col. Clark is expected to accomplish the mission first, but there's more to being a leader than accomplishing the mission alone. In his words, "the army can't cure all the ills of society . . . you still got a mission to do and you can't do it with this guy. He came from society, he needs to go back to society." Somewhere, though, Col. Clark either forgot, or never understood, that the person the Army recruited from society, and then sent off to war, is forever altered by what he or she is asked to do on the battlefield. They aren't the same persons anymore, and many of them need the dedication and help from a leader committed to their recovery.

Lastly, it made sense that the Army, under pressure from the media, decided to conduct an investigation to get at the root cause. What did surprise and astound me, though, was the reaction to the Army's investigation, which highlighted a "failure of leadership" as a major contributor to the events. Many of the soldiers failed to get treatment for conditions that leaders were aware of (some were simply kicked out of the military), while others acquiesced to a cultural code of silence, built on the notion that only the weak seek help for mental problems. When asked whether anyone should be held accountable for this failure of leadership, Col. George Brandt, the head of Behavioral Health at Fort Carson said, "If I had fought this war before and had learned these lessons before, I might hold people accountable."

Let me stop here and take a long, deep breath before I go on. . .

The question was asked of an Army colonel who specializes in Behavioral Health. And his answer was that if only the army "had learned these lessons before?" Hmmmmm ... I wonder if he'd heard of the terms Shell Shock, Battle Fatigue, or PTSD before. If so, does he consider them to be convenient phrases with which to paint, in broad strokes, the suffering of soldiers in the last hundred years of war, but not "this war"? Is there something else at work here? The artist, writer, and veteran John Wolfe wrote in his essay "A Different Species of Time" (for *War, Literature, and the Arts*) about being wounded in Vietnam. At the end of the essay, he reminds us that those who study the human psyche have, for the past hundred years, defined the trauma of war in many ways and that

> each reappearance [of this trauma] is confronted by a psychological community that, though perhaps more sophisticated, is less in touch and familiar with the forces unleashed than our ancestors who painted themselves blue and pranced naked in the snow before Caesar's legions, challenging the absolutism, the dominion, of Rome. There is a criminal, spiritual cowardice in this evasion, because in examining the effects of war, we might well discover just what inveigles humanity to its blackest deeds.

Yes, writers have been telling the world for thousands of years that war consumes those who engage in it, and it is the role and obligation of leaders to understand this. It's why it's imperative that we teach the Literature of War. The lessons are not for the faint of heart, but necessary for those who will one day be in command. When I retired in 2010, West Point didn't have a core English course teaching War Lit to their Corps of Cadets. It was an elective, usually for English majors. I don't know if they have one now or not, but I hope so. When I directed the course at the Air Force Academy, the course motto was expressed in the words of the Greek historian, Thucydides: "The state which separates its scholars from its warriors will have its thinking done by cowards and its fighting done by fools." It's a statement I believe in with every fiber of my being.

Thinking back on "The Wounded Platoon," I realize that if nothing else, the army's report on transgressions by members of the Third

Platoon was spot on, in many respects. There was clearly a failure of leadership, up and down the chain, and if the chief of Behavioral Health needs to learn more lessons, then the failure is more widespread than I would have guessed before seeing the episode. As the poet John Balaban, who served as a civilian in Vietnam during the war, wrote for an essay in the 2010 edition of *War, Literature, and the Arts*:

> In ancient China, generals returning home with their armies re-entered the capital through a so-called Gate of Mourning. This was true whether the campaign had been a success or a defeat, because war is a pollution and ceremonies are required to protect the living from the inevitable spiritual consequences.

While the complexities of this war may be unique, the effects on the individual are not, regardless of how effective the military is at dehumanizing the enemy. This is not a new field—a new science—or a new phenomena in which the individual soldier needs to be studied to discern the emotional toll wrought from killing another human being or watching a friend die beside them. The war poet of this era, Brian Turner, expresses the natural human reaction to accomplishing what is asked of the soldier in this amazing poem. He read it (or rather, yelled it) to my class a few years ago.

SADIQ

It is a condition of wisdom in the archer to be patient because when the arrow leaves the bow, it returns no more. —SA'DI

It should make you shake and sweat,
nightmare you, strand you in a desert
of irrevocable desolation, the consequences
seared into the vein, no matter what adrenaline
feeds the muscle its courage, no matter
what god shines down on you, no matter
what crackling pain and anger
you carry in your fists, my friend,
it should break your heart to kill.

Despite all the education and training over long careers, I wonder how is it still possible for military leaders to deny or minimize the toll that war demands of the individual soldier. After ten years of the proclaimed War on Terror, headlines abound on the problems associated with treating the hidden wounds of war in both the physiological and psychological manifestations.

At the 2010 Association of Writers and Publishers (AWP) conference in Denver, I was fortunate enough to meet two poets associated with the Warrior Writer Project, Lovella Calica and Laren McClung. In short, they've worked with veterans at writing workshops, helping them to impart their wartime experiences on the page as part of the healing process, and they've published the work in a book, *Warrior Writers: Remaking Sense*. Like many, they find that the creative process is a powerful way to combat the effects of war on the individual—creation as a cathartic antidote to the destructive nature of war.

When I learned that Laren and I have fathers who fought in Vietnam—men who both became carpenters after the war, I could understand the shared commitment to our own art and the central role it plays in our life. We know, as the children of Vietnam Vets, that the burden our fathers carry is borne by us, as well. If the nation and its military continues to dismiss, underfund, or minimize the need to address the effects of war on those who fight them, they do a disservice to all of society and especially the spouses and children of those wounded warriors.

As for my own father, I always thought that the act of building and creating things as a carpenter was a way of keeping the memories at a distance, but not a means of confronting or moving beyond them. On trips along the highway, he would point, with a sense of pride, at buildings and tell my siblings and me he'd built that school, house, or church. Over the years, I've sent him copies of our journal, my favorite war books, and some of my own work, all in the hope that I could persuade him to write about his experiences, but to no avail.

When I was finally healthy enough to depart Colorado Springs and attend this year's AWP conference, I received a phone call from my father. He said he was writing some things down about the war. Things he needed to put down on paper and that he wanted to send them to me. It's been over forty-five years since he left the military, and I was overjoyed for him—for finding the courage to sit alone and reacquaint himself with that eighteen-year-old boy who joined the military and lost a part of himself in a war that none of us will ever fully understand.

As a child, I remember him telling me about being a weapons specialist, taught to disassemble and then reassemble any weapon while blindfolded. For some reason that story always stuck with me, and last year when I was reading the poetry from the *Warrior Writers: Remaking Sense*, the words of Nathan Lewis brought that story back to me. Nathan asks a simple question in his writing: "Why did I know the difference between an M-16 and an AK-47 before I could compare a Hindu to a Muslim or a sonnet to a Haiku?" It's a great question, I think, isn't it?

At this year's AWP conference, I met up with several old colleagues from the Academy—those associated with the journal. On our last night together, I turned the conversation to some of my ideas for this essay, and I was reminded about a recent attempt to get the troops at Fort Carson to engage in a writing program. Like the Warrior Writers project, it was meant to help them work through their problems, but it never got off the ground. Evidently, soldiers were quietly dissuaded from taking part in the program. Needless to say, I wasn't surprised.

As for me, I've been back home for over a week now. Between the travel time, surgery, visiting friends, and attending the conference, I was gone for nearly a month. I start therapy in a few days to rehab my shoulder. They say it's the first part that's the most difficult—just getting started—fighting through the pain of scar tissue, getting movement back, and pushing the muscles to remember what they are capable of. It'll take a lot of time and patience before I'll be able to get back to flying, but I will recover.

Shortly after I returned home, the letter from my father arrived in a package along with other mail my mother has been collecting for me. The letter was marked in my mother's handwriting: "James from Dad." At the time, I was outlining this essay, fighting the jetlag and shoulder pain, but also trying to focus on spending time with my wife and kids. I told myself that I'd open the letter once I finished writing this. After a few days, though, realizing how much writing I was doing on this and other projects, I finally picked up the letter and turned it over, prepared to open it. On the back, written in the thick, chalk-like print of carpenter's pencil, are the words from my father: "Correct my spelling and add whatever it takes. I could have said more about what these men went through, but one memory is enough." I put the letter back down, deciding that I needed to finish this before I opened it. The letter has been sitting beside my computer ever since.

As I come to the end of this essay, I realize that ultimately, each soldier ever sent to war begins his own personal odyssey. Driven by the call of a nation or by the desire for adventure, many will be searching to find themselves in the shattered ruins of a life forever altered. Some may never find their way home, while others might cope and assimilate quickly after they return from war. The process can begin well before they go off to fight or it might take forty-five years for a person to start.

Nothing is certain, but a failure of leaders to understand the complexities and repercussions of inaction or to address the problems with honest conviction is both unacceptable and an abdication of responsibility. This mission, though not accomplished on the battlefield, may be the most challenging of all. It may require the military to heed the lessons that the poets offer us, and a new generation of commanders with compassion and a willingness to truly lead. To abandon or marginalize our wounded warriors is to abandon ourselves as well.

You'll have to excuse me now. I've written far more than I meant too, and it's taken longer than I planned. I've got a letter to open.

James A. Moad II is a former Air Force C-130 pilot with 3000+ hours and over a hundred combat missions. He is a graduate of the U.S. Air Force Academy where he later served as an Assistant Professor in English and as a fiction editor for the journal, *War, Literature, and the Arts* (*WLA*). He also holds a Master's Degree in Creative Writing from Southern Illinois University Edwardsville.

Michael Sukach

Veteran's Quiescence

Save the morning flutter and plop of pitched
newspapers littering the tops of our dead end

drives and the flurried chitchat of Miller moths
professing in the tenured pause of their lives

there's nothing I can tell you about this poem,
save that it has suffered forty-two years of inertia

(. . . in between my second coffee
and cigarette when I catch sight

of John waddling up the street
in his robe and loosed combat boots

past the stone bow splitting our roads
into the breathless nowhere of Cheyenne

mountain after his dog, Mabel
(who is still sitting still in his driveway

and already knows he will return—just not when—
but gladder than before he left awakening the air with her name)

because it's not leaving or forgetting
or remembering where you put the key,

under which headstone lies which
of your revenant loves you loved more,

which is really not the question at all
but just the sooty breath of chimeras

who are somehow still with and without
you, wandering around the etching of your life . . .)

and that I don't want to have to bother to have any
epitaph that will scratch in the back of your throat

or anymore titles to poems trying to tell
you where this is and what to expect below.

Michael Sukach is a veteran of numerous conflicts and wars which include Operation Iraqi Freedom and Operation Enduring Freedom. He currently resides in Colorado
Springs and is nearing his seventeenth year of service and teaching writing and literature
at the United States Air Force Academy. Beyond his duties as an instructor, he continues
to write creatively and within the fields of post-modern literature and theory.

Bruce Sydow

Lake Serene

A dappled morning light
peers through a tapestry of mist
creating shadows on the gun rack.

I pull down the M-14
and cradle the stock
and smell WD-40.

Steadying trembling hands,
I inhale deeply
and pull the trigger.

In Quang-Tri,
rifle bong-hits of viscous marijuana
were the resin of my serenity.

I look out back
and see earnest mallards
bobbing beneath the surface.

The loud report
jars me from my stupor
and the spackled morning of silver.

A punctuated calamity
echoes loudly across the lake,
rattling the sliding-glass door.

The fowl take flight
with determined commitment
and hold formation to the last.

And one-by-one they fall,
in startling loyalty,
like fucking Marines.

Bruce Sydow, former Marine and Vietnam Veteran, received his master's degree from the University of Washington—Seattle. His poetry and essays have appeared in *The Evergreen Free Press*, *In Tahoma's Shadow*, *Salon*, and *In the Biblical Sense: An Anthology of Apocryphal Poetry*. Elected Professor of the Year, he is the recipient of the Exceptional Faculty Teaching Award.

Jacob Worthington

Becoming the Devil

A static-jumbled voice comes through the radio. I cannot remember if I imagined the static as a subconscious rejection of what I was hearing or if it was real, but I did in that second recall all the moments that brought us to that point.

Five hundred and fifty meters east of COB (Counterinsurgency Operating Base) Wilson in Arghandob, Afghanistan, sits a temporary watch post established in a thirty by thirty mud hut compound called a Kalot. Our thirty-six man platoon exits at sunrise after being up two hours prior performing pre-operation checks and practicing operation run-throughs. We move out in shifts with as much food and water as we could possibly carry and stay out until we deplete our supplies. The march down Route Philly to the watch post is roughly two football fields long and runs through several rivers, pomegranate orchards, as well as marijuana, poppy, and corn fields. The march takes us two and a half hours in 115 degrees of cloudless weather; we march with about 90 pounds of gear and 30- to 40-pound rucksacks on our backs.

We arrive at the watch post and immediately drop all weight. Shirts off and cigarettes out, we catch up with our friends whom we are relieving from their nine day mission. Their platoon begins packing as we exchange orders and new area information. Once they leave, I take up a three hour guard post at the sandbag-blocked doorway to the Kalot. As I'm getting off guard, a blast echoes from the east. We all look up, disinterest on our faces. We normally hear five to six blasts a day, and usually we only discover details on half of them. We wait for any radioed explanation, and after a few minutes, we shrug it off as no big deal, nothing new.

A static-jumbled voice comes through the radio. Through the static, I can only make out "Break Line Tree fife alpha . . . break Line Four fife echo . . . break Line Niner foxtrot." We can all translate the Army jargon. The message is a Nine Line Medevac Request to the emergency air evacuation dispatcher informing them that five of our friends, two football fields away, are dying. No reaction from the platoon; we are all paralyzed by emotions. Disbelief, sadness, anger, worry, and questions all overwhelm me in a split second. Seconds seem like minutes, until we all realize simultaneously that Line Nine reported a high possibility of enemy in the area. Time instantly rotates on me and minutes become seconds. Sergeants start yelling and privates start scrambling, while I am moving without a purpose and unable to find anything. I shift into fast forward and hurry to catch up with all the others as all the sounds surrounding me became static.

I post up in a guard position on the roof with my adrenaline still pumping, heart still racing, and mind still spinning from all the emotions and thoughts that overwhelm me. I sit there for hours trying to deal with the emotions and figure out what has happened, also trying to maintain security. The entire time, details are coming in bit by bit. There I sit, unable to do anything. I want to run, fight, and rescue. I daydream about saving my friends only to be awakened by updates of who's stable, dying, and dead.

The event causes me to contemplate my own mortality. I realize how easily it could have been me. If their supplies had lasted one more day, the mission that sent them over the IED would have been mine. I decide that my priorities while living at home need to be adjusted to surviving in combat. I decide that, in America, the drive and instinct to stay alive has become the psychological tonsils. They're there and they work, but they're never truly needed. American society has set up a system which allows us to truly never need to try to stay alive, so it has fallen on our list of active priorities below money, sex, and many other comparatively irrelevant goals.

I work out a series of questions that leads me to my combat survival mindset. Through these questions, I must ask myself to remove the possibility of hesitation and distraction that can get me killed. What must I do so I do not get killed? I must stop my killer. How far am I willing to go to stop my killer? If staying alive is my top priority, then I am willing to go as far as needed. These questions remind me of one proposed in the movie *The Boondock Saints*: "The question is not how far. The question is, do you possess the constitution, the depth of faith, to go as far as needed?" I answer no. I do not possess the constitution, the depth of faith to go as far as needed. Through this realization, I decide I will possess it and contemplate how to acquire the mindset to go as far as needed. I ultimately need to be able to take another person's life without hesitation or distraction when the time comes.

You must achieve mind over soul. You must mentally work at turning off your emotions. Through accepting two universal truths, I come to the underlying philosophy behind the warrior's survival ethics. Accept the fact that the world is filled with uncontrollable atrocities. In laymen's terms, shit happens, so deal with it. You must realize that the world always has and always will be filled with murder, rape, abuse, and many other emotionally devastating events and also that you will witness these things firsthand. You cannot allow your emotional response to distract you. The second is a more difficult truth to accept. Accept the fact that to keep your comrades and yourself alive, you will do some morally questionable things. In layman's terms, you shit, so deal with it. You must accept the worst. You will see pain, suffering, and death. You will cause pain, suffering, and death. You must deal in definites, because ifs and buts will get you killed. You must realize the full gravity of your actions. When you kill a person in war, nothing matters but survival. I say person to convey maximum vagueness because in war that person could be anybody. Men, women, children, Muslims, Christians, Jews, Blacks, whites, and browns all fire the same deadly bullets. You will make widows; you will make orphans, and you will destroy families, but your spouse will have you, your children will have you, and your family will have you.

I realize and accept these truths early on and achieve mind over soul. Having to fight these moral and ethical battles in the heat of real battle will distract you and cause you to hesitate, and that's why I always come into battle mentally prepared. I desecrate cultural and religious traditions and laws. I detain, interrogate, and threaten children. I forcefully march shoeless, foodless, and waterless men through miles of detrimentally harsh terrain while they carry pounds of confiscated Taliban ammo, homemade explosive materials, and live anti-tank mines to their inevitable incarceration, and send some to Guantanamo Bay. These Gestapo style tactics save lives through the capture and elimination of killers, the detection of attack locations and details, and the destruction of equipment just like the kind used to kill my friends. I acknowledge that these actions may seem unredeemable to some. I confess to you that those events are actually my lesser wrongs and that there are few who would accept the others, so you have to ask yourself by now, how do I live with it?

A friend, who never achieved this mindset, is a nineteen-year-old non-combat communications private named Daniel Yance. It is his boyhood dream to be an American soldier, but it meant nothing to him if he wasn't a combat veteran. He begs his friend and commanding sergeant to let him go on a mission. Thirty minutes into his first mission, he is separated by the chaos of battle. He is physically and intellectually on par with the rest of the platoon, but because of the sudden mental and emotional distress, he becomes distracted and hesitates. It causes him to lag behind. Over-attention to his mental state distracts him from the surrounding physical state, and he steps on an IED Still alive, yet badly wounded, he is captured. It's unknown to me if he survives long enough to be tortured, but if he did, his knowledge of our secret encryptions and classified networking systems would mean this torture would not be over quickly. His killers then transport his body to Pakistan and on their way leave pieces of him at village squares, mosques, and U.S. funded medical clinics with notes glorifying his murder.

Machavelli wrote in *The Prince* that "The ends justify the means." I did evil things to stop evil men, so does living through the war make my actions justifiable? I sacrificed the responses of my soul for the ability to stop at nothing to achieve my one and only desire. I became the Devil to defeat demons. I lived to regret my mistakes and Yance did not, so does that make it justifiable? No. Bearable? Yes.

Jacob Worthington is a US Army Reservist who was deployed for a year in Afghanistan. He is currently attending Georgia College and State University, while awaiting his next deployment in 2013.

James Wooden

The Flies

They think us soldiers
dead already, seeking out
eyes, nostrils, any exposed
skin, for something to eat,
a place, soft and warm, for eggs.

They seem to time the swipe
of our hands, leap, then twist
a lazy figure-eight, land again,
and again, ink marks black
on our sunburned skin. We hang

fly paper, the long strip
nailed to a cross-beam of timber.
The yellow spiral slowly molds
black with flies. Soon there's no place
to die, the living walk over the stuck,

whose lives are twitch and nerve.
By spring we will be gone, the snow
will melt, and the flies will crawl,
guided by instinct and memory,
from the mud, to dry their wings
on bones strewn by ice and thaw.

After serving in the US Army Reserve and deploying to Afghanistan in 2003, James Wooden returned to school and discovered poetry. In 2011, he received a Master's degree in writing and taught at Johns Hopkins. He now writes in Western Massachusetts, where he lives with his wife.

Leslie Harper Worthington

Army Issue

Sometimes
I wear your green Army socks.
I walk around the house
With a picture of you in my pocket.
It makes me feel
You're just out of earshot:
Just down the hall,
Just playing in the yard,
Just clear of gunshot.
But then it occurs to me
That I can wear your socks
And that actually
They're quite big on me.
Then I count the days again
Till you'll be home.
I count the days
Since you last called.
Is that enough to worry about?
I wonder are you still sleeping
On the cot beside your truck.
Are the bomb blasts,
That you don't really hear,
Still waking you up?
I know the phone,
That doesn't ring,
Still wakes me.

Leslie Harper Worthington is chair of the Department of English at Gainesville State College where she also teaches and serves as an advisor for *The Chestatee Review*, the college's award-winning literary magazine. She holds a PhD from Auburn University with a concentration in Southern Literature and is the recipient of a Brittain Fellowship from the Georgia Institute of Technology and Quarry Farm Fellowship from the Center for Mark Twain Studies at Elmira College. Her book *Cormac McCarthy and the Ghost of Huck Finn* was released in January 2012.She lives with her children and grandchildren in Flowery Beach, Georgia.

Richard Van Beeson

The Life of a Superhero

We left with our dreams: dreams of youth, from youth, for even those beyond spring are young in danger, to the loss of youth, and whatever lay beyond.

We dreamt of different worlds, and foreign adventure; such hopes of making a difference, and putting our stamp on the world seemed our right. We dreamed of what we would be when tested by fire; sometimes we dreamt of the fire, and cried in our sleep. We dreamed of open doors, and the many possible futures, of finding we were who we had always believed we were, and of proving ourselves to each other.

We came home more practically minded. Some of us returned with honors, some with broken pride. Some came home stronger, others scarred. A few returned with ghosts where pieces of their human body used to be. Some came home blind, but we all came home with new eyes.

Some of us didn't come home.

The case of Ben Thurman is an odd one to many strangers, as well as folks from his hometown who've known him since he was in the belly.

Ben dreamed of being a hero, not just your run-of-the-mill soldier, fireman, or astronaut; Ben dreamed of becoming superhuman, with skills and attributes to conquer those situations that cause heroes to give up. But, in order to be superhuman, he first had to acknowledge he was human, and nothing brings us closer to our divine material state than the threat of losing it. That peril danced with Ben Thurman, and ended his friend; bits of twisted metal, flying through smoke, striking random places at great speeds were Ben's magic ring, his radioactive spider, his yellow sun.

And so it came to be that Ben Thurman acknowledged his humanity, and thus, came home with a Superpower.

After his convoy was struck by an IED on a crowded city street, Ben became all too aware of the gaps his eyes were not sharp enough to see, the spaces concealed by physical barriers or shadow, and from that real-ization, he discovered the secret to his material flesh, a secret most of us never realize. For the human body is nothing if not an antenna.

After the shock of that attack, Ben began to feel the hidden nooks and crannies around him, to sense the areas beyond walls for threats. His body's natural electricity became a radar system, sending his own energy out in pulses that returned to him with vital information.

There's just one problem with such hard-wired special abilities. Once they've been switched on, sometimes, we can't turn them off.

We've grown up, or, for some of us anyway: we've been grown up. Been shamed and beaten down for believing in our fantasies. But it may be the odd case of Ben Thurman is not as unique as you may think . . .

"Thurman, I'm dead."

Awake!

Ben's body was a live antenna. His senses shot outward, forming the shape of a giant bubble, encasing the house and the area around it. As his senses found their limit, the bubble began to shrink, its edge dragging sky and ground, touching everything, categorizing each object and its status on its path back to him. He felt, and recognized, each tree near the house, the frigid air between branches, and the space between each blade of grass.

A sliver of moonlight shining past the edge of the skylight's curtain revealed every shadow cast by the window. His eyes probed the darkness, searching for an imminent presence the hairs on his arms assured him was there. The folding white closet doors remained in the half-open position he had left them. The bathroom door—shut.

The bubble's edge raked the birdbath, the two dead stumps on the east side of the house, and the small wooden bench on the west side; dead limbs lay strewn about the yard in all directions, and he felt their decay. It touched the dilapidated railroad tie landscaping holding the hill off the house, the porch, the natural slope and curvature of the land. All, he sensed, as it should be—all still, all dormant.

Shadows leaned off the vanity and dressers in the same direction, forming dangerous pits of darkness. He acknowledged his pounding heartbeat then put it out of thought. Unable to slow his breathing, he flared his nostrils and opened his mouth, quieting the sound of it. He waited for his eyes to adjust.

His senses continued their trek back to him, sweeping the deck on the west side of the house and the driveway out front for threats and ir-regularities.

His eyes adjusted. He scanned for movement between the dressers and found none.

Outside, the air was cold but not biting; nothing stirred. His bio-radar told him there were dead things out there: dead limbs, dead bugs, dead trees rotting on the ground. The feel of their decay came to him on invis-ible lines, irritating his skin, massaging his bones, and filling his stomach with smoke.

Ben Thurman's mind continued its magic trick: alternating between scanning his moonlit enclosure, to feeling the world blocked from his view, so rapidly it felt as though both were occurring at once. The sphere's edge dragged rocks and worm-filled dirt. His eyes adjusted again and re-swept the room in a clockwise motion.

The beagle lay at the bottom left corner of the bed. His wife's body faced the north wall, her breathing—steady and calm. His eyes zeroed in on an unfamiliar pale object resting in the shadow of the closet doors and waited for the abnormality to move. His nostrils flared wider, and the skin around his eyes contracted, until the image sharpened into the long, white snake of his wife's robe belt. His mind quickly resolved its story—the overlapping arrangement revealed it had fallen from the closet's small doorknob, where it had been haphazardly hung—but his eyes remained locked in, waiting for his body to acknowledge its lack of threat. All the while, peripheral shadows crept in, becoming alarming. He ceased focus on the belt and adjusted his eyes to take in the entirety of the room. Nothing was moving or out of place.

The edge of the collapsing dome his senses created floated through the walls with nothing to report. It swept over the roof and through the other rooms of the house, confirming no threat was at hand, then collapsed through the bedroom.

His senses returned to him gently. No foreign presence, no movement, no noise lurked outside. The bare trees in the window remained blatant and calm against the moonlight. The sum of all these familiar digits was calculated crisply: Georgia, autumn, Tuesday. Safe.

The hairs on his arms lay down, the electricity under his skin faded.

Ben rolled right and turned the glowing clock on his bedside table to face him: 1:33AM. He reversed onto his back and squeezed the blanket tighter around his shoulders. The cold air outside was no issue. The shadows filling the mass of space between his body and the walls no longer mattered. His senses were now fully encased within his flesh. He became aware of the heat radiating from his wife's body.

He lay facing the ceiling for several moments before the sharp tingles in his mind began to recede. His wife was a furnace; the beagle was snoring.

Safe.

The feel of warm, comforting water rolled over him, then through him as his muscles relaxed, and his consciousness sank into sleep. As his eyelids fell, he shot one last pulse through the room. It returned affirming all was still, and where it should be. He let go.

Calm and comfortable, aware of nothing, he floated on the current through the warm rushing water.

The face loomed over him. Its black skin, once so dark it was almost purple, was now caked in sickly white. The lips were strangled blue, the eyes urgently dull and blank.

"Thurman, I'm dead."

Ben sprang from the deceitful water into the massive blank space of his bedroom. The bubble shot out and began collapsing over the trees, the grass, the birdbath, and the wooden bench: all familiar—nothing out of place. His mind flew around the room like a hurricane searching for a threat; his body remained stiff and alert. Invisible lines of feeling brought him the status of the dead stumps and limbs, the railroad ties, porch, and deck. The closet doors remained half shut, his wife's robe belt coiled like a snake beneath them. The sensory dome marking the limits of what he could feel and assess collapsed on the house: roof, basement, attic— nothing stirred. The stairs, the living room, and the kitchen remained quiet and watchful. Caesar was snoring at the foot of the bed. Each visible detail of every dark inch of space was confirmed.

He took a moment to congratulate himself on waking in a half-sitting position.

"Hey baybuh . . . Whatsa diffuh shuh. . ."

She was out again.

Ben remained half-upright in bed, feeling the dark empty spaces between the bedroom furniture become more comfortable. He checked the clock on the bedside table: 3:32 AM. Thirteen minutes passed before he could feel the warm water teasing him again. This time he would remain in the shallow part.

Dark black skin: strangled purple and powdered white. Rot. Decay. The eyes blank and knowing.

"Thurman, I'm dead."

Ben was on his feet cursing. His body cut through the cold empty space between the walls. The electricity under his skin began to fill the room then shot out further. Trees, grass, landscaping, closet, bathroom, porch, roof, basement, stairs, vanity, living room, kitchen—same as before.

His eyes were taking an eternity to focus. Something in the darkness between the two dressers caused old, dusty cobwebs in his upper back to stretch uneasily. He found the switch; a moment later, light was there. Caesar's body sprang to life.

It was well past four in the morning. The back of his mind was a noisy clutter of old conversations that had never happened. The forefront of his mind was concerned with work. A few fucking hours of sleep weren't going to cut it. He needed to be alert, dammit.

"Baby!" Tammy's voice struck an urgent chord in his spine and sent ghosts flying through his head. His mind swam, and his body became dizzy. A moment later, one terrifying idea solid enough to hold onto presented itself—*I forgot her medication yesterday.*

She hadn't said a word about it, but now it was surely coming. She had taken her last pill before bed, and was doomed to a day filled with the pain of her strained back, all because he hadn't remembered to pick up her relaxers.

Caesar was sitting at his feet, asking questions with his eyes. He had forgotten dog food as well. It was so hard to remember things these days.

An unwelcome song began playing in the back of his head, something by Buddy Holly. Dog food and medication, problem and solution, shame and practicality turned over each other in his mind, fighting for dominance. The more his thoughts turned to Caesar's forgiving eyes, the more the large room around him became real.

From the corner of his eye, he noticed Tammy sitting upright in bed, her hair was a mess; her face looked like her breath probably smelled. The left shoulder ribbon of her pink gown hung loosely above her elbow.

"What the hell?"

Ben was pacing now, trying to fill the room with his energy and feel the space around him, as the noise was growing louder in the back of his head.

"Hey!" she yelled.

The volume dial on the radio in his head turned from five to seven.

She doesn't understand, fucking idiots don't understand. It's all on me now; I'm alone, except for the ghosts.

Ben Thurman stood on the edge of three worlds: the world of his dreams, the world of his bedroom, and the intensifying noise in the back of his mind, each one struggling to overtake the other. From the depths of his subconscious came images of Baghdad, the desert, his friends, laughter in the chow hall, the superman medallion he had worn around his neck along with his dog tags. They came with smells and feelings, most of them comforting and light. But somewhere buried in that slideshow was the face, and the face was trying to tell him something. The senseless voices of his conflicted mind fought, like heroes, to drown the pictures out, and as the images were buried deeper and deeper, the physical world around him began to overtake his dreams. His shoulders and lower back began to relax. A cloud of tenderness and peace began descending on the room in a shy manner; the noise was fading. . .

"BENJAMIN! What the hell are you doing?"

The volume knob turned from seven to eight. The pink, blonde blur on the north side of the room threw back the covers and jumped to her feet.

"Baby!"

Ben struggled not to see or feel the ball of anxiety approaching from the bed, and the noise in his mind was delighted to help. The cloud of warmth and safety was slipping away.

"Oh, shut up, Tammy, just shut the fuck UP!"

As his temper rose, he felt power pulse from his body, ricochet off the surrounding walls and return to him. He marveled for a moment at the smaller size of the room. Clean, electric light filled the dangerous places between: the gap between his dresser and hers, the gap between the vanity and the bathtub, the gap between the bed and the wall: all filled with a glorious soothing glow.

The pink, blonde blur was in his face.

"What is this? Is this the P . . ." she stopped, confused, "P.T. . . ." She couldn't remember the letters.

"Don't start with that shit."

"Baby, I think you're having an episode . . ."

The volume knob on his mental radio rotated another notch. The tempo of the music in his head was grinding and steady. Somewhere back there, a movie was playing as well. In it, this conversation was different; Tammy understood the seriousness of the situation and wasn't threatening the safety of his bedroom with her bullshit.

"Leave me alone."

"Ben, you're changing. You're becoming something I don't understand. You feel too much."

Dead limbs, dead bugs, dead trees lying on the ground.

"I feel everything."

"Just turn it off, baby. Dr. Chattergy said your mind may act like this, he said. . ."

"I can't."

"But—"

"I can't dammit! I can't fucking turn it off!"

Buddy Holly and The Crickets were playing "Brown Eyed Handsome Man" in the background, and the more Tammy talked, the more the background struggled to become the foreground. Ben heard her over the drone, but found himself unable to register some of the words she spoke.

It was the noise: the music, the alternate conversations, and pleasant memories—some real and others fabricated. They all kept his synapses from firing on the tangible things of the here and now.

His eyes caught the glint of something silver behind his wife. On his dresser sat a black box with a window for a top. Under the glass were his medals, his dog tags, and the medallion. A triangular silver brooch with a symbolic capital S stamped in the middle. S for Superman. Ben hated the arrogant prick that had worn that god-dammed thing to the desert. He brushed past his wife, ripped the symbol of his naiveté from the shadow box, and threw it against the wall. When it landed unharmed, he rushed forward and smashed his foot down on top of it, grinding it with his heel.

"Baby, please."

"Shut the fuck up, Tammy."

"No!"

The star in the movie in his head said something cool and strong, and the movie version of Tammy complied. He had walked himself into a corner to stamp on the necklace and now felt the juncture of the walls closing him in. He turned to retreat, only to find his wife blocking the way out. She laid her hand on his shoulder.

"Baby," she said, "just turn it off."

In his cluttered mind, her words seemed to be suspended in mid-air, opposite a giant aquarium filled with water. All except for one: just.

Just turn it off.

It cut through the noise keeping him detached from his memories; it infuriated him, made him want to punish her for her ignorance. Extinguishing the well of violence swelling in his belly proved effortless when he looked into the emotion on her face, but he was left with the heaviness of the smoke it left behind.

"My mind's falling apart. My head's going . . . it's going—"

"Shhhhh, what's in your head, baby, hmm?"

"The noise, so much noise. Can't shut it off. It won't leave me alone."

"What noise, honey?"

"Noise!"

"Look, Dr. Chattergy said this may hap—No, no, no, NO! Don't you turn away from me! Listen, Dr. Chattergy said this would happen. You're sick—Ben! Please, come back. No, no. . . . You're not sick, you just— Your mind is trying to protect you, honey, it's trying to protect you. Look at me."

He allowed her soft hands to turn his face toward hers.

"If you can't turn it off, turn it down just a little."

The volume knob in his head slipped a notch.

"I love you, baby. My hero. You're not there anymore. You're here. You're safe here."

Ben felt his body let go; the burden of those empty spaces began slipping away, as his senses retreated to rest within his flesh.

"I love you," she said.

Locked away somewhere, in a stronger compartment of his mind, was the face. He acknowledged it, affirming it was not in his world. The light in the room became softer. He was now holding his wife by the back of the neck, the same way she held him. He marveled at her beautiful, sweet smile, then watched as it turned to a wince.

The pain would be at its greatest intensity soon. He struggled to blame it on the noise—the noise wouldn't let him remember her meds—but his grip wasn't tight enough to hold on to that one. The adoration in her face brought to him the shame of his failure.

The radio blared.

"Get away from me!" he yelled, and pushed her away.

"Baby, what—"

"Just get. . . . Get the fuck away from me! I have to go!"

The pharmacy in Terlington was open 24 hours and only 40 minutes away. He could dress, make it there and back before work, but he would have to concentrate.

"Ben, please—"

"I have to go goddammit, can't you see that? Can't you just fucking listen?"

Tammy limped out of the bedroom. When the door closed behind her, the radio in his head quieted down to six. He sighed in relief.

Ben Thurman crossed the room and entered the walk-in closet. The radio was still playing Buddy Holly; the movie theater showed clips and scenes of himself acting with dignity. A preacher with his voice shouted theories and opinions on politics, the world, and people in general. It was hard to focus under all that noise. The clothes hanging directly in front of his eyes refused to stay still in his mind. They ran quickly through, slipping on its slick surface, then fell out. The space outside the closet was becoming more and more burdensome, and it had something to do with Tammy. He could feel her sad electricity out there somewhere. He closed the closet doors behind him and shut it out, then sank to the floor as the noise washed over him like rough waves.

One minute . . .

Two minutes . . .

He would have to concentrate to get from the closet to his truck, and to the pharmacy and back. Thoughts of his boss and co-workers joined the mess in his mind. He was beginning the second day of a new work-week with a fatigued body and only one quarter of his mind. He was letting them down.

His jeans from yesterday still had a belt woven through their waist loops. He put them on. A few moments later, he scanned his shirts again. They darted from side to side in his head. He swallowed his failure to sleep, and waited for the preacher in his mind to pause for breath. When it came, Ben was able to find a shirt fit for the weather that matched his belt.

Another piece of noise came shouting at him above the rest of the din—*CAESAR's FOOD!*

Ben squeezed his eyes shut and fought the madness in his head long enough to make that point stick. Concentrate. He wasn't going to let her down again. Focus. He couldn't afford to put being late for work on top of his list of current failures. Take Charge. He needed to get moving.

Time was closing in now, creeping like a shadow, and everyone was counting on him.

Richard Van Beeson served fourteen years in the Oklahoma Army National Guard and is a veteran of the Iraq war.

Tim Leach

Cloud Fishing

i

Mirrors of irrigation laid down clouds all around us
in a patchwork of pools, reflections of sky almighty
pierced by spear tips of rice shoot. An ancient army
aiming for ambush came to mind. Impervious, imperial
and unrepentant, our juggernaut rumbled down levy road,
churning more horse power than Custer's cavalry.
We four rode shotgun up top, flack-jacketed, helmet-headed,
heavil -armed, and armored, our sweat a glaze of arrogance.
Proud as football heroes on a homecoming float,
drunk on fumes of diesel thunder, we fancied ourselves
Centaurs of mechanized armor; deputies of manifest destiny.
We bore authority's badge, the white star branding the side
of our one-five-five millimeter self-propelled howitzer.
Cruising prickly waters dragonflies saw reflections as
multiple lovers, to be seduced by a zigzag of come-ons.
Swallows strafed mosquitoes, and imperial cumuli glided
still waters like sun-gilded galleons. Rice spears did not
impale or impede them. The threat of our fire power
did not intimidate, dissuade, or delay them.

ii

But when the mud road sank our tonnage to a quagmire crawl,
pistons pounding, low gears whining, our bellicose moods dissolved
in simmering heat to fear. At steam-roller speed, we neared
three old men fishing, 50 yards off. Clad in peasant black, natural
as charred stumps, and still as herons, each branched a bamboo pole,
line taut, spent lead for sinkers no doubt,
barbed and baited hooks unseen—inverted questions, glossed over,
by cloud where sunfish lurked.
Broad coned hats veiled the ancients in shadow; edited them into
a prickly calligraphy of reed and sprout no soldier could decipher.
Perched like a plough bird on war's tractor, an Alabama farm boy
shouted, *"Any luck?"*
We expected a red betelnut grin, and back-home's mute answer,
the lifting of a stringer.
Would the chain, if raised, hang heavy with carp, clouds, rainbow

trout or Alabama farm-boy scalps? Aloof as ink on silk,
they fished on, weathering our piston-driven passage
as if an afternoon monsoon blowing through.
Our tank treads stirred mud thick as putty, heading for higher ground.
Looking back, now and again, we saw there was still no answer
invaders wait for. Armies advance faster than age or wisdom, slower
than cumuli drift. The big one, clouded in myth, never takes the bait.

Tim Leach

Prisoners of War 1965

Government gray were the ships, sea, and sky and so seemed the gaze
of cynical sailors, even the pier as long as an airport runway. Disrupting
this nocturne of dawn's early light, olive drab troops tumbled out black-ass

ends of olive drab trucks—war's inventory. Coded by numbers on bills
of lading, we were cargo signed for and delivered for transport from Boston
in World War II rust buckets to Asian war. Ours was not to reason why.

Free thought, erased by training like chalk, uniformed to conformity,
we milled about numb as sheep until ordered by officers who strutted
and crowed, then herded by barking sergeants to form up for roll call.

We wore the weight, if not yet the guilt, of war, each slumping under
an 80-pound duffel, backpack, flack jacket, steel pot, entrenching tool,
gas mask, canteen, and M-16. We were a brigade of "light infantry."

Like drunks focused on a straight line, our challenge was stability,
moving out single-file, on many feet shuffling, a body of men twisting
like a Chinese dragon. The gang plank was so steep we hunched

our stagger like stoop-shouldered apes, to balance the backward drag
of a year's worth of laundry and gear. Then sea swell made the walkway
see-saw, so we teetered, queasy with fear that one false step

would bowl us all over like rowed dominoes to be sunk by stuff supposed
to save us in war. Once on deck, the badgering brass backed us by welded
ladder down a muzzle-black hatch, our slung and buckled gear aiming again

to kill us. Tentative feet felt for unseen rungs, and wary hands retreated
from boot soles landing on the rung above, as down three manholes
by ladder, two decks below water, we descended to whalebelly bottom.

We understood soon after that we were prisoners of war already, sentenced
to 40 days and nights of collective passivity—trained killers dying of boredom,
hunting ways to kill time between meals, letterwriting, and poker mostly.

At night we shelved our bodies in morgue storage, sacked out six deep,
two across on canvas racks, sheeted by thin sleep, sucking breath from miasmas
of sweat and flatulence, all of us slippery and twitching like caught fish.

Orders to pack up sprung us from stupors of tortoise-like torpor.
We hoisted ourselves to the hatch of sun, fumbling up a tunnel of light,
awkward as deep sea divers, surfacing on deck, fully-loaded.

Then, under orders, we heaved ourselves like lemmings over the rail,
bag and baggage, feeling for footholds in webs of rope edging down
the steel hull, dropping, at last, into landing craft.

Tall steel walls were all we saw until the front wall dropped open like
a startled mouth, revealing a tropical beach, and a local brass band
butchering Sousa. Vietnamese girls draped trumpet-flower leis

on grinning officers as a mayor welcomed us in broken English.
We gathered our gear not hearing him, tuned instead to a frequency
of orders, high-pitched with urgency calling for movement by feet

by now automatic as heart beat. The band played on fading behind
as we slogged to an airfield, then through tail doors into a cave dark
of Flying Boxcars, Korean War surplus resurrected to ferry us
to War Zone C.

After a tour in Viet Nam with the 196th Light Infantry Brigade, Tim Leach embarked on
a 45-year writing career in journalism, public relations, and advertising. A 2010 *Pushcart
Prize* nominee, Tim won the 2009 Russell Grant Poetry Award from the University of
Missouri–St. Louis MFA Program. He has been a finalist in annual *River Styx*, *New Letters*, *New Millennium*, and *Winning Writers War Poetry* competitions. Tim's poems have
appeared in more than 20 literary journals, including the *Atlanta Review*, *Southern Poetry
Review*, and the *Potomac Review*. His work has been included in four local and regional
anthologies. He lives in St. Louis.

Philip Renner

A Letter Home from Fort Bliss, Texas, 1918
(printed with permission from his daughter,
Mary Elizabeth Renner Saalfeld)

November 4, 1918

Dear Folks,

I am on guard again, went out last night and I had a fine night, not very cool and was clear—nice. Well, things look better all the time. It's now up to Germany to see what she can do. There are rumors out that

there is not going to be any more men sent here. Then I hear the new bunch would be in about the 18th. Yesterday an order came out to have every man write the four following words, sign their name, and hand them in. Gallon, Trunk, engine, and filling. I just drew an idea that they wanted to pick out the best Scribes to help with the work when the new bunch comes in. A couple of other boys and I went out for a walk in the woods yesterday. I found a couple of fat squirrels in a tree, borrowed a gun from a[n Italian] boy who came along and killed them for him. Also we helped kill a ground hog. I have not heard a word from home for nearly a week. Well, I guess this will be a busy day for Jim. I sure hope he gets elected. Wish I could have been at home while Georgia and Billy were there. Say, did they disapprove my furlough papers or just sent them back without either approving or disapproving them. Well, from all prospects I will be home planting, come next spring. I hope the flu is getting better down there and hope you all are well now. Must stop as it is about time for me to go on guard again. It will be my last shift. I hope so anyway. Last night a few of us were out here at the Y. We popped corn and had cider and ginger snaps. I ate so much I was really uncomfortable. I have been playing bank again for the boys. Tuesday will be pay day so I have loaned them 50¢ and a dollar. Until then I have about $15.00 out. I had a lot of fun yesterday. Two that I don't like asked me for a dollar a piece, put up a good story about they can't get use to just having $24.00 a month to spend when they were making $30 per week before they came into the army. I [bartered?] them rather hard. I told them I did not get but $8.50 per month and never did make $30.00 per week, but I knew what I was coming into and saved a little money and brought it with me. That I would let them have the money this time, but I wanted them to show me how good they were to pay their debts instead of telling me. One of the Sgt. was standing near and heard me throw it into both of them; he said, I would not have had nerve enough to have taken it. I just wanted to see how they would act about it. It is right funny the way some act. They are your best friend when they are broke. None of our Sgts. got to go in the bunch that went to the O.T.C. Our Top Sgt. [thought] that he was going to up until about two hours before they left. I will tell you why when I get home, [. . .]of things that I had better not write. I get to stay here I think I can get a pass home about the last of this month soon after the new men get in and start to work. May be I will be shipped out, but I hardly think so. Must stop now.

Phil

from 2:30 to 4:30 then hang around until 6:15 and I am done for 5 or 6 more days.

Phil

Just got your letter awhile ago I am going to talk to my Leiut. [sic] tomorrow or this afternoon if I get time and see what the chance will be to get 10 or 15 days off about the last of next week. I will take what ever [sic] I can get. May be I will get the same I got before. Nothing. If I can [. . .] hunting tomorrow afternoon.

Phil

I will bet there was almost as much rejoicing as mourning at Posey Moseley's funeral.

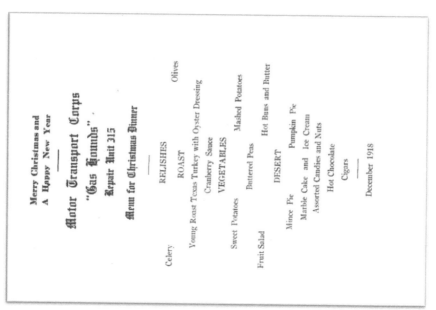

Merry Christmas and
A Happy New Year

Motor Transport Corps
"Gas Hounds"
Repair Unit 315

Menu for Christmas Dinner

RELISHES

Celery   Olives

ROAST

Young Roast Texas Turkey with Oyster Dressing
Cranberry Sauce

VEGETABLES

Sweet Potatoes   Mashed Potatoes

Buttered Peas

Hot Buns and Butter

DESERT

Fruit Salad

Mince Pie   Pumpkin Pie

Marble Cake and Ice Cream

Assorted Candies and Nuts

Hot Chocolate

Cigars

December 1918

Christmas, 1918

Motor Transport Corps
Machine Shop 315
Fort Bliss, Texas

William Philip Renner served in the U.S. Army as a private from 1917–1918. He was trained as a mechanic in the motor transport corp at Fort Bliss, TX. After he was discharged, he worked as a farmer, owned a farm implement business for a short time, and sold and appraised real estate property and farms. He and his family lived in Cape Girardeau, Missouri, most of his life. His daughter, Mary Elizabeth Renner Saalfeld, submitted his letter and photos for this anthology.

204

Jason Sansburn

What We Leave Behind

I'm still there
Pacing the house always on guard
Fear that they've broken through
crushes me like a vise, panic rising

Fourth of July,
others celebrate our independence
the basement is my home, my bunker
each firework, each explosion
a memory, a shot through the heart

That time of year again
to board the big grey bird
for a world away, tattered by war
buried under a millennium of bodies and sand
to reclaim myself

body's going back, the soul stayed there
zero dark thirty
the plane grinds to a halt
shadowed figures sigh to my left and right
ghosts hit the tarmac at a dead run

sirens begin their familiar wail
dive for the bunkers
concussion of mortar impacts
debris turns day to night

Months go by, blistering heat, winds that blind
A-10s rain fire, children die in minefields
bullets ricochet off boulders, tracers burn the sky
blood on the ground, friends die in my arms

What brought me here?
A world away from those I love
to this hell hole, this foreign land

Time to take stock
innocence lost, trial by fire, loss, shame
pieces of our souls left to blow in the sand

Two months left the freedom bird is near
to leave this hell hole
but I'll be back next year

Jason Sansburn served eight years in the United States Marine Corps as radio operator.
He served in Afghanistan in support of Operation Enduring Freedom with 6th Marine
Regiment, CJTF-Stonewall. He currently resides in Bay City, Michigan, with his wife
and three children while attending Delta College in pursuit of a degree in English.

William Lusk Coppage

In the Salmon's Eyes
September 15, 2001

A day after my enlistment's end and I am blending with Seattle, drunk on
  dark ale and bliss.

Twenty-four hours before I was across the Pacific—knee-deep in camouflage and combat boots, wailing base sirens
and flight lines filling with missiles and men.

I do not hesitate on war's images, blasting across America's face. I do not
  worry of delayed flights that eventually
take me home.

It is today I have no home, but here, watching tribes dance in glory on
  the banks of Puget Sound.
Their tanned skin, beaded, reflects the surrendering Sun with each spin
  and kick. Behind them, the Nation's canoes
fill the waterway to create a floating bridge deep into the purple horizon.

As if to conduct the crowd, a turquoise-faced man lifts his hands and
  begins to chant in pentatonics.
Welcome the new Moon, welcome the Salmon, farewell the good Sun.
  Canoes paddle towards darkness illuminated only by
their celestial ancients and crowds leave.

But before trekking back across the port city, I watch the decorated men
  box up their drums
and rattles, then strip their deerskins to reveal jeans and t-shirts. The
  men, joyous of the day, all embrace, and the
waxy sheen of black feathers tied in their hair, flickers in the moon like
  an open blade.

William Lusk Coppage

Furlough, May '99

While my uniform sleeps on a chair-back
next to unpolished boots, I barrel deep
through broken roads, far away from R.A.F. Mildenhall.

I call out tongue-heavy signs of English countryside
the same way tourists back home parse Tishomingo
and Kosciusko. My date, laughing at my accent,

asks about America, then New York
and Hollywood. Asks of the war. She asks if I'm lost
and then of other things that I know nothing about.

"America's not lost," I say, "only losing," and she crosses her legs.
My tongue continues to play its roadside games
and half an hour later, we are in the club's parking lot.

Inside there is the dance and stout pints,
the endless rows of shots and shots until my voice slurs.
Music is felt from the ground up,

the heat from her skin radiates and twists
with mine. This is when I forget war's stars
and unraveling stripes. But as house lights flash

and the heavy bass retreats, the DJ calls out to us.
Drenched in sweat and new sadness, I raise my hands,
surrender to the night, scream, "no more, no more."

In this absence of sound, the burden of tomorrow exists.

After serving in the United States Air Force, William Lusk Coppage completed his MFA in poetry from McNeese State University in Lake Charles, LA. He now lives with his wife in Carolina Beach, NC where he enjoys surfing and playing music. His poetry has appeared or is forthcoming in journals such as *Oxford American*, *Passages North*, *The Greensboro Review*, *The Pedestal Magazine*, *The Pinch*, and *Cream City Review*.

Velda Goodgion Brotherton

A Red-Haired Rosie

I was very young when my mother went to work at Boeing, Wichita, during WWII, but I do remember that the one big change was when she began to wear pants. I'd never seen her in pants until she started working on the B29 bombers at the defense plant. And she tied a bandana around her gorgeous red curls before leaving for work.

"That's to keep from getting my hair caught in a drill," she explained.

At the time we lived in a housing development built specifically for families involved in the war in some way. Many women whose husbands were overseas fighting lived there, as well as people working at the plant. It was just Mother, my brother Fred, and me. Dad was serving in the South Pacific as a radio man (sparky) on the *U.S.S. Attu*. She worked third shift, I learned from papers she'd saved, and earned 70 cents an hour.

My mother had always been a stay-at-home Mom, though we didn't call it that back then.

In those days she was a wife and mother. Simple as that. She loved to cook and garden and can and sew. She made pickles, too, just as I was doing the day l began to think about what I could write for this essay. The smell of the sweet spicy vinegar filled the house and brought back every detail of her as a young mother. Her smile, the red, red lipstick she always wore, the freckles on her pale skin, and most of all that tumble of red hair.

Landing that job gave us the income we sorely needed while Dad was away at war, but it also changed her. She went from a farm wife living in the Ozarks to a working city woman overnight. Gone was pickle making, canning, gardening, and all that went with it.

A photo in one of her many albums shows her and Daddy, him in uniform, standing beside a car. She wrote, Ray home on leave. He was soon to go overseas where battles raged, and where he might be killed, yet both were laughing in that picture. He left and she went back to work on her beloved B29s. She clipped and pasted news articles about those bombers on which she worked.

Going through her scrapbooks, one thing jumped out at me. She diligently saved clippings, photos, and articles about my Dad and the war in the South Pacific, but only a few concerning Boeing and the B29s. Tucked amidst my dad's Navy paraphernalia, I did find a sheet about rivet sizes and how they were to be used. I think the women were so ac-

Georgia Goodgion

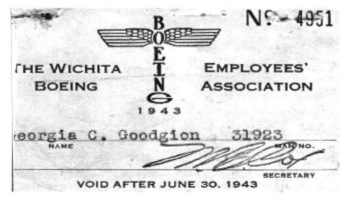

Georgia Goodgion's Boeing Employee Card

customed to the secrecy necessary regarding what they saw and the work they did that they simply had nothing to say about their jobs. Ever.

Two newspaper clippings: July 4—A photo of 20,000 Boeing Wichita employees gathered at Boeing Plant II to unveil the names of two B29 Superfortresses bought by them during the fifth war loan drive. One was named "Eddie Allen" after a Boeing chief test pilot, the other named "293" after the original B29 of that name lost in the first B29 raid over Japan, June 15. No year on clipping.

Another clipping tells of a B29 that crashed six miles east of Wichita Municipal Airport and burst into flames. Pilot, copilot, and two civilian passengers escaped injury. The plane caught fire while in the air, and as the pilot was forced to crash-land across a hedge, one of the motors dropped from the plane. Less than two hours after the crash, another B29 made a belly landing at the airport. No year was on either clipping.

I saw my mother change during the war years, and now as I look back, I understand more clearly that she was moving from a rural life to a woman embracing a new place in society. She began to style her hair and wear lipstick and smoke. All indicative of her move into the role of a working woman.

These women did not see themselves as heroines. As they always had, they were doing what was necessary at the time. I never heard her complain about the job or working, or for that matter that Daddy was over there fighting the enemy. Looking back, I'm sure she cried at night in the dark after we were asleep, but not once did she shed a tear in front of us. And as a child, it never occurred to me that she might be sad. She made the best of every day.

We didn't see Dad again until the war ended in 1945. He was away a bit longer than two years. Mother received a letter from the Navy with a huge headline on it. He's Coming Home! it shouted. She pasted it in her scrapbook along with ration books and his discharge papers.

In later years, Mom went back to doing all those things she loved so much. After the war she quilted and crocheted and went to work selling Avon. I suspect that every jar of pickles I open this winter will be another reminder of Mom and how she became someone different out of necessity, yet kept in sight the things she most loved to do.

Once it was over, she never referred to those lonely war years again, but that was her. On the other hand, Dad told us many stories because he was a born storyteller.

He told of an enemy Zero that crashed on the deck of the ship, and it gave me shivers to think how close he'd come to being killed. One of his cousins was on board a ship that was torpedoed, and he floated on debris for 15 days before being rescued. Dad said he was never the same again. At the time I didn't understand what he meant, but today I do.

Ray Goodgion, U.S. Navy *USS Attu*

RIVET INFORMATION SHEET

ALUMINUM RIVETS

NAME OF RIVET	SHAPE	CALL NO
COUNTERSUNK-35°		AN425
ROUND HEAD		AN430
FLAT HEAD		AN442
BRAZER HEAD		AN455
BOEING SKIN HD		BAC1345
COUNTERSUNK 78°		BAC1341
JACK RIVET 78°		BAC1340

DRILL SIZES TO RIVET SIZE	
No. 51	1/16
No. 40	3/32
No. 30	1/8
No. 21	5/32
No. 11	3/16
F	1/4

ALLOYS AND MARKING
APPLIES TO ALL NAMES OF RIVETS

ALLOY	TYPE	MARK	HOW DRIVEN	HEAT TREAT	DEGREE OF HARD AFTER DRIVI
2S	A	PLAIN HEAD ON END OF SHANK	AS RECEIVED	NO	SOFTEST
53S	NO TYPE	POP HEAD ON END OF SHANK	AS RECEIVED	NO	SOFT
A17ST	AD	⊙	AS RECEIVED	NO	STRONGEST OF
17S	D	⊙	ICE BOX	YES	HARD
24S	DD	⊖	ICE BOX	YES	HARDEST

HOW TO USE FORMULA AS IT WOULD APPEAR ON A BLUEPRI

EXAMPLE
AN 430
AD 3-4

AN430=ROUND HEAD, ARMY AND NAVY STANDARD
AD-A17ST ALLOY
3-DIA. OF RIVET IN 32NDS
4-LENGTH OF SHANK IN 16THS

PLACE MANUFACTURE
HEAD NEXT TO THIN
MATERIAL

BLIND RIVET
CODE SIGNA
1 TAP-MORE DRI
2 TAPS-GOOD RI
3 TAPS-RIVET T
FLAT

Boeing Rivet Records

213

Ray Goodgion's Plank Certificate

Georgia Smith as born in Montana and raised in Arkansas where she met and married Ray Goodgion. When WWII broke out, she and her husband Ray moved to Witchita with their two young children. In 1942, he enlisted in the Navy and served for approximately two years in the South Pacific, while Georgia worked at Boeing on the B29s. Their daughter Velda wrote their story. Georgia's sister Milfred served in the WACs during the war, and Ray's youngest brother, Alton, served in the Navy and was witness to the A-bomb tests. He died of cancer at the age of 32.

Carl Palmer

Green Card Soldier

seasonal migrant worker
unwed mother in Arizona
temporary work visa expires
sent back across the border

she allows her teenaged son
a chance to have a better life
than his first eighteen years
to stay and join the U.S. Army

he fights to become an American
becomes an American fighting man
offers his life for this country and
becomes a citizen . . . posthumously

incoming

daughter pops bubble wrap
laughs as Daddy dives to floor
while on mid-tour leave from Iraq

Carl Palmer spent his 20-year military career as a non-commissioned officer with the United States Army on HAWK missile systems throughout Germany, Korea, Fort Bliss, and Fort Lewis. His son, Major Jason Palmer, is presently serving the U.S. Air Force at Offutt AFB after multiple tours in Iraq and other overseas stations.

David S. Pointer

Smedley Butler's Disciple

Mike didn't want
destabilizing democratically
elected governments on the
other end of his sniper rifle,
so he took his place
unemployed   watching
lines grow like lions' tails
watching   his boys'
video games making over
their easy going masculinity
into serviceable product, and
the post traumatic stress
          disorder diagnosis
following him around had
nothing to do with war time
atrocities, or a well-placed
shot, rather being deployed
by upward mobility
          mapmaker bureau
so far down range at home as
to be a fringe area non-factor

David Scott Pointer was born in Kansas City, Missouri. He served in the United States Marine Corps from 1980–84. His son served in the military from 2001–2005. In 2009, David was declared a winning writer in *Empty Shoes: Poems on Hunger and Homelessness* anthology.

Susan V. Meyers

The Cost of Memory

The March In

The heat sticks to us like butter. Air so thick it feels like something you could reach out and grab onto. I can feel it breathing next to me: it's like something alive. Already, I have the terrible feeling that we are being followed, even though our scout swears the enemy is dug in on the other side of the island. He looks at me—knows that I am a man with ranking, and that I will have some responsibility once we arrive. So he issues his warning in a low voice, and once only: *Of the dangers out here, nature rivals the enemy.*

The jungle is green and unforgiving; it has its own kind of violence. We pass burn marks and battle scars, but we can hardly make them out. The forest swallows them up and goes on without us. This island doesn't care who lives or dies. Things just keep growing and growing: palms and clumped bamboo shoots staggering twenty feet into the air, blood red flowers larger than a man's head. Birds shout like sirens. The dry pampas grasses cover us to our waists; in other places, there is mud thick enough to swallow a soldier's boot to the knee.

Finally, we find a place and dig in. The scout who brought us here is gone. He knows the island—works at moving men around between stations. We might see him in another week, when the next ship docks full of young GIs. In the meantime, we are building our camp: pup tents and the long, square storehouses covered in camouflage and mosquito nets. The most elaborate are the medical and mess hall tents, and mine: the supply. The boys work hard. They like this work; it is exhausting, and safe. It is something they can believe in, watching our camp grow daily: concrete and human, in the middle of this godforsaken jungle.

After three weeks, we have seen no sign of the enemy. We are still waiting for orders. Camp is mostly built, and the boys are beginning to relax. They trace kickball diamonds in the shade and laugh over dirty magazines. Everyone is taking snapshots to send home: soldiers in the jungle; heroes doing their duty. They are quick, sweaty pictures of boys smiling, feeling victorious already. Nobody knows where the front is from here; for the moment, nobody cares. It is only the nights that are terrible for us: dark and invisible. Already, we've heard stories about what the enemy is capable of; already, they don't seem quite human. The boys swear they're ready to go out and fight them. *Go lick those Japs!* But they are so terribly young, these boys. They don't know what war is—and truthfully, neither do I. But I do what I can. I try to teach them to be strong and careful—to become men as quickly as possible.

The Supply

"Hey Joe!" He calls all the men Joe; if he calls you anything else, it means he likes you. "Hey Joe! Come and take a walk with me."

Commander Jones is the man we have been left to serve under. He never meant to go to war. It is rumored that, before Pearl Harbor, he held a desk job in Washington. Now he is a leader of men in the South Pacific. His ideas about things are very specific: "You gotta lay off these men here, Joe. This ain't no workhouse."

"It's a war, Sir, and I'd like to see it over as quickly as possible."

Jones shakes his head. "Ah, Joe." He sets a hand on my shoulder—a hand in a white kid glove. Before we got here, he was burned with kerosene. Now he bathes his hands in imported cream and covers them with cotton gloves. "Wars got their own internal clock, like a woman. You gotta treat 'em just like that. Court 'em a little, flirt with 'em, lead 'em on. No point getting to the punch before you're good and ready—you got me? Else you'll spoil the whole thing." He picks his gloved hand off my shoulder and slams it back down again. This takes effort because he is much shorter than me. "I'll tell you what, though, Joe," his voice gets lower. "We're gonna win this thing; you just gotta give it some time. Every man to his job, and to every job, a man." He pats the side of my face then, and I can smell the hand cream: that light, floral scent. "Just keep to yours, huh, Joe? One job only. Don't be trying to win the whole damn thing yourself."

I nod. My job is to keep the supply in order, but this is not an orderly war. Not like Europe's war, with its cadre of soldiers in uniform marching off against a united front. This is another kind of war entirely: a war in the jungle, in the pampas, in the heat. Already, I have heard about some of our boys, not quite dead—in the dark, shells still going off—waiting to die. And someone helps them—someone finishes off the job. Back at the supply, they come and take what they need; they don't apologize. This is not a uniform war. The land does not permit it; the heat does not permit it; the enemy does not permit it. So the men take what they need; and the dead give back what they have. Where we are, there are no cities and no civilization. Time and again it seems there is nothing here to destroy or be destroyed—except ourselves.

Before

Like so many of these men, I got married right before the war— *be-*

cause of the war. Of course, I loved her; I probably would have married her anyway. We understand life in the same way, Maxine and I: ferocious hard work; don't step off track; rely on yourself more than anyone else. She is a strong woman. A woman, I knew, who would withstand a war.

But in lovemaking she was still new. I would teach her, I promised. I had been with other women—though only in quick, dirty ways—and it was enough, I thought, to help me guide her. To make her understand pleasure.

But she was shy or coy or both. "Oh darling, women don't go naked in front of men; it isn't nice."

She slipped into bed, and I followed. I thought it was a game. I pulled at her and pleaded: "Please, Maxine. I want to see you." She giggled as I began to undress her—like a fish in the sheets, squirming and giggling. It was like taking off her skins, layer after layer. I had never wanted a woman like that—so adoring and desperate and wildly unsure. But all I could see of my wife were pieces: a nipple; the soft underside of a breast; that dark "v," and the red inside. I fell over her, panting, trying to uncover her, being just as seductive as I could be: kissing each small toe and lifting the sheet a little higher over her leg, past the sweet calf, the tiny round kneecap. Her thigh. But as I was moving here or there, she had slipped back into the blankets someplace else. "No, Gerald," she insisted. "It's not nice to look at naked people." And I laughed; I thought it was a joke. A sweet, nervous joke from my sweet, nervous bride.

There were other ways she surprised me, too. She was passionate. When she came, it was with a ferocity that I hadn't expected: screaming out loud and grabbing onto me in a way that I didn't know women did. She didn't apologize or explain. Passion, I guess, doesn't require explanation.

We had six months together, and things never changed. I loved her, but she was never fully mine. I continued to laugh and to tease her, but nothing worked; she would never let me see her fully. At moments, she was so sweet or so lusty that I forgave her. But the truth is, it worries me still, knowing that I have married a woman that I can never fully possess.

A Year In

This place is dirty. The natives live dirty, and we live dirty. In the dry season, the dust is insufferable; it covers over everything. When it is wet, the rain stings like hail, and the mud rises. It is difficult, sometimes, to remember what is real. In the beginning, the evils of this place were easier to ignore. We were busy digging in and laying hold to our station. But now the days have gotten longer—and the nights, too—and memory slows down. I notice each thing more.

A year in, and there is more time. Too much time. The black market offers a few distractions. We gamble and drink, if anything is available. Women are almost always available. The country is poor. Families send their daughters to camp carrying papaya or sugar cane as gifts. That is enough of an invitation.

We are on a different island now, but everything looks the same: the trees, the mud, the camp. The boys—some have died and been replaced—are still so terribly young. Nineteen, twenty years old. They have come to war to avoid churches, families, marriages. They want adventure. They get by the way they know how: being loud and raucous, working hard. Finding what satisfaction they can in the women that are here. But the nights are still dangerous and long. Once, a boy goes out and does not come back. We find him the next morning, face down in the mud. No one can tell how he was killed.

I have a lot of nostalgia, like we all do. We think about home; we read and write letters. My wife writes nearly every day. This is something that the men respect: a woman who is waiting for you. Their jealousy reminds me that I should feel lucky. That I should feel *something*.

There are days when I still believe in what we're doing. There are days that this war makes sense—when we advance, or the boys come back from the front and not too many of them are missing. We win battles, shift islands. We push slowly forward against the enemy. Other days, though, I can see right through the bitter machinery of this army, and I know that very little of what we do has any consequence. Our unit is holding ground; that's what we're doing. In other places, other men are up at the front, doing the real work of this war. I am not an educated man, but I'm not foolish; I know that most of what we're doing is just for show. There are men at the top sending down orders, trying to keep us busy—with anything. And here is my guilt: I'm grateful for that. I am not an important man in this war; I am not doing important work. And that means that I will probably survive.

A Prisoner

How quickly can a man react? I wasn't hardly trained to kill. A few weeks with a gun at the camp in Missouri, and after that, I've spent more time lining up the supply shelf than considering the strategies of combat. I am no kind of hero.

The prisoner falls over onto his knees. I've seen Japs before—most of them dead—but this one is so small, I think he must be younger, even, than the boys who have dragged him into camp. "Look what we found snooping around," they laugh. "Fucking spy."

It is hard to be afraid of him, he is so small. His bones are so thin and his skin so smooth, he looks almost like a woman. His head hangs low. A gurgling sound comes out of him; he looks miserable. The boys kick dirt and laugh some more; they are waiting around for something to do. We get bored out here—bored and scared both. "Move!" one of them yells, shoving the prisoner in the back with a boot. But he won't move anymore. He falls right over onto his stomach and just lays there, barely moving, in the mud. "Stupid chink."

Most of his clothing is already gone. What is left makes him look like a poor grandmother: a white sheet wrapped around him, full of holes. I could almost feel sorry for him, except that he is Japanese. I wonder again about his age, but it is impossible to guess. These people aren't like any I've ever known; it makes them easier to hate.

So he is a man down, and he is ours. But he stays calm; I do notice that. It is nerve-wracking, the way our enemy never reacts to things; it can certainly make a man feel useless. But this one lifts his head now; he is looking around, studying his surroundings. We are damn close to the middle of camp, soldiers all around; there isn't any hope for him at all. A few yards away, some of the other boys are playing kickball; the officers' tents stand up ahead in neat little rows. The boys drag him closer in: the intruder, the fucking-gimp-Jap-jinxie-spy. He'd come to scope them out, but they'd caught him, like taking bait. And now they have him, mother-fucker, and they are going to bring him in to the commander, to show off what good, smart soldiers they are. *He's a caught duck*, they laugh again. *His goose is cooked*. Except that there is a little movement left in him: a hand reaching down inside his tunic, carefully, down close to the crotch. And then that hand comes slowly back out. How many of them notice this? We are damn near up on officer's row, now. And the hand inside the prisoner's robes has doubled in size; he is bringing something out. Something round and hard and metallic. Quickly now—the other hand is reaching for the pin. Except that a bullet sails through him just then, so he sags instead and tumbles face down into the mud.

Then things get real quiet. The boys have stopped laughing. They look at their prisoner: the grenade lies a few inches away from him, the pin partly extended. The mess hall and the officer's suite are just a few yards away. There are soldiers everywhere. "Motherfucker-goddam-fuck-in-traitor!" somebody yells. Another boy starts kicking the dead man, jumping up and down on his dead legs and his dead back. Somebody else fires some more bullets into him. But who has saved them? Who noticed the hand reaching into the tunic? Who fired? Later on, I can remember the gun in my hand. I remember gun powder in the air, the dead Jap, blood oozing out into the mud. But I don't remember feeling anything. Nobody thanked me; I just stood there, looking around. Boys were swearing and kicking the corpse; officers were scrambling out of their tents. So I don't know what it feels like to kill a man; I don't remember that part at all.

The Visitor

The women on the island don't speak English. Which meant that they don't speak. They come to us and lay themselves down. Someone else makes the arrangements ahead of time. Money exchanges hand: man to desperate man.

And we are satisfied with that; we prefer women who mean nothing. Except for the youngest ones, most of us understand the importance of a nameless body: a woman's body that doesn't have anything to do with what she means to anybody. Carnage. Out here, that's all any of us are: just bones and flesh doing a job, filling up space, hour after bloody hour. Besides, it's easier to think about your wife when the woman whose body you're filling up doesn't say anything for herself. And there are other times when I don't want to think about my wife—when I just want to fuck something. Sometimes I want violence. Most of war is waiting—a man can get sick of it. Then I am just a man fucking a woman because he can.

She came to me every week for three months. The portion of money that I didn't send home to my wife, I told her I'd spent on cigarettes. In all the time I saw the girl, I never learned her name. I called her Maxine. Her skin was soft and a dark copper color; her hair and eyes were shiny black. She was probably pretty, but I tried not to think about it; for a man at war, prettiness hardly matters. "Maxine!" I would groan into her ear, like it was a secret I wanted her to keep for me. It wasn't personal. She would have to understand that, I told myself. What a man has to do.

I used to imagine that I knew what it meant to be a hero. I was a foolish young man then, and so many of these boys out here are even younger, stupider. They get ideas; they talk about love. And war. They think they can do something—or that there's some kind of meaning to all this. But that's the most terrible thing about it: there isn't any kind of meaning. One of them dead and then another one. And you learn—you learn to stop caring about them individually. The same way that you stop caring about the girls that come to you: fourteen, fifteen years old. She comes in and lies down on her stomach. She doesn't move or speak. When I am finished, she waits, lying there under me, my weight exhausted on her; and she feels like nothing more than a worn-out roll of fabric, a flattened inner tube. She gets smaller and smaller, until I almost believe that I can't feel her there anymore at all.

Night

My brush with death is so much quieter than I had imagined. Like so many things here, the danger had passed before I even knew that it was there. One single explosion: a grenade lodged in the middle of the night. I woke up staring at shrapnel, lying there on my pillow. A quick beam of moonlight shot through the hole it had torn in the tent lining. There was a smell of burnt cotton. Silence.

And what more is there to remember, really? The quick slash of air that woke me, the shouts of men outside. It was over almost before it had begun. And I was still alive. That's what I had to keep telling myself: over and over, until I could finally move again. When I picked up the twisted metal, it was still hot. Like some other living, breathing thing.

After the midnight attack, I become a different man. It is an experience that I can't shake—mostly because it wasn't at all what I had expected. Because isn't it wrong to die without even knowing the danger that killed you? Without ever hearing the pop, the click, the laugh? Death, I had thought, should be something dramatic. But so often it isn't—not for the one who has died. All these quick, brutal deaths: you turn suddenly, grind your heel into a mine, and go up in a flash of light. Or get laid out under some invisible bullet: one moment you are all adrenalin; the next moment, you don't exist. Gone. The medics come down afterward to check for the ones with vital signs. But it is the sudden deaths that seem worse—unannounced, almost painless. The quick ones. Those are the ones that bother me most.

The Enemy

Japan is a halfway time. A long pause after victory, after the shouts and tears of relief. We have spent several months here—in Tokyo, Kyoto, Kobe—cleaning up the fallout of war, taking our time with things. It leaves my wife distraught; she can't understand what is taking them so long to send us back. But wars aren't like storybooks, I remind her. There are no clear endings.

And the truth is, I am grateful. It doesn't hardly make sense, but I am terrified, finally, of going home. A man who has been to war knows that he will come back changed. There are certain things he won't be capable of. Tenderness, for one. Or sympathy. War shuts off whatever emotional stuff we had to begin with, so we come back rougher, meaner, covered up.

But we will go back, of course. And until then, I try to enjoy the things that are worth enjoying. Women, mostly. I watch them walking by, painted white and red and dressed in elaborate kimonos more like art than women. Such careful beauty, it begins to give you hope again. And the Japanese are such small people, like my wife. Their features are narrow, but they are much more fine and fair than the women on the islands. So it is easier to pretend, here in the Gion, lying in the arms of a small, painted woman. I don't kiss her: her face is still shiny and white like the moon. She has a dress like fish scales; it is thrown across a chair. She is practicing her English, "You are marry? In United State?" Not all of the women paint themselves up this way, but I have chosen this one—not for any aesthetic reason, but because it makes things seem less real. She is an actress; she wears a mask. And as we move through the motions of love, I tell myself: *I am doing this for you, Maxine.* I am trying to remind myself how it is to be with a woman. What gentleness is. And affection. I whisper to the woman that I love her. Her name is Hasuko; she is extremely beautiful. "Thank you," she says. "You are ve-ry kind."

Home

It is still so far away: a whole ocean between us. My wife continues writing—her last few letters ecstatic. I can imagine her lips moving over the words: the date of my departure from Japan, the name of the ship, the estimated two-month crossing. Already, she is going over to the calendar hung by the window, counting the days until my return. She is taking the bus into town, cashing her unemployment checks to buy smart new dresses and fresh linens for the bed. She is planting flowers in the garden and gossiping over tea with the other ladies in the neighborhood. When she sleeps, it is me she dreams of: the man she used to know.

But she is worried, too. There are stories, she says: some of the men coming home damaged, deranged. They won't talk about the war; they won't talk barely at all. "But you won't be like that," she insists in her letters. "Not you—such a good man. Such a good, strong man." *Of course not*, I write back. And I promise to tell her things: whatever is important. Whatever I can remember clearly.

But it has gotten difficult, in the end, to remember the exact details of things: which events came first, or later. The hunk of metal that I keep wrapped now in a handkerchief—did that come before or after the girl in the woods? Was she the only one, or were there different girls each night? in different camps? Was the commander one man, or many? Who shot the prisoner? Who took the credit or the blame for any of it?

These are not difficult questions: just brief, historical facts. But a man's brain gets crowded: women in the Gion with white arms like doves; mud-covered Japanese boys, their skulls split open on the battle-field, collecting rain. In the end I don't feel anything—not love or hate or anything at all. I'm a stranger to all of it. The only thing left is memory, which I don't trust, either. Things that happened, or might have happened; things I did, or might have done. We spend most of our time forgetting. And it is better that way.

So how can I hope to explain this to her, when I can barely explain it to myself? My job was order, but there was disorder everywhere. Three years of violence, stillness, and fear. But we weren't just waiting ducks—how could we be? There is some choice in everything. That is the terrible part: the boys on the battlefield, begging for death; the girls with their papayas; the piles of bodies that, on occasion, I had a hand in burying. The war, the blood, the cost of it all. This is what I have to find a way of explaining to her. To myself. We are done with order now. It is over, finished. And it is better, in the end, not to think too hard about things. Better not to siphon out: this I did, and this they made me do.

A Seattle native, Susan V. Meyers has lived and taught in Chile, Costa Rica, and Mexico. She earned an MFA from the University of Minnesota and a PhD from the University of Arizona, and currently teaches at Oregon State University. Her work has appeared in journals such as *CALYX*, *Dogwood*, *Rosebud*, and *The Minnesota Review*, and she has been the recipient of several awards, including a Fulbright Fellowship.

Search Team

The boys didn't know, thought
death was about to swing
its hammer at their heads.
Tears scythed through dust-caked
cheeks. Every lesson had taught
them men with guns will
take and take and take,
then give back with the butt
of a rifle. Or its muzzle.

One soldier pointed his M-16
at the boys while another
said, "Ell-ah-ess-fell,"—*down*—
and pushed them to the sand.
Bodies became brown leaves
rattling on a branch
beneath winter's breath.

Hands raced through their task,
scooped pockets, patted flat
dishdasha's white cotton.
Thumbs-up to his buddy
before lifting children, sending
them to their mother. Then on
to the next frightened family
lined up beside the adobe wall.

Bill Glose

Clearing a Room

"Clearing a room" sounds courteous,
inconsequential, so much like
clearing a table, as if the term could steady
your hands, allow you to rush into
a room smiling, as if what you're doing
is as simple as searching for dirty napkins,
removing dinner plates. But no one
ever lost his legs bussing silverware.

Do antiseptic terms fool anyone?
Not the brass, who spoon them
like strained veggies to a teething child;
nor media, who pick at statistics
like tender scabs; but maybe mothers
ensconced in recliners, heating pads
pressed to smalls of backs, frightened
by what the nightly news might bring.

For them, "movement to contact"
connotes beef-fed boys marching
on manicured parade fields, white gloves
saluting. Because truth repulses.
Who wants news of tired men scurrying
over open sand with only smoke
to ward off flying steel? Jabbing
at bee's nests with bayonets to see
what flies out. Truth must be sanitized
before consumption.

To "clear a room," men form lines
and cascade past one another.
Luck lingers in the rear where comrades
in "overwatch" promise vengeance
if required. A hand signal means
it's your turn, then the current
pulls you in. Blood thrums in ears;
mind tells legs to stay put.

Yet you run, you point, you run
and hope your aim is true.
Run round corners and decide
in the half-moment it takes to squeeze
a trigger whether the starving, shattered man
in dusty rags is springing to attack
or raising hands in surrender.

Experience has taught you to squash
sudden movements like a niggling fly.
Survival instinct screams, "Engage!"
that oh-so-genteel word that really means
"kill." Stained teeth in a spurt of light.
Black smear on a wall. Stand
shaking in a cyclone of dust.
Later they will feed you the salve
of "collateral damage," which
will nestle in your stomach and rip
claws through its lining for years
of nights to come. Right now, though,
regret is a concept as foreign
as the land beneath your feet.
You stare at what is left and cry out
in stunned joy while the image
brands its place in memory.

Daniel D. Bradford

Moment Two

The September mission had been plagued from the very start. The night before our departure a heavy fog had set in, and by 0800 hours the morning of our departure, it was difficult to see our large aircraft sitting only one hundred yards from the terminal. As the heavy, misty fog drifted slowly past the terminal window, the image of the plane would fade in and out as though it were a large, gray ghost. Even the brilliant California sun could not cut through the fog. The sun appeared as a dull, silver orb. Because of the fog, our takeoff was delayed nearly an hour. The delay in the takeoff produced one problem after another all the way across the Pacific. We added a total of six hours to our crossing time. The longest delay came at Wake Island because the air crew that was to take my plane from Wake to the Philippine Islands had to fly another plane to Japan to pick up wounded.

We landed in Saigon just in time for me to be rushed off to the Command weather briefing at the Saigon Hilton. The Hilton was a palatial hotel in downtown Saigon. At the height of the war, the hotel had been converted into officers' quarters and Command Headquarters. After seeing all of that splendor, it was hard to imagine there was a war going on just outside the large front doors.

There was no time to rest after the briefing. I was introduced to my assistant and quickly led to a small dining room just off a small bar reserved for NCO's. The only thing on time was the truck in front of the hotel at 1930 hours. As I pulled myself into the back of the truck, I was directed to two large packs with all of my weather equipment and an M-16 rifle.

The tall thin private who had been assigned as my assistant seemed to be all thumbs as he handled the equipment. I only hoped that it would withstand his examination until we needed it. I shouldered my pack and helped the private with his. The choppers were warmed up and ready to go when we rolled onto the mat. Somehow, the private had climbed into the wrong chopper, and we didn't have a chance to go over what we would do once we got to the drop site. The two-hour chopper ride with all of its sharp turns and rapid changes in altitude made me sick to my stomach. As soon as the choppers landed on the deserted road, we all jumped out and dove into the ditch on either side. I slammed a full clip of ammo into my M-16 and flipped the control to fully automatic.

The moon was nearly full that night, and the light breeze made the shadows move mystically. We crouched in the muddy ditch for five or ten minutes before we formed up single file and started into the jungle. Our guide was a Vietnamese sergeant who had grown up in this area.

We had been walking single file for about a half an hour when the Master Sergeant behind me whispered to me.

"How are you doin'?"

"Good."

A few steps farther and the column stopped. We all sat down on the side of the narrow trail. I leaned back and whispered to the Sergeant who was the last man in line.

"Is the jungle always this noisy?"

"Yes. If the birds and the bugs stop making noise, hit the ground."

"How long you been in Nam?"

"This is my second tour," he replied. "You been out like this before?"

"Yeah! Lots of times, and I hate it more and more every time. The odds are against me."

The signal was again given to move out. We had been walking for about a half an hour when I became aware that the Sergeant behind me had slowed to the point of almost stopping. All of a sudden it hit me like a ton of bricks! THE JUNGLE WAS QUIET! I stopped dead in my tracks. My blood was on fire. The Sergeant took one more step and was now standing a foot behind me and slightly to my right. What happened next was as though it were in slow motion. The Sergeant and I spun around at the same time. Standing in the trail behind us, plainly visible in the moonlight filtering through the trees was the silhouette of a small loosely clad figure. The left arm was down at one side holding something long that I could only assume was a rifle. The right arm was cocked high overhead as though to throw something. The Sergeant and I fired our M-16's at the same time. The figure lurched and jumped as each bullet struck it. The rifle flew up and off to one side. The object that was being thrown exploded, spraying us with dirt and debris.

I dropped to the ground, more from fear than the explosion. From where I was, I could see the flash of the enemies' rifles. I heard one of our guys yelling. It was the Captain giving orders.

"Get your ass down. Who's got the damn M-79? . . . Sergeant, get some grenades into them."

There were three rapid, ear-shattering explosions right in front of me. I raised my M-16 and fired until my clip was empty. I quickly slammed a second clip from my belt into the chamber. There were several flashes about forty yards in front of me. I could hear the bullets slashing through the brush just over my head. Before I could raise my rifle to return the next short burst, a heavy weight slumped over my shoulders forcing me to the ground. At first I didn't know what to do. I didn't have to look to know what the weight was. It was the Sergeant. As I eased him off my back and on to his side, I could tell he was really hurt. I quickly crouched over him and raised my M-16 to return the fire. As quickly as it had started, it was over. We had walked right into a V.C. patrol. The Sergeant wasn't moving.

"Captain," I called out. "The Sergeant's been hit!"

"Is it bad?" He rushed towards me.

"He's not moving. I just can't tell."

"Corpsman, get down here. Someone get on the radio and get us some help."

"Did anyone else get hit?"

"Scope took one in the leg . . . and I'm afraid your private bought it."

My stomach became tight. A thick, wet feeling swelled in my throat. A cold sweat crept over me and I got sick.

"Your first time?" the Corpsman asked.

"Yeah." I got sick again.

"It doesn't get any easier. You just learn not to lose your guts."

"How's the Sergeant?"

"He took a bad one in the shoulder."

"Will he make it?"

"It's hard to tell in the dark, but I think if we can get him out of here quick, he'll be OK."

"Can I help?"

"Find me a couple of poles for a stretcher."

A couple pair of pants, two belts and we had a stretcher. As we eased the Sergeant onto it, the Captain informed us that the help would be waiting at the drop site. All we had to do was get there. The march out took us about forty minutes and without any more enemy contact. We each took turns carrying the two litters. Our only casualty was brought out by the Captain. I think he must have known the kid because he refused to let anyone else help him. Every man there was a volunteer, except me. There were no two men from the same unit. We weren't to talk to each other about anything personal and had to disappear when our mission was over. Most of what we'd done was top secret and we'd never be able to tell anyone.

The pick-up choppers were waiting as we entered the clearing that ran along the edge of the road. We loaded everyone into the choppers with a slow, sluggish pace that can only come from complete mental and physical anguish. We'd lost a friend, two more were wounded, and our mission had been a failure. As the choppers lifted off, in the same sluggish progression, the impact of what had taken place hit us all. There were no lights in the chopper, so I couldn't see who was sobbing. I could only feel sympathy because the tears were slowly roaming down my cheeks.

Sometime later, I felt the landing gear of the C-141 jet transport drop from the belly of the plane. In about a half hour, I'd have to face my family and pretend as though nothing had happened. It had been nearly impossible after the first mission, so this time it would be easier. I needed to remember to leave the sling in the plane when I headed for the terminal. I couldn't have anyone asking questions. This was supposed to have been a checkout ride. My stomach was in a knot. I wished I could have just kept going . . . kept going . . . kept going—just put this plane back in the air, and kept going.

Dan Bradford is a retired engineer and project manager who spent eight years of active duty in the military. He has written and published two chldren's books, *Akabish's First Christmas* and *Akabish's Long Journey* and has a science fiction novel on the way. He has three grown daughters and nine grandchildren. Dan currently resides near Duluth, Minnesota.

Dario DiBattista

Sonnet for Killing

In Husaybah: the men in pixel gear
And bullet-jackets occupy the town
With armored trucks, ammo, and brawn. On clear
Evenings after curfew, they sneak around
Like ebony beetles. And IEDs
And snipers lie concealed around their base
Like scorpions waiting to sting. They freeze
In place, eager to murder Marines. Place
These fighters in another city (say
London or New York) and exchange their guns
For legal tender, bullets for buffet,
And give them skills they can bequeath their sons,
And then you'd find that peace is a quack's pill.
In Husaybah, men fucking love to kill.

An Iraq War veteran, Dario DiBattista is a graduate of the MA in Creative Writing Program at Johns Hopkins University. His work has appeard in *The Washingtonian*, *The New York Times*, *The Washington Post*, *Connecticut Review*, *World Hum*, *Johns Hopkins University Arts & Sciences Magazine*, and other places. He is a frequent blogger for www.notalone.com, which is a resource website for returning veterans.

The Cargo

Nothing but the wind churning up dust and sand. And from the cockpit, sitting on the ramp, we can't tell where the ground ends or the sky begins. Outside, the dust storm is gaining strength bit by bit, and so we wait, hoping it will clear soon, but like everything in Afghanistan, the weather is unpredictable and violent.

Overhead, the roar of another plane's engines tells me everything I need to know. It was Rodeo 22's last attempt to land, but the visibility is close to zero, and they never had a chance to get on the ground. I can hear the thumping sound of propellers fade in and out as they climb, corkscrewing upward to avoid the small-arms fire and Stinger missiles hiding in the mountains all around us.

I envy Rodeo 22's escape, and I'm angry at the wind and sand conspiring to keep us here the ground. Absurd, I know, as I resign myself to waiting for the storm to subside and for a radio call—a new directive from command post that I don't want to hear.

I glance over my shoulder toward Nick, our navigator, both of us understanding what's ahead. We won't be going home as planned. We're the only aircraft available now, and we'll get tagged to pick up the rest of Rodeo 22's mission. Although I've never done *that* mission before, I've been instructed on the sensitivity and procedures for carrying *high value targets.*

Intel briefed us on a riot yesterday inside the compound here—a former Russian military base during their decade-long war. The makeshift prison held a few hundred Afghan fighters, and when the food ran out, things got out of control. Somehow they managed to detonate a few grenades, killing a young guard and an interrogator. The riot was cut short by a group of special forces troops—*snakeaters* who've been working and dying alongside the Northern Alliance since the invasion last fall. The Afghans who survived—the worst of them—were locked in metal cages, but rumor has it that the leaders will be moved to a secure site. This can't happen again, the Intel guy said. Not again.

"Looks like it's our show now," my loadmaster Skinner says over the intercom from the back of the plane. "They got some bad mother-fuckers to fly out, and I'm thinkin', *tag, we're it.*"

"We'll see," I say, not ready to commit to anything. We should've been airborne two hours ago, but our cargo was late, keeping us on the ground as the storm rolled in. And it's the waiting—the uncertainty of what's next, coupled with the sound of RPGs and small-arms fire that's keeping my whole crew on edge. One or two properly placed mortars and we're all history.

This isn't how it's supposed to be. We're just a reservist crew who volunteered to fly support missions, play our part for a few months and go home. Rodeo 22 should be the one to carry these guys to Ashgabat, the air base in Turkmenistan, where they'll be conditioned at a secure site for interrogation. We were here to just pick up the bodies, a pair of Human Remains—*HRs*—as Skinner always corrects me. He runs the show in the back of the plane, and as a nicotine and Mountain Dew junkie, his mouth is always running ahead of his brain. Fifteen years my senior and the only member of our squadron with any Vietnam experience, he makes sure to use proper term: HRs—the code we use to designate whatever's left of the dead. Sometimes I still say *bodies*, even though more often than not, it's just body parts iced up inside silver boxes for the long trip home. They're onboard now, strapped down and ready to go.

We're not supposed to combine missions and carry the dead on those *High Value* flights, but standard ops keep being waived for necessity. Deep down I'm thinking Skinner's probably right, and I can feel any illusion of control slipping away. It's March 19^t, and I imagine the whole crew is thinking about what they'd be doing in a few days if this really is our last mission, and we get to go home. In moments like this, it's easy to lose focus and get ahead of ourselves, to forget the real reason we're here.

I'm as guilty as everyone else, already thinking about being home, what it will be like to settle back into old routines and put everything behind me. Usually I'd be getting the lawn mower ready this time of year, changing out the oil, putting in a new spark plug, and sharpening the blade for that first cut. I can see myself in the garage methodically going through all the proper steps to get things right. I miss all the old rituals and the sensations of spring at home—the smell in the air, digging out my old green-stained tennis shoes, and brushing off the wet grass from my skin as I take in the view of a perfectly manicured yard. For a moment I'm almost there, and I imagine my son Chase coming home from baseball practice—his spikes and glove being tossed on the back porch as I finish up and guide the lawnmower to the garage.

But that's half a world away—a completely different life from what I'm taking part in. Here, we're all just waiting in the dark, wondering what's next, when Nick taps his boom mike twice—a hint for me to make eye contact. There's something he doesn't want the whole crew to hear. We lock eyes, and he holds up the folder of flight pubs, opening it to show me an empty slot. The approach procedures for Ashgabat's runway are absent, and without the right instrument procedures, legally we can't fly there. My expression lets him know we'll solve that problem if we get to it.

"I'll have to reconfigure things back here," Skinner says. "They like to strap down these Haji fucks good and tight."

"Hold on," I say as my copilot and I catch a glimpse of a green truck turning onto the ramp. Barely visible through the blowing sand, I recognize an old Soviet transport truck moving away from the hangar.

"I'd like your take on things back here," Skinner goes on, but I'm only half listening as I watch a dozen armed soldiers surround the truck with their weapons raised in anticipation. I can see their bearded faces and the civilian clothes beneath the outer Afghan garbs. Five of them are wearing combat boots—more *snakeaters,* I think, as they force three handcuffed men in orange jumpsuits and bags over their heads down onto the tarmac. One prisoner fights to stay upright before being hit in the head and driven hard onto the pavement. The wind shifts once again, obscuring the view, and I stop breathing for a moment, feeling the hair on the back of my neck rise to attention.

"I'll come back in just a second," I tell Skinner as I open the cockpit window and strain to hear or see a little more through the blowing dust.

The scene is a reminder of what's waiting for us out there. It's why we keep our engines running after we land, upload our cargo, and depart as quickly as possible. We didn't expect to be here this long, and my crew is mostly silent, their eyes scanning the edges of the airfield as we wait. We're big green target, after all, a bull's-eye in a sea of gray and tan just waiting to be hit.

We've been lucky so far, and our missions have become routine, maybe a little too routine. Seeing the caskets onboard and flying out the wounded is about as real as this war gets for us. From the sky, it's easy to become distanced from the reality of everything on the ground. We see the villages and the bases from the air, the fragmented cities and the bombed out buildings, but I seldom see the people. At times, I imagine the enemy hiding in the mountains, waiting in the shadow of the white, jagged peaks filling the horizon day after day. I can feel their presence, like the statues of ancient warriors watching us from a place we can't see or touch—somewhere out there amid the great Hindu Kush—the defiant mountains climbing upwards of 24,000 feet, nearly two miles higher than Pike's Peak.

Straining to see and hear what I can, I imagine the scene unfolding behind the dust clouds, just a hundred yards away. My copilot looks at me—wide eyed without saying a word. *I don't want to do this*, I'd like to say, but I'm in charge, and those are words I can't speak. I'm playing my part and doing what I've been trained to do: keep us all safe, get the mission done, and bring everyone back home alive. Today was supposed to be easy, our last flight in country—my final combat mission—short enough for us to get back and catch the weekly rotator flight to Germany, and then onto the U.S. If everything went as planned, I'd be home to catch Chase's first baseball game of the season. He turned eleven a few weeks back and is scheduled to pitch the opening game.

It's been six months since we arrived here, and it's moments like this, the times waiting when I think about my last few conversations with him. He felt betrayed and angry when I volunteered to deploy, or, as he put it, *leaving us all during the holidays.* I can't recall how or why things escalated between us, and it's the idea of not understanding what went wrong that still eats at me. We didn't speak for days, and on the night before I left, he stopped me in the hallway and held up the model of a C-130 I'd given him years before. Painted in a camouflage green, we'd built it together, glued the pieces in place, and played with it as if we were flying our own missions together across the globe.

"Dad," he said, looking down at his feet and then past me, as if he was trying to find the right words, searching on the periphery of his own imagination for what he hoped to convey. He kept tapping the airplane nervously against his leg as I waited in silence. But the words didn't come for either of us. In the end, we did our best to hug away the distance. "Be good, listen to your mother, and do the right thing," I managed to say, holding his shoulders in my palms and finding his eyes.

"How long will it be?" He wanted to know.

"I'll be back in time for baseball season."

"That long?"

"It'll blow by before you know it," I said, realizing that for a young boy, six months might seem like an eternity.

"Okay," he said with a quiet doubt in his voice—a doubt that lingers with me still.

Over the last few months, I've wondered about how he must have grappled with everything—a young boy with thoughts and ideas evolving and taking shape in my absence. Although we'd sheltered him from the reality of 9/11 and the details of this new war, he knew we were hiding things. He wanted answers to questions he didn't know how to ask . . . a degree of certainty—something to cling to so it would all make sense.

On the ground here, I can feel the wind beginning to die down, and I glance at my watch: 12:05 PM—not enough time to do both missions and catch the flight out. The shuttle back to Germany only comes through once a week, and I can feel the opportunity slipping away from me. If they tag us with Rodeo 22's mission, I can decline it, though. Our rules say we can't depart for Ashgabat without the instrument approaches onboard, and that just might be my ticket home. For a moment, I cling to that possibility.

"I'm going to the back," I say, unstrapping my flak vest and setting it at my feet. I catch Nick's eyes and sense his stress as I descend down the ladder into the cargo hold. His job was to make sure the flight pubs were onboard, and it's uncharacteristic of him to make that kind of mistake. He knows he'll be the one to take the hit if we don't do the mission. It's the kind of thing that can bring a career to an abrupt halt, and I ponder the consequences of my own decision.

Nick's quiet and solid, a guy you usually want making sure the details are right. He's doesn't play along with our navigator jokes. No matter how often we remind him that navigators are a dying breed, replaceable by GPS, he just smiles and gives us his version of reality.

"A GPS can't read the stars when the power goes out or tell you where you are when the system overheats and shuts down," he likes to remind us. "If you lose track of where you are, then you can't know where you're going."

It's a favorite line of his, one we all laugh about, but quietly accept. Out here, if something goes wrong with our navigation system, the only backup is what Nick has learned long ago—a way to plot your place in the world by understanding where you are in relation to the stars. Only from there can we determine which direction to proceed.

In the back of the plane, Skinner's sitting on one of the silver boxes reading the cargo manifest. The cold from the metal floor works its way through my boots and up into my legs as I approach him. He's smoking, halfway through a fresh pack of Camels, and I can tell something's bothering him by the way he avoids my eyes. He's been quieter than normal lately. Without acknowledging me, he drops the cigarette into a soda can and smashes it with his boot. Smoking inside the plane is against regulations, but I don't say anything. Without nicotine and Mountain Dew, Skinner's a mess. His hands tremble and he loses focus, so we all look the other way. During long flights he sits on the cargo ramp near the outflow valve. The smoke gets vented overboard, but he can't hide the stink of it on his breath and flight suit.

"I'll have to reconfigure everything," he says, tapping the coffin. "Ain't supposed to be any of them ragheads on the plane with these guys. We need to separate 'em."

"Looks like there'll be three," I say, looking around at the pile of cargo chains and tie down straps. It's rare for me to be in the back on these flights, to leave the cockpit in the middle of a mission, and Skinner can tell I'm out of my comfort zone.

He nods and hands me the cargo manifest to review and sign. I look at the silver boxes, but I don't feel anything. No emotion, just HRs in a box. It sounds heartless, I know, but this is my nineteenth mission with HRs onboard. You adapt pretty fast. Cargo in—food, bullets, newspapers, grenades, toilet paper—anything and everything, and then the cargo out: empty pallets, miscellaneous equipment, and of course the bodies, warm or cold. There's no point in losing myself in the details of everything going on around me. It won't help me get the mission done.

Outside a series of gunshots rattles off a little closer than I'd like. "Jesus!" I stiffen and look toward the back of the plane. The cargo door is open, and the loading ramp is resting on the pavement, ready for a quick upload. In this configuration, we're the most vulnerable, and everybody, including the enemy, knows it.

"AK-47s," Skinner says, unfazed as he thinks out loud to himself, wondering how to arrange all the cargo. I can't explain it, but seeing him trying to solve the problem relaxes me. He's been in the Reserves for over twenty-five years, and we've flown on hundreds of missions together. I know him better than most, and despite his experience, I can tell this situation is troubling him. Over the years, we've shared many late-night conversations, and I know about his divorces, his difficult children, and the months he spent in rehab. Once he confided in me the biggest mistake of his life: a fight with his only son after the kid came home drunk. It ended with a punch to the boy's face—a hard, tooth-breaking fist to the teenaged son he loves more than life itself.

These are the stories we carry with us, the ones we unpack slowly behind a beer or two and reluctantly share in the weeks and months on the road. At times I've marveled at Skinner's resilience over the years, and how he coaxed his son back home and pieced their world back together. Nothing was ever the same, of course, but Skinner managed to salvage what he could from the relationship, keeping it alive, and staying in his son's life despite the odds against him. Standing here, I begin to think that maybe what I want more than anything is a sense of perspective—to know that despite all our mistakes, everything will work out in the end. Watching him struggle to solve our cargo problem, though, I wonder if it's possible to find that now—here in this place and time.

"I'll put the HRs on the cargo ramp. It can hold their weight," Skinner says, finally finding what he's been looking for. "What do you think?"

"It's your call," I say as I take off my gloves and set them next to the troop door. Flipping through the cargo manifest, I find myself reading the detailed information on the HRs—a twenty-seven-year-old sergeant and a nineteen-year-old private. The private was the one who caused our delay. He was expectant—alive, but without any hope of living. A few pieces of shrapnel penetrated his skull, and the internal bleeding slowly killed him. Beyond a few extra shots of morphine, the medics couldn't do much. It just took longer than everyone thought for him to die, and we had to wait.

"Is your son gonna play ball?" I ask, trying to talk about something we both care about—baseball—anything but the mission at hand.

"No," he says looking toward the silver boxes. The short answer tells me all I need to know—something happened, something he's holding close and doesn't want to share.

Before I can answer, a succession of fresh gunshots makes me drop to the floor. Close—too close for me. Skinner doesn't move, though. He just stands there, and his eyes meet mine for a moment in silence.

"He's joining the fucking Army," Skinner continues, pausing to analyze the sound of the gunshots as I stand up and dust off my flight suit. "An M-4 or maybe an M-14," he adds as he bends over, grabs a tie-down strap, and stretches it from one side of the plane to the other. "He e-mailed me the other day. Says he wants to serve."

"Did you mention the Air Force?" I say, but as the words leave my mouth I want to reach out and take them back. His son would never pass the entrance exam. It's the truth, but it didn't need to be said. The Army will take any warm body to fill its ranks, but the Air Force has the luxury of being picky and sticking to their standards most of the time. I feel awkward and a little rattled by the gunfire, but Skinner bails me out.

"He wants to do things his own way," he says. "Ain't nothing I can do about it, anyway. It's a done deal."

I find myself searching for the right words to say, something to ease the tension, but I don't have anything to offer. Instead, I sign the cargo manifest and hand it to him. For a moment our eyes meet, and I finally understand Skinner's silence over the last few days. I can feel a kind of distant sadness and pain working through him—a reminder that maybe the consequences of some mistakes can't be reversed.

He takes the clipboard and taps the coffin next to me. "They usually promote them to corporal, you know . . . posthumously."

"What?" I say, catching a glimpse of Nick climbing down from the cockpit.

"The privates who die," Skinner says. "I guess *corporal* looks a lot better on a tombstone than private."

240

"I guess so," I say, as Nick motions for me to join him.

"The guards will help me get things configured," Skinner says before I step away. "It won't take long." His voice has a tone that makes everything seem like an ordinary mission, as if this was all simply part of our normal routine.

Up front, Nick tells me what we expected—command post officially tasked us with 22's mission. "The weather's perfect in Ashgabat. No ceilings—clear and a million," he says, meeting my eyes and conveying a silent agreement that he's already signed onto. "The storm's starting to blow over."

Nodding, I resign myself to what it all means. "Okay, let's do it," I say, knowing that the clear weather means we can fly a visual approach into Ashgabat. No approach procedures necessary. It's not legal, but what's probably expected, and besides, I'm not putting anything or any of my crew at risk. We'll be halfway there before my copilot figures things out, and at that point, it won't make sense to turn back. As for Nick, he can feign ignorance, and I'll laugh it off, reminding everyone just how useless navigators really are.

"I'll let command post know," he says. "The cargo's ready to load."

Following him into the cockpit, I turn and notice Skinner in the back of the plane. He's kneeling by the right troop door talking to one of the *snakeaters* who'll be escorting our cargo. The soldier is holding his M-4, and he leans in toward Skinner, his worn face and beard almost touching him as they whisper words I can't hear. *Ghost passengers*, I remind myself—no paper manifest to mark the presence of anything or anyone except the two HRs already aboard. Nothing left to sign or do back here, I think, as I climb up into the cockpit.

Outside, the old Soviet transport-truck begins to move, circling slowly toward the back of the plane. Two Humvees are following behind, and I tell myself that it's just a few more flights—just another week and I'll be home. It'll all be over soon.

Missing Chase's game is a small thing, nothing to get worked up about, I remind myself. It's insignificant, but I can't help thinking about his disappointment and how things must have changed over the last few months. He knows I didn't have to go away. I could have stayed home and done a staff job instead, but I like to think that someday—years from now, he'll have a whole new perspective on everything.

These are the ideas I take with me as I strap on my flak vest and get comfortable in my seat. It can't last forever, I think, as I put on my helmet and start running the checklist. By the time I'm finished, a quiet optimism begins to settle over me, a hope born from the thoughts that we're getting the mission done despite everything working against us.

"Pre-flight checks are complete," the co-pilot says as I look around for my gloves.

Nick's on the radio, talking command post. "The cargo's secured," he says. "Just waiting for Skinner to get back on headset and button up the ramp."

Realizing I left my flight gloves in the back, I pause and consider not wearing them. I don't actually need them, but there's a comfort in flying with gloves on, a secure feeling on the yoke—a sense of control that isn't there without them.

"I left my gloves in the back."

"I can grab 'em," Nick says.

"That's okay," I say, climbing out of my seat and then stepping down the ladder. In the back, I'm caught off guard by the scene before me. A cat's cradle of tie down straps and chains are stretched out, connecting one side of the plane to the other. I've never seen the back configured like this, and I'm unsure of what to think. Two hooded prisoners are tied to the cargo floor, their bodies intertwined with the straps and chains. I start looking for the third prisoner when I realize Skinner is sitting on the floor in front of the other two. He's smoking, exhaling into their hooded faces and quietly speaking to them—words spoken too softly for me to hear or understand. Before I have a chance to react, Skinner jumps up and moves toward me with my gloves in hand.

"Here you go, boss," he says. "Got 'em both strapped down good and tight."

"Aren't there three?"

"Umm . . . they only brought two." He shrugs, half-grinning, as he looks back over his shoulder.

"Just two?" I hesitate, uncertain about everything as I glance at the men standing beside the troop doors on the right. Their dark, tired faces meet mine, unfazed by the implications in my questioning gaze. Their eyes are the eyes of dead men, and I wonder for a moment about all the things they've experienced in their short time here—things I can't begin to imagine or understand. I look away, pushing back against the images taking shape in my mind. "Is it safe? I thought they'd be chained down in the passenger seats," I ask, defaulting to old instincts, everything I've been taught, as I consider the safety of everyone onboard—the prisoners, too.

"They're not going anywhere. Don't worry about 'em. . . . We're safe," Skinner says.

"We are?"

"Yep," he says, his voice wrapped in a quiet urgency, pressuring me to get back into the cockpit.

"I guess we are," I say, putting my gloves on and then climbing the ladder.

Up front, I pause and take a deep breath as the storm continues to subside.

"Looks like the we're going into extra innings," my co-pilot says. "Sorry you have to miss the opening game."

"It's okay," I answer. "It's just his first game. There'll be more."

Outside, the clouds are breaking up, and I can see the mountains taking shape all around us. The early afternoon sun is reflecting off the bits of dust and sand lingering in the air. Squinting to read from my checklist, I brief our tactical departure to the crew—a tight turning spiral above the airfield to get as high as possible in the shortest amount of time. It will keep us relatively safe from small-arms fire. Beyond that, we'll have to rely on the chaff and flares to defeat any shoulder-launched missiles.

"We're ready to button things up," the engineer announces as he switches on the hydraulic pump and clears Skinner to raise the cargo ramp.

"The flight plan's loaded," Nick says.

The weight of the plane begins to shift as the ramp starts closing and then locks into place.

"Everything's secure," Skinner says. "Let's get the fuck out of here."

My co-pilot stifles a laugh and shakes his head.

Pulling my visor down, I can't help but imagine the silver caskets on the cargo ramp—the dead soldiers concealed inside—and those hooded prisoners facing them. But most of all, it's Skinner I can picture so clearly. It's as if I'm right there, standing beside him—seeing a cigarette dangling from his bottom lip while he paces nervously back and forth, maneuvering somewhere in between the two.

Up front, I realize the whole crew is waiting for me to start the engines. I hesitate, though, feeling the weight of my co-pilot's gaze upon me. He's so wrong, I think, as I turn to meet his eyes. Dead wrong. This isn't extra innings. It's a whole new game.

James A. Moad II is a former Air Force C-130 pilot with 3000+ hours and over a hundred combat missions. He is a graduate of the U.S. Air Force Academy where he later served as an Assistant Professor in English and as a fiction editor for the journal, *War, Literature, and the Arts* (*WLA*). He also holds a Master's Degree in Creative Writing from Southern Illinois University–Edwardsville.

Fred Rosenblum

tree line

you could feel
a resistance in this jungle
as bamboo sores
and leeches
in chest deep creek
could attest

a resistance
where lasers of light
refracted in a cathedral
of flora
thick with mosquitoes
& muggy air
that choked the shit out of you

. . . then fucked you in the psyche
with an insane cacophony
of fauna gone berserk

you could sense them out there
. . . lizards and frogs fell silent
you could smell them out there—
rice and rat meat in their bellies

respiring the humid stench
and rotted breath of jungle

you could sense them out there
. . . angst palpable
with aggression and fear

anticipating the beat of the drum
that would cue the chaos
and a blitz on our positions

Fred Rosenblum was born in St. Louis in 1949 and enlisted in the Marine Corp in 1967.
He later graduated from the University of Alaska—Anchorage with a degree in Business.
He retired in 2001 to the life of a hermit, currently in San Diego.

Jason Poudrier

Sulfur and Moonshine

the sulfur scent
of a case released
unloads
a sound that cracks
you in half:
each

pop,

pop,

pop,

distances you
further from yourself
as rapidly as the lead
leaves the copper
and erases the space
between you,
and, if you're lucky,
the man
who wants
to kill you,

then you taste him,
dry your mouth
and forge your gut

like a shot
of Kentucky Moonshine

Jason Poudrier

What's For Dinner, Doc?

Inside my Coke-can-armored Humvee,
I swelter in my flack vest,
feeling like Bugs Bunny, boiling
in a bathtub-sized pot,
singing along with the dancing little Indian
who is preparing him for dinner.

The solemn Iraqi children
stare at me with
starving big, black eyes
with sleepless, deep, brown bags
on a dried-up palette,
which is accompanied
by their dance,
a synchronized, sombering
movement of the hand
tapping the tip of the tongue.

I tear off the corner
of a bag of Skittles from my MRE
and toss it so it spins
and sprinkles Skittles from the sky
like on the commercials
back home they know nothing about;
they scurry about
collecting the colorful candies,
then scamper off,
leaving subtle dimples
in the sand.

I ask my BC
where their parents are;
he tells me
they're awaiting us
behind the dunes,
and I wonder if
I made the right
turn in Albuquerque.

Jason Poudrier

Picking up the Slack

After I awoke him,
his eyes remained shut,
but his brows and cheeks
picked up the slack,

lighting his face,
just as my flashlight's red
glistened off his eyelids,

complementing
his thin lips that smirked
as I let him know

it wasn't time for his guard shift, yet,

and he rolled his head
to the side—asleep
before his smile left his lips.

Jason Poudrier was deployed to Iraq, wounded in action, and awarded the Purple Heart in 2003. He completed an English degree at Cameron University. He has authored two collections of war poems: *Red Fields*, Mongrel Empire Press 2012 and *In the Rubble at Our Feet*, Rose Rock Press 2011. His work has appeared in the *New Mexico Poetry Review*, *Connecticut Review*, *Sugar Mule*, *Goldmine*, and was anthologized in *Ain't Nobody That Can Sing Like Me*.

The Ponytail Palm Christmas

The ponytail palm in the kitchen window is a barometer on the future; my wife believes it has the power to predict whether our son will divorce his estranged spouse. She has a theory, and I would not discount it one whit. I'd be willing to bet the ranch on it.

She understands the thing; it and she are attuned. It does not so much as talk to her, you understand; their communication does not include mundane conversation in any way. No. It is more a matter of feeling. As a crystal ball must for a psychic, her ponytail palm speaks in a language of swirling ideas portrayed in a disjointed syntax she has come to understand; images distilled from a melding mist etched cinematically onto the retina of memory as fully realized as if the events depicted had really happened—or were about to—right in front of her eyes.

Today, calmly, confidently, she informed me that he—our son—will do it. Divorce is in the cards.

"And how have you reached this conclusion?" I managed to ask with a straight face although I knew already; I just wanted to make her admit it. She answered seriously, but with a self-deprecating smile, and I had to chuckle a little. Our son and future ex-daughter in-law have been married for only three years—and fortunately, have yet to make babies—but this ponytail palm has been a topic of conversation for the last thirteen years or more, the duration of his continuing military career.

"Do you know how old this ponytail palm is?" You always ask.

"Why must it always start this way?" I always say.

"Well, do you know how old it is?"

"It's about thirty days older than the last time you told me."

"And?"

"It's as old as Gabe." Our son—that is—and he's turning thirty-one. Jesus, to be thirty-one again. That's what my ninety year-old dad says. That's what everyone in my aging circle says. It's what I say, too, usually. Some days, more frequently now, I simply say no to the prospect of being thirty-one again. Thank you, but no.

"And what is it I always say?"

"What?" She's about to tell me again. It's Gabe's.

"That it's his. It's his ponytail palm. It's a part of him. I can see how he's doing by looking at it. It reflects his well-being; it has ever since he left enlisted."

248

Don't laugh.

My wife, like my mother, often knows exactly what the hell she is talking about, even if it sounds odd to you or contradicts your own experience. Who're you gonna believe, her or your lying eyes? More often than not, you'd better go with her; you'll be right if you do.

Our youngest son—Gabe—is Army. Regular Army. Real Army. Noncom, as in Sergeant First Class. Over the last thirteen years and more now, he and his fellow combat brothers-in-arms have been in harm's way more often than a vicious flea on the vulnerable underbelly of a sharp-toe hound.

Christ.

Every time he turned around somewhere someone shot at him—our son—or lobbed grenades, mortar shells, or rockets. Under enemy fire he has advanced, running in assault, and withdrawn, running in retreat. That shit gets old. It can change a man. Losing brothers gets old. Survivors are changed forever. Every time you turn around, another good man gone or good man changed, sometimes for the better, as more mature personalities less marred by braggadocio emerge. . . . And sometimes not so much. Sometimes a good guy is just FUBAR—Fucked up (Army speak) beyond all recognition—either physically, emotionally, or both. FUBAR. "Fouled Up," in this PC world.

Desert Storm—The Stormin' Norman Era; my last war. Viet Nam, my first.

Brothers down. Brothers gone. Brothers gone-gone.

I've aged. . .

That shit gets old.

That shit tells on a ponytail palm, too. That plant came near to dying throughout his every deployment. The Balkans. Korea. Iraq. Iraq. Afghanistan.

From the first, that boy—Gabe, that is—has been at extreme risk in extremely dire circumstances; at age nineteen—Kosovo—Serbia. Beyond brutal. Under grueling close range exchanges over protracted hours with hostile forces, far beyond an international boundary they'd been expressly forbidden to cross. Names crossing the president's desk. Christ. And everyday, his mom could tell the state of Gabe's mind and body by looking at that ponytail palm; she watched it wither and flourish, ebb, and flow. In step with him.

Like his father—me, that is—our son is not a spiritually oriented person. He is not conversant with the soul. At thirty-one, he is hungry for sensual life, for being alive—and knowing it, vibrantly. He demands proof of life coursing through his veins, often disguised as adrenaline, sometimes masquerading as alcohol in mass quantities; sometimes as nonstop sex. He wants it all; it is his due.

I remember that.

A four-year Korean vacation along the DMZ, eyeball to eyeball. Special Forces. Black Ops. Black eyes. Two for flinching. He knows towns in North Korea firsthand, only I am not permitted to speak of it. Neither you nor I am permitted access to that information; we have no need to know. The jury is to disregard the previous assertion by the prosecutor.

What the fuck? That shit gets old.

Iraqi Freedom, a.k.a., Desert Storm, Part Deux.

Gone, changed. Gone-gone.

He's aged—Gabe—that is.

Afghanistan tied an old record. Euphoria and Pain. Constant boredom and low-grade fear, punctuated by abject terror, and intense action. Dust. Dirt. Cold. Weekends here and there on base. Beer. Video games, Skype and telephones. Beer. That shit gets old. That ponytail palm withered down to a few scrawny brown shoots on a bulbous main trunk.

Worry is for citizens. Us. Next of kin, a.k.a., beneficiaries. For him—Gabe—it's first one rush, then another. Always in queue for an officially dispensed fix, legal—when possible, illegal—if commanded. That's if things are going well. If they're not, well. We don't talk about that. The 3:30 a.m. phone calls that happily all turned out to be him, okay, not calling from a hospital. The unforgettable call in the night that ended with me in terror, listening helplessly as a mortar assault began on his position. Rounds exploding close by, I listened to him running with full pack, calmly telling me repeatedly not to worry. Concussion distorting the telephone. Finally, reassuring me, saying he had to go; his voice sounding so young to me, as if he were still in Little League, excited that it was his turn to bat. The forward-deployment Army life and mission are his drug, deadly as any other, and potentially even more debilitating. He doesn't do it for love of country, to protect us, or to protect our freedom, so much, although it's all that, and more. But really, it's about the rush; it's about his brothers, his Army brethren; his chosen family. When his brothers are in harm's way, he'll be there—our son, Gabe—he'll be there. He doesn't worry and doesn't want us to worry either. I remember. Worry is for citizens.

The old in-out; the old in-out quick, and nobody gets hurt; the old in-out quick, and everybody gets hurt.

Disavow all action. That shit never happened, soldier.

We never knew. We never will.

Iraq. Afghanistan. Pakistan, Iran, but you didn't hear it here. South America. What the fuck?

That shit gets old.

He's different, now—Gabe—that is. He's forgotten how to smile, I think sometimes, but then I realize, it's not that. It's that he doesn't know how or doesn't remember how to take humor in the little incidents; the invisible threads running throughout our days; the minor details aligning and underlying the major events in life; the little things propelling the whole big thing forward, all according to the unknowable ineluctable workings of the infernally ruthless mechanism; the wheel of life. Around and around the lugubrious wheel. Vast and eternal, and if not infinite, then something that will do just fine until the infinite comes along. He—our son, Gabe—never stops to smell the roses. He says he has learned to focus on falling into buckets of shit and coming up smelling like roses.

Now that is a major life skill, I think admiringly; one I wish he would teach me.

Shit yeah.

Eternity. "I don't want much," I said aloud under starlight last Wednesday night. "Just a minor miracle will do." Several lifetimes, if not eternity to spend with you in a mountain cabin with everything I've ever wanted to read waiting on shelves stuffed full, and all the time I need to git 'er done, with a special window upstairs in our bedroom looking out onto magical vistas, ever changing. First, a dramatic ocean view, something from the Oregon coast; then the mountains, Rockies, Appalachian, Adirondack; followed by a spell alongside a gently flowing river in the lazy summertime; a babbling brook at dawn; a full moon on foggy moors, fragrant heather-coated landscape of darkly silhouetted castle crags frequented by Heathcliff and Cathy. Dang, it was cold that night. Dang, the stars were bright, so bright.

Jesus. Your eyes, I said. Portals to the soul, you said. Windows, I said. Windows to the soul, I said. Oh, you said. What the fuck?

Gabe's eyes, sometimes he conceals behind mirrored sunglasses and a tough-guy persona. That, too, gets old.

Back in the real-world, he fell into a civilian bucket of shit three years ago; he married a beautiful young girl, when instead, he had hoped for a woman, a grown-up woman of a certain maturity extending beyond the train of her wedding gown, but that train derailed. It got old real quick. It happens. Men and women; we use the same words, but we mean different things. . . . In the battle of the sexes, it's a wonder any of us are left standing.

That withered old ponytail palm had been looking bad. My wife is concerned.

Parents, now relegated to occasional holidays-only, don't see much firsthand, but now, we have reason for optimism. Last month, that old ponytail palm began a strong resurgence; new growth; new branches, curling green strands, new leafs unfurling upwards, arching beautifully toward the ceiling—before looping down to find the floor—suddenly that long!

Last night I dreamed of my longed-for cabin in the mountains, the cabin with the special bedroom window; I was on the porch overlooking a wide turn in the slow-moving river, warm at the end of a perfect summer day, reclining in our forest green Adirondack loungers with a favorite book opened across my lap as I looked up to inhale fresh-scented air reaching me on an evening breeze transporting tales of new-mown hay.

Christmas is next week—and Gabe, our son—is coming home, and he's going to confront his young ex-wife to be. She knows why he is calling; knows what he will say. She will not answer her phone when Gabe calls to make a date to see her over the holidays. During over three years of marriage, they've spent fewer than six months together, usually for only a month at a time, sometimes only hours. On leave. On training. Deployed.

Gone, but not gone-gone—Gabe—is coming home in just a few more days.

I wish you could see our kitchen; she just finished—my wife—that is.

Have you ever seen a ponytail palm dressed for Christmas? Well, now I have. She knew how handsome it would be, ever so festive, decked out for the holidays. "It seemed to suggest decorations for a holiday homecoming," she said. She repeated and varied the theme throughout the house. It's never looked better. The ponytail palm has predicted an extremely handsome soldier will appear, when Gabe crosses our threshold. It knows. They know. She told me—my wife—that is. And now, I know, too.

We'll celebrate Christmas when he gets here, but tonight, we'll turn on the holiday lights, light a candle, and maybe pop a cork.

Deck the halls. Fa-la-la-la-la-la-la-la-la.

Writer-filmaker-photographer Mitch Duckworth is the proud father of a career Army professional with over thirteen years of distinguished service. As a corporate communcations, B2B marketing, and public information specialist in business, Mitch is privately engaged in a dedicated pursuit of the craft of fiction. This story was born while traipsing deep woodland trails accompanied by two huge fans, both smart dogs. Happily, the undecorated ponytail palm still thrives in their tall kitchen window.

Kathleen Willard

Their Letters

He wrote to her from an obscure country in Asia
        she wrote back of my frilly dress for Easter
of traveling up the Mekong in sampans, advisor to armies
and of sorrow and assassination, the empty saddle on the black horse, the
  entourage

The blue envelopes from APO San Francisco bringing assurances
        she waited in Georgia drinking cocktails
that he was recently alive and thinking of their children
        among military wives marking time with rounds of bridge, other
  diversions—

He tells of his first night in Saigon, a bomb exploding a fuel depot, the
  fire
        and sometimes she described pill box hats, the white gloves
flooding his quarters, an instant inferno
        she wore to Mass or our eating okra and peach pie at Morrison's
Cafeteria.

Someone shouting run, the city charring
        while she watches their children practicing backstroke
he runs nude into the dark streets, seconds in front of the flames
        and can their daughter and two sons take horseback riding
  lessons,
could they afford it.

Yes, purchase the jodhpurs, thank you for Dad's Brag Book, mentioning
  geography
        she cannot imagine,

he marches deeper into the jungle, up the Mekong, training citizens to be
  soldiers,
        jots down troop movements in a small notepad
and she waits much too long for his next letter,   Dearest Jim,

This week I took the children to the Chattahoochie County Fair.
We walked the midway in the evening eating cotton candy.

Your daughter much too eager to see the freaks on display inside the
   canvas tents.
This week there were cake walks at Halloween parties.
This week our children dressed in riding clothes, cantering and clinging
   to their ponies.
This week a school bomb drill and math homework.

This he is reading while he salts leeches that cling to his calves killing
   them, and dries
his boots soaked by swamp water.
This he is reading before sleep as the monsoon begins its weeping, the
   frog croaking
amplifies.
This he is reading as he puts on his flak jacket, blackens his face.
This he is reading after he cleans his rifle, visits the priest, posts another
   letter.

Love to you and the children
Jim.

Kathleen Willard grew up as a military brat and watched her father, a West Point graduate, serve two tours of duty in Vietnam—in 1962 and 1970. This experience impacted
and defined her family, and she continues to write poems about their time in the military.
Thirty of her poems have been published in literary magazines and anthologies including:
*Bombay Gin, Journal of Kentucky Studies, Monserrat Review, Dry Creek Review, Flint
Hills Review, Colere, Icarus, The Teacher's Voice, Matter,* and *Pinyon Poetry* (featured
poet). She two advanced degrees: MA in Literature from Middlebury College and MFA in
Creative Writing from Colorado State University. She received a Fulbright-Hays Fellow-
ship and a National Endowment for the Humanities grant.

Michele A. Boyle

Just One Smile

The halls are filled with many. They walk in all sizes, shapes and forms. Hair has grayed, or some still hold the remnants of the 60s long hair from the rebellion of the hippies after life in the "War."

Some have canes, wheelchairs, and need assistance. The sights and smells of the heavily populated halls of the Veterans Hospital gives off a charismatic feeling. So many stories quieted by time, such sad faces. Aging men with so much to say, yet quiet in their own thoughts.

I am a people watcher. I come to the VA and wait for my love and think, do others see him as I do? Do others see how many of these brave souls were once so young, handsome, and virile?

I look at him and don't see him as old, balding, or overweight. And when he looks at me, I see the glimmer in his eye that brings me back to the first time I saw him in his uniform some forty years ago. So handsome, so stunning in the crisp, pointed creases of his shirt and trousers of the Marine uniform he so proudly wore and made me feel safe.

A young girl sits impatiently waiting for her dad or grandfather and scoffs at some gentle soul trying to make conversation with her. I want to shake her. Can't she see that this man was once someone she would have sat up and took notice of? That you just don't become old? That he used to sit in her chair? That all it takes is just a simple smile to make their day? That this man gave his life for you!

All it takes is a second to bring them back to their youth and the sadness of their fate forgotten briefly when a pretty lady walks by and smiles. Time has escaped their pain, if only for a brief fleeting minute. Their hearts skip a beat; they forget what day or time it is. That smile takes them back to their youth, when they were dapper in the proud uniform that made others stand up and take notice of who they were.

These are the youths from long ago, where time has passed them by, yet where hope of a future stills beats in their soul by that one smile.

Michele Boyle is married for 38 years to a United States Marine Vietnam Veteran who suffers with PTSD and the ramifications of Agent Orange. Michele wrote this as she sat in the VA Hospital waiting for her spouse and observing others. She has three sons and works as an Office Assistant, but has always written personal journals to help her get through the tough times.